Harbor City / Harbo
Los Angele
68 24000
Los Ang

MW00874914

OCT - 4 2006

View From The
Top of the Mast

by

Bungy Hedley   2006

Happy Beachcombing!

Bungy Hedley

Bloomington, IN   Milton Keynes, UK

authorHOUSE

172464647

AuthorHouse™
1663 Liberty Drive, Suite 200
Bloomington, IN 47403
www.authorhouse.com
Phone: 1-800-839-8640

AuthorHouse™ UK Ltd.
500 Avebury Boulevard
Central Milton Keynes, MK9 2BE
www.authorhouse.co.uk
Phone: 08001974150

© *2006 Bungy Hedley. All rights reserved.*

No part of this book may be reproduced, stored in a retrieval system, or transmitted by any means without the written permission of the author.

First published by AuthorHouse 7/20/2006

ISBN: 1-4259-4430-2 (e)
ISBN: 1-4259-4410-8 (sc)

Library of Congress Control Number: 2006905906

Printed in the United States of America
Bloomington, Indiana

This book is printed on acid-free paper.

Feel free to drop me a line...

Bungy Hedley
Box 101
Ledbetter, Texas 78946
<bungyh@cvtv.net>

ACKNOWLEDGMENTS

I'd like to give many, many thanks to :

* My parents, Eli and Malcolm Hedley, Beachcombers, who showed me that life was an adventure!

* My dear sisters, Flo, Mare, and Ba... having sisters like you makes life a great trip!

* My wonderful children, Ballan, Seaward, and Hedley, for all their encouragement for this project, over the years. Especially Ballan, who, whenever I started to talk story about past adventures, would put her fingers in her ears and say, "Don't talk it! Write it!"

* Larry Hartshorn, my dear husband, who has gone to that Island in the Sun, for his loving support and encouragement over the years for ALL my projects!

* Kay Taylor who helped me pull all this together, and was so happy doing it! In fact, she had her dove sitting on her head most of the time she was at her computer!

* Peggy Huffman ... what a writing teacher! All your grand help was greatly appreciated!

* Carolyn Edwards for all your dedication and research to this project!

* Anne Ruthven, who shoved me in the right direction!

* Leon Callaway for historic photos of San Pedro and my life!

*   All you wonderful friends and relatives who have helped make
     my life such an adventure!

*   All those Tall Masts, and the View that I have had from them!

May the wind be always at your back!

Bungy

FORWARD

My official name is Lady Weldon Bungy Hedley! An old sun dial motto states, "I Record Only The Sunny Hours," and this is exactly what I have tried to do in *View From the Top of The Mast*. This is a record of only the first two of seven decades of my life, so far. It's an account of adventure and fun in old California. Sailing, swimming, beachcombing, movie stars, and more, make up this real life tale of 1940's and 1950's history.

Living right on the Pacific Ocean, in a 2,000 foot Cove that had once been the Royal Palms Country Club; dancing on an outside dance floor under a full moon; beachcombing with my family up and down the west coast (this was our job!); crewing on sailboats to Hawaii, Mexico, and French Oceania; being escorted to my senior prom by Raymond Burr; serving tea to Gary Cooper; sailing in the first San Diego/Acapulco Yacht Race; managing family owned shops in Disneyland when it first opened. These and many more adventures make up *View From The Top of the Mast*.

Today, my adventuring keeps on! The last few years, I have re-learned how to board surf; taken scuba diving lessons; cruised the Caribbean and Greek Isles; catamaran sailed and snorkeled the Hawaiian Islands; and white water rafted down 210 miles of the Grand Canyon.

I take great pleasure in volunteering at church and in my community, and have just taught 100 kids how to hula!

My next big adventure will be who knows what, doing who knows where!

If you like this book, I may start on the next five decades. This is dedicated to you, the Reader, in hopes that it inspires you to start adventuring, too!

NOTE:

To all you sailors and yacht-persons: I have tried to explain nautical terms and happenings in layman language, so all can understand what is happening in this book. Forgive me!

To all you readers: Remember! This happened over fifty years ago and it is all from pure memory. So go easy on me if my "facts" are a bit off!

Fair Winds!
Bungy

TABLE OF CONTENTS

NOTE:
These chapter titles are lines from old songs!

Chapter 1

♪ *California here I come!* ♫

"Dear Okie, if you see Arkie, tell him Tex has got a job for him, pickin' up prunes out in Califorttey" was a hit song.

The Grapes of Wrath, starring Henry Fonda, was a box office success, telling of the migration west from the Oklahoma/Texas dust bowl during the great depression.

Nelson Eddy and Jeanette McDonald were singing, "Sweetheart, Sweetheart, Sweetheart" to each other.

The year was 1937, and I was three years old.

Mother and Daddy decided that there must be opportunities somewhere, so they sold everything they could, packed up and headed out from Seminole, Oklahoma, with us three girls, to seek their fame and fortune in beautiful California, Land of Dreams.

Our first stop after driving across the newly opened Golden Gate Bridge in San Francisco was "Carmel By the Sea," where the ocean pounded in on golden sands and the sunsets were more colorful than any we had ever seen. The smell of the Monterey Pines, wafting along on the cool Pacific breezes, was pretty close to heaven. Our littlest and last sister put in her appearance.

Mother used to say, with a puzzled look on her face, "She was always crying as a baby, but there didn't seem to be anything wrong with her." Because of this, we always had to be kind of careful for that little sister while we were growing up. In writing this book, I started remembering a lot of stuff. One was a memory of me at three, crossing a big expanse of varnished floor, getting to my sister's crib, grabbing the bottle of sugar water or milk, drinking it, and throwing the bottle back into the crib. She was probably just starving, with mother thinking she had already drunk her bottle. I am particularly nice to my darling sister these days!

Jobs were hard to come by in this gorgeous dream of a village, so we packed up once more, and headed to sunny southern California, eventually making our way *home* to the flavorful fishing town of San Pedro, right on the huge Los Angeles Harbor.

Bungy, Mare, and Flo having their first photo op in California.

We found a little, rundown house that sat on the top of a tall cliff, with a magnificent view of the Pacific crashing into the rocks below. The house needed a lot of work, but we set to with a will because we loved being right at the top of that cliff. I slept on a trundle bed, which was pulled out each night from under a bigger bed. There was a little privy about a hundred feet from the house, and on a dark night, when the wind from the sea blew out my candle, I was out of there and back to the house in two seconds flat!

The family consisted of Daddy, Weldon Eli Hedley; Mother, George Malcolm (Yes! That was George! She was going to be a junior.); first in line, Flo Annie (Flo); second, Marilyn Dorothy (Mare); third, me, Lady Weldon (Bungy, pronounced Bungee. I was also going to be a junior, hence the "Weldon"); and last, Charlotte Elizabeth (Ba, as in Bay, or sometimes The Elf).

We started combing the beaches for things we could use in the house, and Daddy started finding a wealth of materials to start his career as a beachcomber. He started collecting and selling beautiful, white driftwood, shells, fish floats that had floated in from Japan on the currents, lots of old fishnets and other flotsam that washed up on the shore.

Actually, Daddy had really become a beachcomber the minute we hit the California coast. Only now, he started seeing the commercial side of it. He found that the movie studios and big department stores in Hollywood wanted his combings and they began to pay the bills. His official title from then on was, "Eli Hedley, Beachcomber."

The Little House served us well until World War II got underway when the Imperial Japanese forces attacked Pearl Harbor, Hawaii, on

3

December 7, 1941. President Franklin D. Roosevelt signed Executive Order #9066, establishing a military zone on many parts of the west coast. It authorized the removal from that area, by the army, of "any and all persons." This included our American-Japanese neighbors and playmates, who owned farms around us. And us, who lived right on the best location for an army lookout over the whole ocean. The army patrolled the entire coastline around us, day and night, against an invasion from Japan. We were told that several Japanese submarines had been sighted right off the coast, and the Imperial Japanese Navy shelled an oilfield up the coast, near Santa Barbara, causing damage but no casualties.

Hedley Family taking a break from beachcombing on rocky coast below Little House.

4

On March 30, 1942, the first forced removals of Americans of Japanese ancestry began all over the Los Angeles Basin. Soon our school chums were put on military truck convoys, Pacific Electric Red Cars, or school buses, and taken to Santa Anita Race Track. They were given converted horse stables to live in. Others were taken to Texas, Arkansas, and Arizona relocation camps, where most lived out the duration of the war.

The Kawashiris, who lived right across the road from us on their farm, were told they had a week before they had to go. I was really sad because there was a boy just my age. We were good friends and had spent hours playing together. Games of marbles in the dirt road were our favorite. I admired him greatly because when he had a cold, his runny nose dripped down about a foot or so, or so it seemed to me! I watched in awe as it stretched longer and longer. Just before it had a chance to fall, he sniffed it back up his nose! I tried for hours to do that, but the most I ever got was about an inch before it fell. When the bus came to take our friends off, we all stood in the road and waved a very sad goodbye. The kids had all been born in the United States and were as American as we were.

Flo started a club called, "Super Sleuth and Mr. I Find 'em Detective Club." This secret spy club aimed to help the war effort. We built the club in the big old pepper tree in the front yard, and started spying on Joe's Hamburger Shack, right down below us on the beach. He was a Japanese from Japan. One day, the army came and hauled him off. It turned out that he really was suspected of being a spy! I'm glad we hadn't told Mother exactly whom we were spying on.

High on the edge of our cliff, near our house, stood the remains of an old gun turret. Daddy admonished us not to go there at all. But spies needed a perfect place to watch for enemy submarines, so we often crept through the tall grass to our spy room anyway.

Every Tuesday, while the war continued, all the kids at school tried to bring a dime to class to buy a Victory Stamp. We pasted it in our little savings books, until we had enough to buy a savings bond. Each time I licked my little stamp and pasted it in the book, I felt as if I were really doing something to help our brave, fighting soldiers. And, of course, we were, because that was one of the ways that the war was financed.

In order to purchase things like sugar, gasoline, tires, and other such necessities, families had to get ration stamp books. Without these stamps we could not buy these scarce items, and with them, we could only buy a certain amount. Our supply of sugar always ran short. My favorite snack food, butter and sugar sandwiches, were curtailed.

Each family was required to register, with birth dates and all the pertinent information. Mother went down to our school, where the government had set up an office, and proceeded to fill out papers for all of us. When I was eighteen, and I wanted to get a passport, I sent away for my birth certificate. All of us girls did the same. My sisters discovered from their birth certificates, that she had mixed up all the birth dates. They had been celebrating them on the wrong days for all these years.

I had the worst problem, because it turned out that the doctor who brought me into this world forgot to register my birth at all.

I had no birth certificate! Thank goodness I managed to find him after all that time. And I forgave him when I found out he was an honest-to-goodness, three-quarter Cherokee Indian, and owned a buffalo ranch! How exciting!

"Oh, Bungy Hedley! Of course I remember when you were born. You were such a beautiful baby, your daddy and I decided to celebrate the appearance, and did so. I must have just plumb forgot!" he told me.

All of us had been born at home so it was easy for him to forget to fill out the documentation for me. After all the intervening years, he naturally failed to recall the exact day. I had to get certified letters from him and from my first grade teacher to verify that I had really been born, in order to get what they called a delayed birth certificate. As a result, I have felt kind of free, because I do not know on what day I was actually born, and never will. Consequently, I can celebrate whenever the time or spirit calls for it.

When I was six, we were still living on the top of the cliff, high above The Cove, in our little house. One fine day, Flo decided to try smoking, so naturally she got us all together in her nefarious plot. Mischief always breeds better in a mob. We ground dried walnut leaves and fig leaves together for tobacco. Even at that age, Flo had plenty of creativity. She sent me in the house for newspaper to roll the tobacco in. I guess she thought that with my innocent look, no questions would be asked. Unfortunately, as I made my way back outside with my little arms filled with pages and pages of paper, Daddy causally came over and asked, "Where are you going with all that newspaper?"

I stammered and hemmed and hawed. Shifting from foot to foot, I finally managed to mumble, "Umm ... well ... uh ... see, we're working on a project ... Flo needs it for something."

Daddy looked down at me for a moment as I shuffled my feet nervously, trying to avoid direct eye contact. "OK," he finally said, and let me go on.

We fixed up the "cigarettes" and proceeded to smoke to our heart's content. Or at least we smoked until we all turned green. No doubt, Daddy knew what the results would be and he just let us believe we got away with something. Anyway, we had learned our lesson, and none of us ever smoked again after that.

Mare had more of a feel for dramatics, instead of adventure. She organized us into a game we called, "The Boys."

The players included my friend Betsy and me, along with little sister Ba and Ancy. Ancy was an imaginary friend of Ba's who had somehow become a real part of the family. Occasionally Daddy even invited Ancy to dinner. Mother put a plate on for her next to Ba, and we all talked with and to Ancy, just as if she were really there. She lived in a huge century plant at the end of the driveway.

Under Mare's direction, we played the role of "The Boys," secret spy agents for the U.S. Government. We played this game a lot, but I only remember one scenario. We were trapped on a tropical island loaded with palm trees, and had to survive on coconuts and bananas. We had a parrot that we kept trying to get back to our government, because he knew the enemy's secret code.

Unfortunately, the enemy soldiers captured and tortured us, trying to get the parrot. Finally, our leader, Mare, said bravely, "Well,

Boys, this is it. I guess we'll have to give them the bird!" At which command, we all stood bravely in a row and gave the imaginary enemy a huge raspberry. This act of heroism so astonished our captors that we took advantage of their temporary paralysis to run to the walnut tree, climb up it, and escape over the privy roof with the secret plans and the parrot still in our possession. General McArthur would have loved us.

In the bay, at the foot of the cliff, we always built rafts to "set out to sea." One day, Flo, certainly the bravest, looked over the cliff, and shouted, "The tide is in! And our raft is floating out to sea! We have to save it!"

Since I was the only one nearby, she grabbed my hand and dragged me to a torturous path leading down to the bay. This path was so dangerous we never *ever* used it. Flo started leaping down this rugged path, and since she just expected me to follow, I did. Running and jumping and sliding as fast as I could, I still fell behind my big sister. About three fourths of the way down, however, I began to catch up by slipping and taking a tumble. I somersaulted the rest of the way down, over rocks, on top of broken bottles, past pieces of broken lumber and twisted, rusted metal. When I finally came to a dust-filled stop at the bottom, my lower lip began to tremble as I reacted to all the scrapes and scratches I had accumulated on my flight. Flo caught my arm, jerked me up, and said, "You don't have time to cry! We have to save the raft!"

Well, put that way, I could see that we certainly did not have time to cry, and we certainly did have to save the raft! I ran after her as fast as my little six-year-old legs would carry me, without even

9

brushing myself off. We ran on to our little bay where we did most of our swimming, and sure enough, we saw our raft headed out to sea. Flo leaped in, and swam with all her might until she got close enough to grab a rope we had attached to the raft. Then she tugged and swam and tugged, and when close enough she threw the rope end to me to help her pull, and we returned the raft safely to shore. We regularly saved rafts during our time at the Little House, high on the cliff.

Daddy taught me how to swim in that bay when I was five. There was a big tin box, about five by five feet, around seven feet from the beach. One day, Daddy waded through the water and put me up on it, waded back to shore, and urged me to jump in and swim to him. And I did! I can still remember how proud he made me feel, and from that point on, I loved the water.

One time, I found him out in the back yard, digging a huge hole. Actually, it was going to be a cesspool, but what did I know? I was only six. I watched patiently for as long as a curious six-year-old could, until I finally gave in and asked him where he planned to go with his hole. He paused a moment, leaning on his shovel, and said, "I'm digging to China. It's on the opposite side of the world, and if you will just be patient, very soon you will see lots of Chinese!"

I stood over him for what seemed like hours, waiting and waiting for each shovel full of dirt he threw up to uncover lots of little Chinese people with pigtails and conical hats, which, thanks to Hollywood, was the way we pictured the Chinese in those days. No one appeared, and I finally gave up and went inside to get me a peanut butter and jelly sandwich.

Whenever we could get enough gasoline with our ration stamps, we went camping up the coast all the way to Monterey and Carmel. We stopped to picnic in the woods, and Daddy always looked around carefully and whispered, "Shh! Be quiet, or you'll scare away the elves!"

So all of us tiptoed around as quiet as mice, as Mother said, until Daddy suddenly pointed behind us and shouted, "Look! Did you see them?" We turned around as fast as we could, but the elves had always disappeared! Kids!

The army patrols were stepped up, and it was a short time later that we were told we had to move off the coast, *now*, away from our beautiful ocean.

Chapter 2

*♪ You're the only star in my blue heaven,
And you're shining just for me! ♫*

Mother and Daddy moved us to Hollywood where Daddy started a business he called the Trade Winds Trading Company, a tropical South Seas nautical shop on La Cienega Boulevard, right in the midst of all the movie stars.

He and Don Beachcomber met and had a little feud over the title of *Beachcomber*, but they finally resolved the problem when Don moved to Hawaii and they both remained *Beachcombers*. Daddy became the most famous actual beachcomber ever, on the west coast.

He also became known as a South Seas Island Trader. He acted as a broker for others who went to the South Seas and gathered shields, masks, beaded hula skirts, carved swords, shells, and lots more, and sent them back to the States. I got so excited whenever a big load arrived from Fiji or New Guinea or Tahiti. The interior of the boxes always smelled of exotic scents. I got to help unpack the huge wooden crates and bring up all the treasures from the packing stuff. What an exciting job! My imagination ran wild, especially when we unpacked a real shrunken head from New Guinea.

Sometimes, I went to the shop after school. While Mother and Daddy waited on customers and took care of business, I explored the treasures.

The first room had a nautical theme. Giant ships' wheels and fish floats of all sizes and colors, with and without nets, covered the room from floor to ceiling. One day, I hit one of those floats with a croquet ball and completely shattered it. I do not remember why I tried playing croquet inside, but that got me into just a little trouble!

The next room, my favorite, was the South Seas Island Room. We filled it with colorfully painted and hand carved masks and tikis, hula skirts, palm trees, grass huts and anything else that came from the islands. I loved to sit on a big tumbled pile of nets, smelling the wonderful odors of the South Seas imports scattered all around me, and do my arithmetic homework.

Well-known customers wandered in and out all the time. Our shoppers included Ronald Reagan, Jane Wyman, Tyrone Power, Clark Gable, Mickey Rooney, Vincent Price, and lots more of the old stars, which were new stars at that time. For years we treasured a guest book that Mother brought out occasionally, and we all oohed and ahhed at the names.

Some Saturday mornings, after we opened up the shop, Daddy and I left Mother there to take care of business while we went off to make a delivery or run some errands. We always ended up at a little chili joint operating out of an authentic old railroad car, with little booths along each side. We boarded it just like a real train. I had to reach up for the iron handles at the door and pull myself up the steep metal stairs. The chili came in big bowls, with lots of soda

Trade Winds Trading Company Chrismas card, 1944. On flat piece of driftwood; words written in small net mending string; anchovy net bow; real star fish upper right corner.

crackers and a big Coke. The café owner, like Daddy, came from Texas, and everyone, naturally, called him *Tex*. He always wore a huge dirty white apron and a chef's hat.

Each table had a miniature jukebox on it. Daddy always gave me a nickel and I slipped it in the little slot. Then came the best part, choosing the number I wanted from the songs listed on the pages. I always took my time and read the name of every tune as I flipped through the music menu by turning a knob at the top. Once I made my selection, I punched the corresponding buttons at the bottom of the miniature jukebox, and my tune began to play from the colorful big jukebox standing in the corner. Tex's jukebox played only Jimmy Rodgers, Sons of the Pioneers, Gene Autry, and all those good old cowboy tunes.

Decades later, when I moved to Texas, it took me a long time to figure out how I knew so many of those wonderful old western songs. They had burrowed down in my subconscious all those years.

Another shop, next door to Trade Winds Trading Company, belonged to Igor Stravinsky's second wife, Vera. She brought us hair ribbons and chocolate bon-bons. A warm, wonderful woman, her heavily accented voice simply wrapped us in love. Occasionally, Mr. Stravinsky, the famous composer and conductor, came by. When he talked, his long, flaying arms gestured excitedly and his long, white hair flew all over. I'd peek around a corner at him, awestruck.

Across the street, Elsa Lancaster ran the Turn About Theater. Each Saturday morning, children from all over Hollywood, sat in individual chairs, and when the puppet show began, we watched at one end of the theater. When it came to an end, Elsa came out from behind the puppet show sets and announced, "Now, everyone, stand up and stretch! Pick up your chair and turn it around to face the other way!"

As soon as everyone had changed around, we watched the show at the other end with a different scene. Ms. Lancaster was so funny, with her wild hair and wonderful humor. We adored her. Beginning in the 1930's, she played in lots of movies, including *That Darned Cat, Mary Poppins, Bell, Book and Candle,* and *Bride of Frankenstein.*

The war affected our lives in many odd ways. Rubber was a scarce commodity during those years. So much so, that not only did tires get rationed, but we never had enough elastic for our underpants. We all had to wear ones that buttoned, and woe unto anyone whose panties were just a smidgen too large. I had a girlfriend on the chubby side, and her panties always drooped down. Since her mother always put her in these short little dresses, we called her Droopy Drawers. She was certainly a good sport.

Before the war, chewing gum was made out of real rubber from trees in Central America. Because of the shortage of rubber and the demand for rubber tires in the military, scientists developed an artificial material to make gum out of. We were never allowed to chew gum in public. It was not nice for young ladies to do this. Whenever I was able to buy a pack, I had to chew it in my room!

The war also led to the invention of margarine, to replace butter. The new white substance came in a plastic bag with a little drop of coloring in the middle. I liked to take the bag and squeeze and squash it until the white margarine turned evenly yellow - just like real butter. We installed blackout curtains on our windows, and put black tape on the top half of the car headlights.

It seemed like everything was rationed, but gasoline and tire rationing hit us the hardest. How could we go beachcombing if we had no gasoline?

We walked a lot, and rode streetcars a lot, and saved up our gasoline coupons. And one fine morning daddy would say, "Boys! I think it is time for a beachcombing trip!" It wasn't possible to go very far, so we usually went up the coast to Carpentaria and Santa Barbara, where the beaches were still free and bon fires were possible.

One trip, we took my friend, Betsy, and we all climbed in on top of each other, in our little sedan. Just beyond Santa Monica, we had a flat. Daddy changed to the spare. A few miles more, we had another flat. He got out the repair kit, took the tire off, put a patch on it, pumped it up with one of those hand pumps, and we took off again. The next flat, we just took the tire off and limped into Carpentaria on the rim. There were three flats before we reached our destination! Tires were so hard to come by that not only us, but lots of folks ran on threadbare ones and kept their repair kits handy, along with a hand pump.

Carpentaria was always loaded with driftwood, so it made our work easier. In the summer, we slept out on the beach, under the stars, and in the winter, Daddy rented a little old store that sat right on the beach front, and we camped out in that. There was a paved circle at the end of the road to the beach, and Flo taught me how to ride a bicycle there. Once I got the hang of it, they couldn't stop me from riding around and around. One visit, we got a hotel room at the old two story wooden hotel a few blocks from the beach. Mother and I were in the room when the chandelier in the ceiling started swaying and jiggling. Ho hum! Just another California earthquake!

The family rented a big, old, rambling three-story house on a cul de sac called Vista Crest Drive in the Hollywood Hills, somewhere above the Hollywood Bowl. Once settled in, Ba and I were put into grade school, Mare in Jr. High, and Flo in Hollywood High School, where she immediately became an activist, starting drives for aluminum, and serving the servicemen coffee and donuts at the famous Stage Door Canteen. You know the song! *I left my heart at the Stage Door canteen!* Ba and I assisted the war effort with a school Victory Garden. Once a week, all the students lined up in straight lines, and walked a block down the street to the garden to pull weeds. I did not care much for that job. But, as the year wore on, we got to pick and eat two strawberries each. Then, pick some more for the cafeteria. I did not mind that at all. One bad boy cheated and ate as many as he could stuff down.

One time, he stole my books and I fought with him. He got a bloody nose and I got a black eye. I stood only somewhat repentant in front of Mother as she gave me a lecture on how to be nice and loving. This boy had already been to reformatory school, and his home life probably wasn't as happy as mine...so...wouldn't it be nice of me to try and make him feel like someone liked him. I did, and he and I became OK pals!

In sixth grade, I finally won the honor of tetherball champion. Some of my fingers to this day remain crooked from hitting that ball. My fingers swelled up and got black and blue, but I did not

There's nothing shiftless about Eli Hedley, yet his business depends on what the sea casts up

He Picks Up
a Living
ON THE
BEACH

by R. Wilson Brown

THE BEACHCOMBER, according to fiction writers, is a shiftless fellow who never knows where his next dollar is coming from. But Eli Hedley of The Beach, San Pedro, California, has upset the classical theory by operating a $50,000 annual business.

Just as it is for other beachcombers, the sea is his source. But from the flotsam and jetsam of the Pacific he fashions unique wares that are now handled by the super-swank Bullock's of Hollywood and many other big and little stores. In addition, he supplies special props to professional photographers, movie companies and interior decorators.

If you would do business with Eli, just drive out to Trade Winds Cove, three miles above San Pedro, and look down to the beach for his brilliant scarlet shirt. You'll probably find him appraising a prime stack of oyster-white driftwood, laid neatly on the sand.

He stops now and then as he ambles along, selecting small twisted pieces and casting them out of the larger piles. Later he will gather them in a wheelbarrow, take them to his shop which hugs the cliff ten feet above shore line, and in an hour will have them fastened together in a large frame, destined for a Fifth Avenue shop as a show-window centerpiece.

Eli is about 50, yet wiry and quick-moving. "Some of the furniture I have designed you might call modern," he says. "But the emphasis is on the natural qualities and conformation of the wood."

He points a lean brown finger. "See those saki bottles? Some of them were washed ashore by the Japan current. I score them with a saw about halfway down, and tap gently until top and bottom part. Then I plug the mouth with sealing wax, imbed it in a piece of old bleached cork, and the result—a goblet.

"Samuel Goldwyn, the movie

78

Coronet Magazine Article on Eli Hedley's beachcombing success

producer, ordered 550 sets of six of these saki goblets as Christmas presents for friends. I packed each set in old fish netting and enclosed them in boxes made of driftwood."

Eli makes more than 100 items, including driftwood ice buckets, boat-oar garden gates, ship's-wheel chandeliers and Japanese fish-float lamps. A salt-bleached water cask turns into a beautiful salad bowl in his competent hands; old strips of bamboo washed in from the South Seas become an attractive bar front, and worm-eaten wood from a wrecked ship is fashioned into jewel boxes that look as though they belonged to Captain Kidd.

His catalogue lists items from "Starfish, 75 cents to $1.50" to "Ship's-wheel table and two chairs, $285." The catalogue itself is something of a curiosity. Bound in what appears to be aged parchment, it has a bit of old fish net and a piece of driftwood attached to the binding.

HOW DID THIS UNIQUE business begin? In 1936, Hedley owned three grocery stores in an Oklahoma oil town. "Just got tired of the smell of crude oil and the taste of red dust," he says. So he sold the stores, loaded his car with the family and a trailer with his possessions and headed West.

Neither Hedley, his wife nor their three daughters had ever seen the sea before they reached California. But it fascinated them, so they moved into three old sheds on a cliff north of San Pedro, where sea, sun and wind are ever present.

Promptly the family decided to decorate the new home with driftwood, shells and rocks from the beach. The result was surprising. As new friends dropped in, they commented on the originality and good taste of the rooms. Eli was urged to market some of the items he had devised. Finally he agreed to tackle one of the most exclusive markets in the United States—Bullock's Wilshire department store on Los Angeles' "Miracle Mile."

When he entered the big store's carpeted office, his sneakers, corduroys and scarlet shirt seemed sadly out of place.

"What can I do for you?" asked the buyer in a patronizing tone.

Somehow Eli explained the reason for his visit.

"Hmm," was the answer. "And where are your samples?"

"I've got a trailer on the parking lot," Eli answered miserably.

When the buyer saw the trailer he turned to Eli and said, "Wait here a minute!" He returned quickly with the advertising manager and window decorator. After a quick conference they asked in chorus, "How much of this stuff can you bring us?"

They fired questions. Could Eli make a driftwood frame six by eight feet? He could. The advertising manager wanted to know his trade name.

"Eli Hedley, Beachcomber," he said simply.

"A natural," whispered the ad man almost reverently.

Eli left the load with Bullock's and went home. Three days later, when he returned, a crowd was standing before the shop windows. One of the Hedley daughters shouted, "Look, daddy, it's yours."

Eli Hedley, Beachcomber, was made, for the windows were filled

Coronet Magazine Article on Eli Hedley's beachcombing success

with his work—the largest display ever devoted to the products of a single company by Bullock's. Inside the store, orders were piling up. Eli, his wife and daughters have been busy ever since.

Today he works the beach from Oregon to Mexico. "The most beautiful and substantial driftwood comes from the Oregon coast," he says authoritatively. "It is carried down the river by the current; out to sea by the tide. There it is seasoned and saturated by the sea's brine until it is finally washed ashore. After some weeks of bleaching sunshine, it is ready for collection."

On a business trip Eli attaches a trailer to his car and follows the coastal highway north. When the family spots a likely beach, they pull off the road and explore.

On a typical trip they gather a railroad carload of material on which to work. Eli has plotted the best beaches for particular species of shells and coral. He knows that certain parts of the Oregon coast will furnish specific types of fine driftwood, and that on others the Japan current will bring varicol-

ored glass globes from Japanese fishing nets to shore. He even thinks he has the location of a sunken Jap submarine spotted—just a stone's throw from his house.

His list of regular customers looks like a seating arrangement for an Academy Award dinner. For Deanna Durbin he made all the furniture and fixtures for a 16th-century French wine cellar. For Myrna Loy he makes lamps. Twice an attractive young woman came to him for items, signing her checks Ingrid Lindstrom. It wasn't until her third visit that he realized his customer was Ingrid Bergman.

Eli has furnished many Hollywood night spots with decorative material, and does a thriving business with movie studios, to which he sells or rents props representing old ships, water-front cafés, tropical dives and other "atmosphere" spots.

Eli now runs both a wholesale and retail business. Besides himself and family, he employs three regular helpers and three part-time. All of them, like Eli, marvel at the way in which the sea can be an endless source of profit, provided you know how to work its wares.

Try This One

If you want to avert the paralyzing shock of ducking into cold sea water, first douse the back of your neck and then both your wrists before taking the plunge.

If you hold a pin or a needle in your mouth while peeling onions, you won't shed tears.—From *Thoughts While Shaving* by NEAL O'HARA, published by WAVERLY HOUSE

Coronet Magazine Article on Eli Hedley's beachcombing success

care about the pain; I was tetherball champ! Those fingers became my badges of honor, just like the broken noses and cauliflower ears of old boxers.

Mother used to wash my hair every Saturday. She undid the long braids that hung down my back, and carefully brushed out all the tangles. Then, she prepared a big pan of warm water and a bar of soap. We had no such things as shampoo in those days. After washing and rinsing, out came the bottle of vinegar. She gently poured vinegar and water over my head for the final rinse, and the vinegar cut through all the left-over soap, and made my hair all shiny and squeaky when I ran my fingers down the strands. Every time I open a bottle of vinegar today, the sharp scent sends me drifting back to the way my hair smelled after a washing by Mother.

One day I came home from school to find her ironing with the radio on. I did not really pay much attention to what she was doing, but the next thing I knew, she was crying. She just kept on ironing and crying. "What's wrong, Mama?" I asked.

"Oh, Bungy, dear. President Roosevelt has died."

Franklin D. Roosevelt was one of Mother's heroes. She admired what he had accomplished by bringing the country out of the Great Depression with projects like the WPA (Works Projects Administration). The WPA put unemployed men to work constructing public buildings all over the country. The government paid them, and people had food on their tables again. The WPA men built my high school and junior high school in San Pedro. The beautiful structures still stand today. They built libraries, schools, government buildings and much more, all over the United States. The structures are all such wonderful 1930s and 1940s period pieces.

Roosevelt also started the CCC Camps (Civilian Conservation Corps), where young men went out into the wilds of America to work on roads and facilities for our national park system. They completed many, many great projects during this era, including the famous old hotel at Yellowstone National Park. Roosevelt had also been bravely leading us through the Second World War, and for these reasons Mother cried when she heard he had died.

Another of Mother's heroes was Abraham Lincoln. She thought he set a wonderful example for anyone to follow. We always had a picture of him hanging on the wall somewhere in our home. Her love of that great president may explain why I can still repeat almost all of his Gettysburg Address.

Mother and Daddy had done a good job teaching we girls to work hard for everything we had. They also taught us gratefulness to God for his provision for us. This attitude came as naturally to me as breathing.

From the beginning, my parents always taught me that God was my loving Father, right there with me all the time. He was like a wonderful friend that I could always trust to get me out of any trouble. That feeling gave me such freedom and I feel for others who have not had this freedom in their lives.

When I had the mumps as a child, my mother cradled me gently in her arms and assured me of God's presence and explained how that meant there could be no unhappiness in his creation. She tucked me into bed, and together we sang a couple of hymns. The next morning, I was feeling just fine and put on my favorite red polka dot dress, to get myself ready for school. When Mother saw me, she put her arms around me, and said, "Oh, dear, you can't go to school today, your cheeks are still all puffed up!" In such a loving way, Mother taught me how God cared for me, and He did! The next day I returned to school completely well.

We kids went to the Christian Science Sunday school in Studio City. The church and Sunday school both met in a great big room above a candy store. We hiked from our house down a long, steep road that led up to the homes high above us, to the streetcar stop. We rode it all the way over the pass, and out into the San Fernando Valley. For the journey, Daddy gave us twenty cents each. Five cents for the trolley and ten cents for the collection. I always used the extra five cents for a package of Walnettos from the store. Those squares of chewy caramels lasted longer than any other candy, so I figured they gave me the best bargain for my money.

Mother and Daddy drove the car over later, and we girls enjoyed our candy while they attended church.

Lots of actors attended that church. Kenny Baker, the first tenor on *The Jack Benny Show* and star of the 1938 *Goldwin Follies* movie with Adolph Menjou, was our soloist. Gene Autry's wife also attended and the Autrys invited everyone out to their ranch several times for barbeque.

Dick Elliot, who played the mayor on TV's Andy Griffith show, and many other character roles, taught Ba's class. We all looked forward to his arrival because we expected him to do something funny for us, and he never failed.

In he came, with his overcoat on. He looked all around at us, took his coat slowly off, and without looking, hung it up on the wall where there was no hook, and just walked away. We roared with laughter as the coat slipped to the floor, Mr. Elliot acting as if nothing had happened. Then he did a double-take at the fallen coat and got another round of laughter.

Sometimes he asked, "Who's your best friend?"

I'd answer with something like, "Mary Smith."

"Mary Smith!" he cried, as if Mary were also his dearest friend, too.

Then he brusquely said, "Never heard of her," and that set us off again.

Daddy served as an usher and Mother was one of the Readers.

In the summer, Daddy wore a white suit and white shoes. During the winter, he wore a black suit with black shoes. Daddy made me a real shoeshine kit because I loved to shine all of our shoes on Saturday night, so they all looked bright and shiny on Sunday. Churchgoers dressed pretty formally in those days.

All our neighbors in our cul-de-sac had connections to the entertainment world somehow. The Haven Macquarries lived right next door. He starred on the radio show *Noah Webster Says.* Whenever we ran short of cash, Mother went on the show and won fifty dollars by getting the definitions correct to all the words they had asked her about. Mother was very smart. She had taught school in the oil fields of Oklahoma before she married Daddy.

Across the street from our house lived Bugsey Siegel, the famous mobster who started Las Vegas. Of course, we had no idea who he was at first. On Halloween, when we kids went trick or treating, his girlfriend, Virginia Hill, invited us in to enjoy their big party. We all bobbed for apples, and they gave us piles of candy. As we left, she gave each of us one of her old teddy bears that she had as a child. She cried so much when she did it, I felt embarrassed for her. The question to myself was, why did she give them to us if they meant so much to her?

A little while later, Bugsey made all the papers by being killed in a gangland shooting. That was when we realized just who our neighbor was.

Next door to Bugsey, one of the Warner brothers, of movie studio fame, lived with his family. One day, all the kids on this street were playing hide-and-go-seek. Mrs. Warner asked if I would watch her little two-year-old boy. She offered to give me a dime for the job. All of eight at the time, I thought I had gotten a great deal. For a dime, I could get two packages of Walnettos, and two packages lasted practically forever. So, off the toddler and I went to join the hide-and-go-seekers. Pretty soon, I got involved in the game and lost track of the little boy.

"Where's the baby?" I called, "Has anyone seen the baby?"

No one had seen him. Desperately, we all started looking and calling for him. "Baby! Baby! Where are you?"

Before long, Mrs. Warner came home, and really laid into me about having lost her son. I started crying, since I felt really bad about having lost him. After a bit, thank goodness, he wandered around the corner from wherever he had slipped off to.

Our neighbor, Mrs. Macquarrie, came out to find out what had caused all the excitement. When she found out why I was getting bawled out, she tied into Mrs. Warner and stuck up for me. "What were you thinking, to leave a two-year-old with another child?" she asked. "And for a measly dime, too!" I felt much better after that.

That ended my career of baby-sitting in one fell swoop. No, wait! Another time, when I was sixteen, a friend with a baby-sitting job asked me to sub for her. Everything went well except that after the two little children fell asleep, so did I. The parents returned and the father pounded and pounded on the door to get me awake. They had forgotten their key. He finally had to climb through a window to get in and then had to shake and shake me to get me to wake up. I decided to find easier ways to get Walnettos.

A few blocks away from us, in the woods, sat this fascinatingly deserted house that we kids decided to visit. The house had a Spanish tiled roof, with a gorgeous swimming pool, much like the mansion in the movie *Sunset Boulevard*. The place was really quiet, and we had lots of fun exploring and scaring each other until one day a car drove down the road and the owner caught us. Apparently the house was not deserted after all. The owner was simply very reclusive. We all ran into the woods, yelling and screaming. We hacked our way through poison oak and other undergrowth, until we finally got home, hearts pounding and gasping for breath. At supper, that evening, when asked what we had done that day, we all said, "Oh! Nothing," with our most nonchalant attitude.

27

About six blocks away, stood what we called, "The Castle." The actor Douglas Fairbanks, Jr. had started building this magnificent stone structure, with great rock fireplaces, sitting high on a cliff above Hollywood. It had no roof, since construction had stopped long before completion. It was just a shell. We enjoyed climbing on top of the foot-thick stone inner walls and walking on them. Soon, of course, we graduated to running on them. They loomed probably ten feet off the ground, but after a while, that got kind of tame, so we tried the much higher outer walls.

The wall along the cliff probably dropped off fifty feet or more and gave me my biggest challenge. The very first time I tried it, my heart pounded in my chest, but I had to do it. All the other kids had been brave enough to do it. I never considered the fact that I was only nine or ten at the time and all the other kids were at least five years older than I. Slowly, slowly, step-by-step, I walked out. I carefully made my way to the middle, and then I froze. I could not make my feet move at all.

Flo Ann started yelling, "You can do it! Don't look down!"

And after taking a couple of deep breaths, I did do it, and felt really proud of myself. Before long, I had grown quite proficient at running along that monster wall. One day Daddy found out how we were spending our time. That stopped our castle excursions.

Our family had planned all along, to move back to the ocean when the war ended. With the war over in Europe and coming to an end in the Pacific, we gave up that house because the owners wanted another year's lease on it, and we knew we just couldn't stand to be land-locked anymore than was necessary. Our parents hunted all over Hollywood for another place to live, but the war had caused a serious housing shortage. The only thing they found was a great big store, its front right on Fairfax Avenue, a block from Santa Monica Blvd. We stacked all our furniture up to the ceiling to make walls for our different rooms. My room faced the big display window in front, where all the cars went by. By this time, I had grown so homesick for the ocean that I pretended the cars passing by at night were waves crashing on the beach. The soft shushing sound helped me go to sleep.

Next door to our abode lived an elderly woman we called Miss Elsie. She baked delicious tarts and pastries for the famous Farmer's Market. Like us, she lived in a store. She had her living quarters in the back, with the bakery in the front, with huge ovens and great steaming pots of blackberries, peaches, and apples cooking on her big commercial stove.

The wonderful scents coming from her place just drove me crazy, so I spent most of my spare time hovering around Miss Elsie. She gave me a dime or a quarter each time I helped her. I had to stand on a stool and stir and stir the fruit while she poured in lots of sugar. I loved watching all that sugar slide into the pot. It seemed so wickedly extravagant. Remember, because of the war and sugar rationing, ordinary families like mine did not get very much at any time. Not only did I earn money at Miss Elsie's, I also got to eat the broken tarts. She never realized I would have worked for those alone.

The day came when I finally earned enough to get me a twelve dollar pair of black and white cowboy boots I had longed for. I wore them everywhere, convinced I looked like a genuine cowgirl. The only place I could not wear them was to school because boots violated the dress code. I managed to break that code anyway, and got sent home for it when Daddy brought me home a pair of genuine, authentic, for real, Indian moccasins complete with turquoise beads and fringe. They were so beautiful that I could not resist wearing them to school. The next morning, my gorgeous moccasins and I quickly ended up in the principal's office, and my mother had to bring me a regular pair of shoes. Schools had pretty strict dress codes at that time. In fact, girls had to wear dresses all the time!

World War II was over! You could feel the future gathering momentum. I felt like I had been stuck in Hollywood long enough, and when Daddy told us he had acquired a ninety-nine year lease on a piece of paradise, right on the ocean in our old stomping grounds of San Pedro, I leaped for joy. In fact, we all leaped for joy!

We began driving over an hour on weekends and holidays, all the way from Hollywood. There were no freeways, and we soon learned the smaller roads with less traffic. Mother and Daddy were busy closing down the Trade Winds Trading Company, and Ba and I continued to go to school in Hollywood, until they hired a nice gentleman, named Henry, as a chauffer. He arrived every morning to pick us up, and off we went from Hollywood down to San Pedro and PT Fermin Elementary. Within minutes, Henry lit up one of his foul smelling stogies. Without air conditioning in the car, (not many had AC at that time) Ba and I had to stick our heads out the window, trying not to get sick. We arrived at school with our little stomachs churning and our faces green. We just about recovered by the time school ended, but then, we had another hour of Henry's cigar on the ride back. That ride home seemed even worse because the afternoon heat made the smell ferment into something truly awful. Ba and I were delighted when the family finally had enough going at the Cove that we moved in permanently and got to stay put in San Pedro, eliminating the daily ride with Henry and his cigars.

Chapter 3

♪ Heaven! I'm in heaven!
And my heart beats so that I can hardly see! ♫

What a magical place, with 2,000 feet of waterfront, right on the Pacific Ocean, just up the coast from San Pedro. This was a land grant that Pio Pico, an early governor of California, passed on from the King of Spain, to brothers, Juan and Jose Loreto Sepulveda, in the early 1800s. In the 1920s, Ramon and Louis Sepulveda, the remaining landowners, turned this choice piece of coastal land into the exclusive Royal Palms Country Club.

High on the cliff above The Cove, the country club proper was a big rambling white structure with an indoor swimming pool and dance floor. Outside, tennis courts were surrounded by palms.

Down below the cliff, they planted rows of stately date and fan palms, with a few royal palms scattered here and there, right smack dab on the shore of the beautiful Pacific Ocean.

We all pitched in to help Daddy build our house from materials found on the beach. At the end of a hard day's work, we climbed into sleeping bags in front of a crackling, colorful fire. We watched the stars twinkle through the swaying palm fronds above, as the moon rose over the cliff, pouring its light all over the ocean. We fell asleep to the sound of the waves crashing against the rocks on the beach.

Trade Winds Cove was heaven on earth! No other family in the whole wide world had ever lived in a place like it. Just a few miles from the booming city of Hollywood, we experienced life as it might have been had we lived on a beautiful tropical island.

Huge wooden gates formed the main entrance. A dirt road led to another gate that Daddy had made of ten-foot-long boat oars. This opened onto a huge oval Dance Floor with an island in the middle, that held a couple of tall, slender royal palms which seemed to be always swaying to the music of wind and sea. Italian artisans had been imported to lay out this light blue and white flecked terrazzo floor.

Trade Winds Cove with Royal Palms Country Club on top of cliff.

Water color of Hedley home at Trade Winds Cove, San Pedro, California, by John Fishersmith.

Hedley home, photo taken from beach in front of house.

Against the backdrop of the cliff, sat a spacious flagstoned patio surrounded by rock benches. We called this area the Living Room. A stone fireplace so huge we could bend over and walk right into it, formed the focal point. Big rocks polished smooth and round by centuries of waves made the chimney, rising thirty feet or more up the cliff. Graceful palms lined this patio, and that is why we called it the Living Room.

From this terrace, four long steps flowed down onto the Dance Floor. A little bridge provided a view right up to the cliff where great vines of *coppa de oro* dripped down a bigger rock bridge higher up. The huge, yellow "cup of gold" flowers poured their scent all over The Cove, making warm moonlit nights on the California coast smell like the lush and steamy tropics.

Across the bridge, there ran a long swath of pink concrete, about the length of a city block, leading up to our house. Palm trees lined the way. Date palms provided a secluded place for owls to nest and send out their mysterious *whoo whoos* at night. Shorter fan palms, which Daddy used in his decorating, filled spaces in between. Four royal palms stood among them all like stately soldiers.

A vast stone barbecue pit stood against the sea wall, along with a massive commercial sink. It was placed so we looked out over the ocean while washing dishes or cleaning abalone.

From here, we leaned over the rocky beach from a little ledge, where we would eat big juicy slices of watermelon, and have seed spitting contests with the guests, who'd never even heard of a seed spitting contest. If it were a really high tide, we would see who could reach the waves with their seeds!

36

A second giant rock fireplace leaned against the cliff in another little place down the way. We called this the Dining Room.

With only a tiny one-room house on the property when we took it over, we had to build our own home. We used the little house as a starter and just kept adding on around it. It stood at the very western end of the property, on a point, where the view seemed to stretch to forever.

Most of the lumber we needed came from the ocean. As far as I can recall, Daddy had to buy only shingles for the roof. About two miles up the beach, the ocean currents ran right into a little cove. 8x10 planks, 2x4s, and other lumber of all shapes and sizes, lost overboard in the winter storms from the lumber schooners that plied between the Los Angeles Harbor and the great forests of Washington and Oregon, washed into that cove regularly.

When Daddy wanted to create another room, he called, "OK, Boys, I need some more lumber!"

Now, four girls made up our family, Flo, Mare, Ba and me. But, he always called us Boys.

Once we got the command, off we went, under Flo's direction, with hammer, nails and rope. We hiked up to the Lumber Cove, and dragged, carried, or end-over-ended whatever good boards, studs, and planks we found, into a pile right beside the sea.

Large, sharp rocks make up the beach along this whole coast, so our lumber gathering was not a nice little sandy beach project. We worked on wet, rough, and uneven surfaces with medium waves breaking constantly on the shore, drenching us with their salty spray, and knocking us down frequently.

Once we gathered the wood together, we started constructing a raft with the rope and nails. Much too heavy to carry, the raft had to be built in the water. Somehow, despite the waves moving the lumber and knocking us down, we fastened it all together and launched out to sea. Each of us grabbed a piece of wood to use as a paddle before shoving off. As we leaped aboard, Flo yelled, "Paddle!"

Using our brawn and the ocean currents, we maneuvered the raft with its load of lumber through the waves, out onto the smoother ocean, and on down the coast, just off the house. We sat there, waiting, silent, our makeshift paddles poised in readiness, waiting for Flo to judge the perfect wave.

As it swept in toward the shore, she yelled, once more, even louder, "Paddle!"

We all paddled furiously, digging our boards deep into the sea, until the raft caught the wave, rose up and surfed toward the rocks ahead. With perfect timing, she shouted, "Jump!" and like rats leaving a sinking ship, we all jumped clear. The wave carried the raft onto the beach, where it broke up and Daddy collected the assorted pieces he needed to build another room onto our house.

Daddy built our home without a square, and without a level, and without a yard stick. He used rule of thumb, measuring by eyeballing it, or using the distance from nose to end of arm. Flo swears he did measure by a tape measure and a square, but I never saw him do it, and whenever I wanted to measure something, I could never find a square, or even a yardstick, in the shop. To this day, I can measure fairly accurately by rule of nose to thumb.

Daddy coming out of front door row boat.

His design started out one way, but in the protracted process of construction, it turned all topsy-turvy. The whole house backed up against the 250-foot cliff, right down to the beach facing the Pacific.

Our front door, set into a rowboat standing on end, had some windows on the top half, but a flat solid piece of wood formed the bottom half. Periodically, Mare, one of the artists in the family, painted a different Renoir or a Da Vinci on that lower half, so we all got to know what a great old master's painting looked like, without even going to an art gallery! Guests invariably stopped and admired the painting *du jour* before coming in. Mare also painted Gauguin Tahitians all over some outbuildings.

An old zither, that everyone loved to strum, was our doorbell. Some of the more musically talented even picked out a tune while waiting for one of us to answer the door.

One day, when the zither "rang," Mare opened the door to find the famous actor, Jimmy Stewart, and his wife, standing on the doorstep. They had come to beachcomb and order some items out of Daddy's catalog. They stood there admiring our front fence, made from an old hawser rope, strung around our front yard in great loops. Later, Daddy got really fancy by making a fence out of a pile of used longboat oars he had found somewhere. He crisscrossed these around the yard. They looked mighty pretty and I used to dream about being a swashbuckling pirate, one of the oarsmen of a longboat, rowing out from a harbor to capture and board an old sailing ship, and sailing off to the Seven Seas, a cutlass held firmly between my teeth.

The front entrance hall was flagstone with large, flat rocks we'd hauled in from the beach. Some of them even had fossils.

The living room and dining room made up the second floor, with a three-sided fireplace in between. The living room had big windows along two sides, with a breathtaking view of the blue, sparkling, Pacific. There was a red stained glass window and looking through it made the whole world outside magical. I had an instant sunset any time of day.

In 1947, Chuck Yeagar broke the sound barrier in an X-1 Rocket plane. Now, this was a brand new thing to happen, and jets would fly over, and a few seconds later, a big boom would make you jump out of your skin. The Air Force had just been made into its own separate service, but the Army was still doing a lot of the flying. So, when a jet flew over The Cove and broke the sound barrier, and the boom shattered our beautiful bay window, Daddy had to go down to the commanding officer at Fort MacArthur, and get them to repair it. This happened twice, and then, I think the laws were made where they couldn't do that in populated areas anymore. 1947 was also the year that sugar rationing finally bit the dust. We were back with sugar in our kitchen cabinet once more, and I got to eat sugar and butter sandwiches again.

On a coffee table sat a huge old leather-bound copy of Samuel Taylor Coldridge's *The Rhyme of the Ancient Mariner,* with illustrations by Gustav Dore. The pictures were in color, both beautiful and mysterious. *Water, water everywhere, and all the boards did shrink. Water, water everywhere nor any drop to drink.*

On another table sat a first edition copy of *Madeline*, the story of that famous little French girl who got into so much trouble. It was given to us by the author, who visited frequently. He signed it, "To the Hedley Children, Love, Ludwig Bemelmans." One day, while we were all sitting around talking, he pulled his pen from his pocket, took up a pretty piece of driftwood that was on the table in front of him, and proceeded to draw a pen and ink sketch of a woman's head with her hair blowing in the breeze. What a treasure that was, until a friend without her glasses, decided the drawing was some dirt, and cleaned it off!

One evening, some guests had just departed, reluctantly. We were always having guests who reluctantly departed, the Cove was such a relaxing influence! Before going to bed, I went up to the living room to blow out the candles and turn off the lights. Outside the darkened room, the full moon was floating high overhead, flooding the whole ocean with its light. The night was as bright as day, only softer. The old console radio was still on. The classical station, KFAC, was playing Tchaikowsky's Concerto in D major Op. 35 for Violin and Orchestra. I just stood there, and let all that beauty flow over me. That night is still with me today.

The fireplace was constructed from the rocks that we gathered from right in front of the house, on our beach. We selected the rocks carefully and made sure we got only the ones with lots of holes in them, to prevent them from exploding when they got hot. We failed to achieve total success in this endeavor. Many times over the years, with a beautiful fire roaring away, a loud pop sent pieces of rock flying out from the fireplace. My family, of course, always took this in stride, but guests, of whom we always seemed to have plenty, got unusually excited when it happened.

A huge ship's funnel served as the chimney. From time to time, after our visitors seated themselves comfortably in the living room having a nice conversation, enjoying a cup of coffee, the wind would shift. The smoke would start blowing right down the funnel, filling the living room. Mother always held out as long as possible, acting the part of the gracious hostess and pretending nothing was happening. But, even she finally had to give in to the acrid smoke.

"Oh, I have a wonderful idea!" she'd say, without acknowledging the coughing and the watering eyes of her guests. "Put on your coats and let's go outside and watch the moon come up over the cliff!"

As soon as Mother herded the guests outside and admiring comments flowed about the beauty of the moon reflecting on the water, Daddy quietly ordered me to "Quick, jump on the roof and turn the dang funnel around!"

I would race out the door and up a winding path behind the house, climb through a bunch of ice plant, scramble onto the roof, creep up the shingles to the massive funnel, put my arms around it as far as possible, and tug it around so that the wind once more came in from behind it. I cannot remember how many times this happened, but it was a lot. The strange thing about it was that I never thought it strange! I think that I just assumed that everyone lived the way we did, and that all chimneys needed frequent turning.

Our furnishings came from various sources, including the beach. We had some 1940s Hawaiian-style rattan furniture, a couple of leather and palm chairs from Mexico, and an authentic love seat, impossible to use. It curved like an S so one person sat on one side and the other sat on the opposite side. Supposedly it provided a safe place for two lovers to sit and carry on a conversation without needing a chaperone. It was very uncomfortable, but it was a good conversation piece.

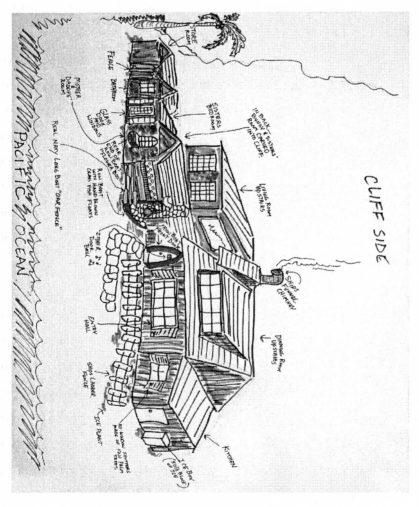

Layout of house, by Ballan Keen.

Daddy had thrown together coffee tables from jetsam he picked up on the beach, and made a desk out of a huge whiskey barrel where I did my homework. He cut the barrel in half length-wise and hinged it with old, graying rope. The top closed over the bottom. Little shelves and cubbyholes built into the top held my pencils and papers, and he fitted the bottom with a smooth sheet of wood for the working surface. This was stained dark brown with a high polish.

He made one of the lamps from pieces of bamboo all fitted together in a circle. The lamp I liked the most was a five-gallon water jug with a whole seascape inside. It had an island with a lighthouse on it. In the water were two ships and a ship's buoy that also had a light. At the top of the bottle was a regular light bulb and lampshade. When you turned on the switch, all the lights worked. Alfred Stave, an old German seafarer, who had sailed before the mast around The Horn, and told stories of being shipwrecked in the cold North Seas, had made this and many more "ships in bottles" that Daddy sold from his catalog.

In 1950, a friend gave us a brand new television set, which we put in a corner of the living room. We lugged a great huge antenna up a path to the top of the cliff, planted the pole firmly in the ground, attached one end of a coil of wire to the antenna and threw the rest of the coil over the cliff. We scrambled back down, found the coil in the bushes, and proceeded to lead it up through a window of the living room. We hooked it up with the television, and lo and behold, we could see a picture!

One day, after school, while I still had on a white blouse and a skirt, I decided to heat up a bowl of chili and beans, take it up to

45

the living room, and watch television. As I was engrossed in food and TV, a car horn sounded. I looked out from one of the big bay windows. This gorgeous guy that I had met along the docks, who lived on a scrumptious powerboat, was climbing out of his brand new black MG! Oh! Joy! I had tried all my wiles on him, and they must have worked, because here he was, calling on me!

I set my chili bowl down, opened the door, and was my most gracious self. "Please, come in!" We went up to the living room and talked for about a half hour. He then said he thought he ought to be going. I saw him off and was just wondering why he hadn't asked me out, when I glanced down, and there, right in the middle of my chest, on my beautiful white blouse, sat a single chili bean! And I thought I was being so perfect! Oh, Well! He was what is called "a stink potter," and I was what is called "a rag sailor," and never the twain should meet.

We always seemed to have guests for tea, which Mother did exceptionally well. One day, the zither rang, and there was the actor, Gary Cooper, wanting to order some items from Daddy's Catalog. He and Daddy strolled out to the beach and up to the shop, with both of them gesticulating here and there. Pretty soon, I saw them both with their pants legs rolled up, searching the tide pools.

Mother said to Flo, "We'd better get tea going, I think Mr. Cooper is staying longer than he thought he would."

Pretty soon, she went out to the edge of the beach and yelled, "Yoo Hoo! It's time for tea!"

They came in and went up to the living room, both of them barefoot and rather wet from the tide pools. Downstairs in the kitchen, Mother and Flo put the finishing touches on the prepared tea and, with one on each side of the big silver tea tray, proceeded to carry it up the steep stairs. The tray was loaded with the gleaming silver service, delicate china cups, cream pitcher, sugar bowl, and platters of cookies, cakes, and tiny elegant sandwiches.

Suddenly, the tray began to totter, they both backed down a step and bumped into each other. Within seconds, a huge resounding crash filled the hall, as all the silver, china, and food clattered to the stone floor of the entry hall. China shattered. Silver pieces bounced across the hall, the lid of the teapot spun noisily on the stone floor, until it finally slowed and stopped. Mother and Flo stood poised on the stairs, looking at each other in that awful silence that followed.

Daddy said later, that Mr. Cooper never gave the slightest indication of having heard anything untoward! He just kept on talking. So, of course, Daddy did, too. Hearing nothing from the living room, Mother and Flo rushed to the kitchen and rebuilt the whole tea in nothing flat. Then, they floated gracefully up the stairs, and Mother proceeded to serve tea to us all. No one ever mentioned or questioned the catastrophe. It was all quite civilized!

We had lots of guests who would say, the minute they got out of their cars, "I can only stay a few minutes. I just want to order some items from your catalog." Daddy always got them searching the tide pools for shells, and the beaches for their own creations. Then, Mother would look at them on the beach, and tell us to set another place for supper, and the "shopper" sometimes ended up staying for two or three days, or longer.

Our home looked large from the outside, but had limited rooms on the inside, so when we had an over-night guest, they were given the master bedroom. Mother and Daddy moved down the hall to Mare and Flo's room. They moved to Ba's and my bunks. Ba moved up to the living room couch, and I took my sleeping bag outside by the ocean!

We finally built a thatched guest house with big wooden shutters that swung open to catch the fresh sea breezes. Being thatched by us, it proved useless for guests when it rained. When we had no visitors, Mare took it over and turned it into her art studio. She often painted from ten o'clock at night to four o'clock in the morning. In other words, she was going to bed, as I was getting up!

Back to the inside of the house. To get to the other side of the fireplace from the living room, we went down two steps to the dining room. Our dining room hung like a balcony over the entry hall. A weathered wooden plank formed a rail along the edge. Originally, Daddy intended the hall to be the kitchen. Instead, it ran beside the kitchen that was originally supposed to be a laundry room. Somehow, in the process of building the house, Daddy's plans changed. After all, he didn't know quite what kind of lumber he was getting each time he "ordered."

Daddy built our massive table out of twelve-foot long planks that had washed up in our favorite lumber cove up the beach. Two huge anchors Daddy had found at the marine salvage store, one of his favorite haunts, formed the feet at each end. The points of the anchors stuck out a bit and guests always tripped over them as they made their way around the table. As they stumbled, they reached desperately for the edge of the table to try to keep from falling flat on their faces. They were just like a slapstick comedy! Meanwhile, because Mother had raised us right, we politely pretended that we had not seen their "act," and tried our hardest not to laugh.

Our chairs were well-polished barrels, with every other stave missing, forming the seats, and the backs were small ships wheels. The chairs weighed about fifty pounds each, and we children got tickled when a charming male guest asked to seat us. "Why, Yes, thank you," we replied, looking up at them with innocent smiles. Then, when they attempted to move the chairs, we bent over laughing so hard tears spilled down our cheeks. Most of the time the fellows responded like good sports about looking like the ninety-eight-pound weakling.

We drank our milk out of goblets that Daddy made from tops he had cut off of wine and saki bottles, turned upside down into corks, and sealed with sealing wax. The saki bottles from Japan had the prettiest colors when you held them up to the candles at night. Abalone shells, the holes filled up with sealing wax, were our bowls for soup. Daddy carved polished pieces of driftwood into unusual serving spoons.

One day, Daddy got a huge ship's wheel and fixed it to hang horizontally from a pulley, with a rope that secured it down in the entry hall and up by the table. He had the whole contraption rigged to come up through the space in front of the balcony. When we were ready to serve tea or set the table, we loaded all the dinnerware on and hand-over-handed the rope until the wheel reached the level of the table, where we tied it off. Then we ran up the stairs and unloaded. Then we lowered the wheel again, and dashed back downstairs, loaded it with the food, and hauled it up to the table once more.

We thought that set-up quite modern, compared to the days "before the ship's wheel," when we had to run up and down and down and up the stairs from kitchen to dining room with our arms full of crockery and food.

We put the new system to the test when Flo, taking a French course in college, decided one day to cook an authentic French meal.

"Everyone gather for dinner at seven sharp!" she commanded.

Well, that sounded good, so at seven sharp, we all settled around the table.

Daddy lowered the smaller ship's wheel candelabra he had installed on another pulley above the table, and lit the candles. We waited in hungry anticipation. Delicious aromas and the sound of pots and pans were heard behind the closed kitchen door. After a while conversation waned. The candles burned down considerably.

Of course, the Hedleys never showed up "sharp" for anything. A huge old grandfather clock Mother and Daddy had somehow hauled with them from Oklahoma kept the time in our house. That clock sometimes struck up to eighteen times without warning. And occasionally, it never struck the hour at all. None of us ever owned a watch. I read in a Girl Scout Manual how to tell time by standing a stick up on the ground and looking at the shadow it cast, as if it were the hour hand on a clock. You had to be facing north in order to get a true reading. Hey! That was good enough for me, as long as I was called for meals!

In about an hour, up came the first course, homemade onion soup. Getting the big, steaming bowl up to the table on the ship's wheel dumbwaiter proved a bit tricky, but it arrived without too much spillage. That soup may have been delicious in its own right, but by that time we had all grown so hungry, toasted cardboard would have seemed scrumptious.

A half hour later a fish course came up on the ship's wheel. And a half hour after that, yet another course came. We finished eating some time after eleven.

Every once in a while over the years, Flo mused aloud, "You know, I really would like to make another authentic French meal for dinner again." The entire family mumbled something non-committal in return and ducked out the door before she could pin us down to an official date.

When Mother and Daddy went out for the evening, Mare usually took over the cooking chores for the four of us girls. She loved doing pork chops with mashed potatoes and fresh sweet peas or green beans. Ba and I set the table nicely and lit the candles. Then Mare brought the food up in lovely bowls and platters. She always included a plate of fresh cut carrot and celery sticks.

We solemnly took our places, properly put our napkins in our laps and passed the bowls around the table, filling our plates with the delicious food. Then the trouble started. Flo inserted the carrots and celery in her ears and up her nose!

"Stop that, Flo!" Mare would shout, furious with her for ruining her perfect presentation, while Ba and I laughed until our sides hurt.

Mother made us set a complete table almost every night, to teach us proper manners. So, up on the ship's wheel came salad plates, bread and butter plates, two glasses (for water and milk), and all the silver needed to accompany that setting. After a dinner of potato soup and biscuits, which we often had when we lacked money, it all got lowered down to the kitchen again. Of course, Mother's system of etiquette education worked, and all of us grew up knowing proper behavior in all social situations. But who uses "proper" nowadays?

Sr. Ramon Bascon De Asumende, who came to visit for the day and stayed a year, was a tall, handsome Basque from the Pyrenees, in Spain. He had a head of gorgeous white hair, and a white flowing mustachio. He took me under his wing, and at night, after we had cleared the dining room table, started helping me with my Spanish homework. Of course, since he was from Spain, he taught me to use the Castilian accent which is full of th's instead of s's. But my teacher at school had learned her Spanish in Mexico, and I had to speak it that way for her. It was a bit confusing.

Many a night, after supper and homework, he and I got out the playing cards and a box of kitchen matches and played poker. He swore he had broken the bank at Monte Carlo when he was young, and so would teach me how to win! We always played by candlelight, and it took me many years to realize that we did everything in the dining room by candlelight because the room had no electricity!

He'd deal, and we'd start betting matchsticks, the pile getting higher all the time until he called me. I'd have maybe two pairs and he'd have three of a kind. He'd grab his white hair with both hands and shout, "Mine Gott! I'm going out in the ally and shoot myself, if you bluff one more time!"

Sitting at the table, we looked out a window at the beautiful Island of Catalina, just twenty-two miles away. A big old cedar tree draped its twisted boughs over the top of the window, framing the picturesque scene. One day, Flo climbed up that cedar tree and was sitting on the little roof above the front door. She was calling, "Bungy! Bungy! Come here!" Now, unbeknownst to her, I had seen her filling a small bucket with water, before she climbed up. I was inside the door, and when Mother, who was inside also, asked me what Flo wanted, I said, "Hmm! I guess she wants you!"

I hightailed it out the back door, just as Mother stepped out the front, and got Flo's whole bucket of water on her head! It was probably the only time I ever got the better of Flo in practical joking. Poor Mother!

When it came to cooking, I was Ramon's sidekick. We'd go to the store to get rabbits, wine, rice, and lots of other stuff. When we got into the little kitchen, he'd say cut this, wash that, clean up here, etc. And presto … we would call the family to a real Basque feast!

The winter Ramon was with us was a very cold one. The gales blowing in from the Pacific found every crack in the house, so the family rented a house in a canyon in Hollywood, where we were all supposed to move up to and be warm.

Go back to Hollywood? Me? You must be crazy! And Ramon felt the same, so the two of us stayed at the Cove, while the rest went to luxuriate in a heated house. It was very cold, with winter gales rolling in from the North Pacific. I had a hard time keeping up with the wood gathering for the fires, but we wore lots of sweaters and, we were free!

Then, the rains came, and came, and we had a landslide down at the other end of the Cove, and it buried the road and we weren't able to get out. Our food supply ran low. So low that all we had left was a big pot of garbanzo beans and another of lentils. We ate this for about a week until a bulldozer came along and got rid of a bunch of the mud, and we were able to walk to the store once more. I still love garbanzos and lentils, because they remind me of that wonderful, free winter.

Everything Daddy made had the flavor of salt water and tropical isles. Down in the entry hall, the doors of the cabinets for our dishes and glassware were wood frames with fan palm branches going up the front. That meant they were beautiful, but not so practical. Dust got in the cabinets through the cracks left by the uneven palm stems, and even today I have a very hard time not taking a glass from the cupboard and blowing the dust out! It became a habit of all of us for many years!

A good friend gave Daddy a bunch of those old-fashioned cellar keys on a big iron ring. Well, Daddy took a look at those, and declared, "Boys! We need a cellar door to hang these on!" So, out came the wall against the cliff in the entry hall, and we took picks and shovels and dug a cellar into the cliff just under the dining room. We cleared out a bunch of rock and dirt, but left one big rock that was perfect for sitting on. Daddy built beautiful wooden doors to enclose the cellar, and to hang the keys on, which was the main reason for this whole project.

Mother declared that she did not like the strident sound of the telephone ringing, so she said, "Eli! Your cellar is perfect for a telephone room!" And that is where the telephone went. The phone would ring, and one of us would finally hear it, dash into the cellar and answer. "Hello!" Oh, my goodness! It was a boy calling for a date. So you closed the cellar door, and sat on a cold rock, in the pitch black, trying to sound fetching! "You'd like to take me to the formal ball on Saturday night? Why, yes, I'd like to go!" But, the placement of the phone pleased Mother, and was only a small inconvenience to the rest of us.

The kitchen was so small that a hole was cut in the wall for the icebox and most of it stuck out into the yard. The door inside was flush with the wall. We went down to the fishing docks every so often, and picked up a fifty-pound block of ice from the icehouse there. An ice pick hung on the outside of the door, and we just hacked off how much we needed at the time. The box looked very modern on the inside, in the kitchen, but kind of odd on the outside, until Daddy built a thing that looked like an observation tower on top of the icebox.

Our kitchen back door was a Dutch door. That is a door cut in two, with a shelf on the bottom half. You could lean out on this shelf as you were drying dishes and watch the freighters ply the Seven Seas. One time when we had a big party, Mare, who didn't like cats much, had set strawberry shortcakes all over the kitchen counters and on the shelf of the Dutch door, while she put big globs of real whipped cream on top of them. One of our cats was sitting outside on the "observation tower" looking down at her. She looked him right in the eye and said, "Don't you dare!" Well, he looked right back at her, and dared, and landed right in the middle of all her strawberry shortcakes and whipped cream. Cream and strawberries flew everywhere. She grabbed that cat and threw him, literally, across the yard. The cat landed on his feet, naturally, and instantly sat down and started licking the whipped cream off himself, very contentedly. Mare was not pleased!

I never minded washing dishes because, that meant that I got to eat the leftovers. After breakfast, as I did the washing and cleaning up, if we had eaten pancakes, I poured all the leftover dough onto the griddle to make one great big one. Then, when I had the kitchen "ship shape and Bristol fashion," I smeared peanut butter and jelly on the pancake, folded it in half, and went merrily on my way. Of course, I had already had about seven or eight regular pancakes for breakfast. When the family got on me about eating so much, I'd say, "Well, If I'm going to work like a horse I need to eat like one, too!"

Lots of times we went through very lean times, although we never thought of ourselves as poor. Despite not having much, we always had lots of guests, and how mother ever came up with the meals she did, I do not know.

We did have a handy family trick of saying, "Pass the word. FHB!" That meant "Family Hold Back." We used it when someone dropped in unexpectedly and stayed for dinner, which happened a lot! With FHB, we children knew we had to go easy on our plates, taking very small servings. Later, we slipped off to the kitchen to make a peanut butter sandwich. The guests never suspected.

Daddy made everything beautiful. Even utilitarian things reflected his artistic bent. A long piece of the prettiest driftwood I ever saw twisted and twirled its way up the stairs to form the banister. The steep steps that led to the dining and living rooms required us to use that banister a lot, and after a few years, our hands had polished the wood as smooth as satin. It flowed down the steps like a stream of silvery, moonlit water.

We built three bedrooms downstairs, all off one straight hall, which backed onto the tall cliff behind the house. Ba and I shared the last room in line.

The area for Ba's and my room was too small for beds, so we dug into the side of the cliff with pick axes and shovels and made a little alcove, or cave. Daddy built a complete room inside this cave with about a four-foot high ceiling, and about ten feet long. We climbed up a short ladder, bent over, and rolled into a couple of recycled Navy bunks that hung from the rafters by some old rope. I had the only window right above my bed, a large porthole from an old sailing ship. I opened my porthole each night to get the fresh breezes from the ocean, before I drifted off to sleep with dreams of sailing being predominant. The two to five dogs, depending on puppies, poked their heads through my porthole to wish me a sweet good night.

Along the way, Daddy got me another iron bunk, but this one had legs. I put it outside and spent most of my life at The Cove sleeping under the stars. If it rained, I had a piece of waterproofed canvas that I pulled over me to keep me dry. If it was cold, the dogs all piled on top of me, and I was all cozy and warm.

One time I decided to build me a palm thatched lean-to against one of the outbuildings we had. It looked magnificent, as if I were on a tropical island, in the middle of nowhere … until a real gale blew in one night! The lean-to lasted for all of fifteen minutes and then the palm-thatched roof collapsed right on top of me. I crawled out from underneath all the soggy palm leaves, gathered up my wet sleeping bag and pillow, and trudged through the pouring down rain, the wind pulling and pushing me every which way. I finally crawled into my inside bunk, and went to sleep instantly, probably dreaming I had been sailing at sea and had run into a storm!

When Ba and I had friends over, we all climbed up on the bunks and started them swinging back and forth the long way, so high that the mattresses, with us on them, sailed across the room and we all landed in a heap. Laughing and pushing and shoving, we struggled with the mattresses until we got them up on the bunks again, and did it all over.

We each had a chest of drawers, and I kept mine perfectly neat at all times. I squared away everything on the top. Every item in each drawer got neatly folded and cataloged. My one pair of school shoes and one pair of tennis shoes stood neatly in the closet. As I grew older and had more things, like a couple of dresses to dance in and a pair of high heels, I still put everything right in its place.

I always liked getting up early. To me, the morning was glorious, something I hated to miss. Exactly the opposite, Ba loved to sleep late, wrapped up in soft blankets on her bunk. I was responsible for getting her up in time for school. We all went together and if one of us ran late, we were all late. Every morning, I reached up into her bunk, firmly grabbing her elbow, trying to shake her awake. It never worked on the first try, and a few minutes later, when I realized she still slept, I shook her again. It often took three or four energetic shakings before she opened her eyes. To this day, she cannot stand anyone touching her elbow.

I liked to iron and lay out whatever I wanted to wear to school the next day. Ba always started to do the same. She ironed the clothes and tried on this outfit and that outfit. After much thought, she made her choice. But invariably, the next morning all her plans changed. It drove me crazy. However, she always looked cute. I, on the other hand, just looked practical.

At thirteen I started a matchbook collection. I often found additions for it on my walks home from school. Soon I had maybe a hundred. I tied lengths of string from the beams above my bunk and hung all my collection over them. Several mornings of every week

I forgot about them and jumped right out of bed and right into my collection, knocking them off the strings. I very meticulously put them all back on the strings, and happily went off to meet the day, only to do it all over a few mornings later. I never came up with a solution to this problem and continued to displace my matchbooks regularly.

Our room had a door that opened to the outside, that led up to the shop about a hundred feet up the beach. This door provided a convenient exit through which all we girls occasionally sneaked off, after Mother and Daddy had fallen asleep, usually about seven in the evening. They stretched out on their beds, slightly snoring, with their books having dropped down on their chests, the classical radio station softly playing.

We waited until we knew they had fallen asleep, and then, at Flo's instigation, slipped out the back door, pushed our station wagon down the road far enough not to awaken them when we started it, jumped in and drove into San Pedro to the movies. We usually lacked enough money to go to the big picture show, but we could always get together the twenty-five cents apiece that it cost to go to the old movie theater that ran the classic westerns like Ernest Tubb's *Fighting Buckaroo* or *Riding West,* or the Our Gang movies, or old Shirley Temple films. After the show, we raced back home, got to that certain point, cut the car engine, pushed the car back into its parking spot, slipped into the back door, and started acting natural, which never failed to wake Mother and Daddy, who pretended they had never been asleep.

The bathroom was the other half of Ba's and my room, which is why we needed a bunkroom in the cliff. It had an old iron claw tub, with pieces of twisty, beautiful driftwood at each end for towels. When we had special guests, Mother put flowers on the branches of the towel racks. Mare painted a Michelangelo fresco on the ceiling!

My two oldest sisters' bedroom was next. They had one whole wall that was floor to ceiling windows, and a glass door. This looked right out on the ocean. After a few years, the panes became permanently frosted from the spray of the ocean waves with the winter high tides. The floor to ceiling windows were actually doors, only they didn't open.

One night Mare, who was a dear and never hurt anyone, except for that time the cat jumped into the whipped cream, was coming home around midnight from a date. Flo, who was always a practical joker, had put herself lying halfway on and halfway off her bed with a knife stuck between her arm and chest with catsup spread all over and her eyes open and rolled up. Mare was humming along as she came into the room. She saw Flo and screamed bloody murder, waking the whole family. Flo and I thought it was the best joke ever. The rest of the family didn't!

One cold winter, Mare had a mouse problem. Over her bed a section of the overhanging roof met the under-hanging ceiling, almost. Remember that Daddy never used a square in the building of the house. The mice wanted to come in out of the cold, so they nested up there in that little niche, right over her bed.

Mother always kept a bunch of unshelled mixed nuts in a large bowl with a nutcracker, on the table in the living room. These mice obviously knew about them, for they regularly gathered up a supply and carried them back to their lair, where they enjoyed rolling them around. It always surprised us to hear how much noise a couple of little mice can make with just a few nuts, especially when we wanted to get some sleep.

Mare began taking stacks of books to bed with her, and carefully setting them on the floor, right within handy reach. When the nuts started rolling around, Mare started yelling and throwing those books at the ceiling. Even though it awakened the rest of us, I always thought she and the mice put on quite a good show.

Then came Mother and Daddy's room. It was just big enough for a double bed, a couple of easy chairs, a chest of drawers, a wood stove, and a wind-up phonograph for Mother, who could never figure out anything mechanical. This room was the core of the family. On cold winter days we'd gather for tea at four o'clock with the potbellied wood stove burning, the classical music station KFAC on the radio, the sound and sights of the big storm booming outside. We played lots of checkers, Monopoly, and tiddlywinks. There was always good conversation, and good reading. I read things like *Mutiny on the Bounty* and *Pitcairn Island* by Nordoff and Hall, or *Sailing Alone Around the World,* by Joshua Slocum. *Robinson Crusoe, The Three Musketeers*, and the Captain Hornblower books, with their glorious and gory battles, held me spellbound.

The *Burton Holmes Travel Stories* for kids, and Arthur Ransome's series of children's mysteries, where the kids sailed the English Channel in their little boat, were among my favorites.

Flo took me to the library weekly, but before I could read any of the kind of books that I wanted, I had to read a "classic" that she had chosen for me! She thought I needed more education! My favorite classic was *Ivanhoe.* I never let on to Flo that I really enjoyed her choices, too!

While reading, I dreamed of running away to sea on a freighter. If I could only get my braids cut so no one would know I was a girl! That is why I took *International Morse Code* in school instead of typing.

My real hero at that time was Richard Haliburton and his "Royal Road to Romance." He traveled around the world in the 1920s, doing things like swimming the Panama Canal and paying the regular tonnage fee, which, because of his weight, was sixteen cents. Or, hiding from the guards in the Taj Mahal until they closed for the night. When he was sure that everyone else had gone home, he silently slid into the reflecting pool and swam under a full moon. My kind of guy!

One stormy day, rainy and cold, the little wood stove was radiating a blast of heat. Mother and Daddy leaned back on their piles of pillows on their bed, reading. The radio softly played Vivaldi's *Four Seasons.*

Meanwhile, Ba and I were beating our way home after school, along the high cliffs, with the wind pushing against us, rain pouring into our faces and down the necks of our yellow sou'westers. We had to walk about two miles, starting along the top of the cliff until we got above the Cove, and then along a road that led down the cliff and into our property, up through the Dance Floor and palm trees, finally arriving at our home at the far end.

As we topped the cliff and started down, a huge gust practically knocked us over. On ordinary days, when I hit this spot, I stood on the side of the cliff, gazed out over the whole Pacific, and recited John Masefield's poem, "Let me go down to the sea again, to the lonely sea and the sky, and all I ask is a tall ship, with a star to steer her by!"

But on this day, leaning practically all the way in half, we made it down to the reasonably sheltered Cove. To our horror, we saw that a huge part of the cliff face had caved in on the Dance Floor. Panic filled us as we slogged through mud two feet deep. Were our parents all right? Was the house still there?

We finally made our way through the tumbled rocks and mud and debris and breathed a sigh of relief as we saw the house, still safely tucked away against the cliff. We slopped through the mud to the upturned rowboat front door, looked up, and saw the whole side of the house on fire!

I ran in, shouting, "The house is on fire! The house is on fire!" Violin strains greeted me in all tranquility, the coffee pot bubbled on the stove. Mother and Daddy sat comfortably propped up, reading, with a question on their faces, "What in the world has gotten into her?"

When I finally made it clear that the house really was on fire, Daddy leaped up, ran outside and got the hose. He stood there in the midst of the storm, with the rain pouring down, holding the hose on the house, and, by golly, it worked. He put out the fire.

In discussing the mishap later, we decided they had added so much wood to the stove to warm up the bedroom that the wall behind the stove had heated to the point that it had caught on fire. Daddy decided to put some insulation behind the stovepipe after that!

The next day, when the sun came out, Daddy went up to the shop for a while, and returned with a beautiful carved piece of wood that fit exactly where the fire had scorched the house! He declared that it made our home so much more interesting.

We had several landslides like that over the years, each creating a horrendous cleanup job. Daddy took long sticks and nailed small boards at one end of each stick. These we used as "pushers" and we literally pushed all that mud into the sea.

We then took the hoses, and washed down all the cement areas, and the Dance Floor. We waited for it to dry, and then reached up into a palm tree, pulled down a frond, cut off the end with the thorns, stripped away enough of the leaves to make a handle for this long sweeping broom, and back and forth we would sweep with these fronds, until we had swept the whole Cove. This is the way we kept the Cove clean and sparkling all the time. The palm fronds not only covered a lot of area in a hurry, it was fun to sweep this way, too.

Mare, Mother, Ba, Bungy, Daddy, Flo, in front yard. Bungy wished ship's wheel were attatched to a boat!

Chapter 4

♪ *I could have danced all night!* ♫

"I can't dance, don't make me," Fred Astaire sang in one of his famous dance routines. Oh, yes, you can *if* you have your very own private outside terrazzo dance floor! The backdrop was an infinite ocean, lighted by candles, tiny lights, and stars. When a full moon came up golden over the cliff, the moonlight spilled onto the dance floor, and the tall, swaying palms kept time to the music of wind and sea.

I can't count the times we had parties for friends and family. When they entered the gates, they knew they had hit paradise. Colored lights twinkled merrily through the swaying palms. Romantic Viennese waltzes played softly. A big fire blazed in the huge fireplace right off the Dance Floor. We served dinner on long tables right in front of the huge, glowing fire, candles adding soft light from their rock perches.

With all the guests full, Mother called out gaily, "I think we ought to have a Virginia Reel." We coaxed everyone to the Dance Floor, and into two long lines. *Turkey in the Straw* started playing. Daddy started calling, " Now! forward and back, bow to your partner!" Some would be reluctant to try this "new" dance, but when that set was over, they were the first to ask to do it again. The Virginia Reel was the ice breaker followed by waltzes, tangos, swing, rumbas, all the guests fast becoming maestros of the dance!

Lots of times, I would lug the portable phonograph all the way from the house down to the Dance Floor, put on a bunch of old 78 Viennese waltzes and polkas, and dance and twirl around all by myself. To have this joy, just me, and the moon, and the sea, was a lot of freedom. Many times, I turned off the light and danced right at the edge of a sea that was filled with the whiteness of just a half moon. On full moon nights, with the tide running full and high, big waves loaded with phosphorus rolled in, one after the other, crashing on the rocky shore. It was just too glorious.

When we knew guests were coming, Flo got her siblings together to create some kind of a *show,* complete with costumes. One time, my friend Betsy came to dinner with her mama and daddy and some other people, so, with Flo's direction, sets, costumes, and music, we put on Ravel's Bolero.

Each of us dressed all in black. Flo had found this door, complete with door jam, in an alley and we'd lugged it home and propped it up on the dance floor. We made a fake fire with red cellophane and put a small light bulb on an extension cord underneath the cellophane, put some driftwood around it, got our audience gathered, and our show began.

The music started - *boom duh duh duh duh - duh* - and one-by-one we came through the real door that was supposed to be fake. Whirling and twirling around the dance floor, then around the fake fire that was supposed to be real, we slowly lowered ourselves to where we were all lying on the dance floor, our bare feet pointing to the fire. As the music boomed we raised ourselves from the waist, one time, two times. The third time we had sticks with marshmallows on them in our hands. They were props and had been lying there waiting for us. We poked our marshmallows in and out of the fake fire to the beat of the music and as the music rose to crescendo, we ate our marshmallows and then jumped up and ran off the stage, holding our stomachs, acting like we were going to upchuck! Flo's sense of humor, at times, left something to be desired!

In high school, my girl friends and I were allowed to give some parties at the Dance Floor. We all counted ourselves very fortunate to have our very own dance floor. I mean, none of our other friends had one! Most of our parties were nice, innocent dances, just as if we were in our own living rooms. But one time, the captain of the football team stopped me in the hall at school and asked if my friends and I would please give a party for the football team at the Cove! I mean, he actually spoke to me! I couldn't believe it, after having been ignored for three long years! I spoke to my friends, who were equally amazed, and then, I asked Daddy.

He said, and I quote, "You may have the party *if* you are sure there will be chaperons and no drinking!"

"Oh! Thank you daddy! We will make very sure!"

I told the rules to the captain, and he said that was no problem! He would make sure everyone knew the rules, and *he'd* take care of getting chaperones.

We decided to have sandwiches and cokes, and if we charged two dollars per person, that would cover the cost.

So, the big night arrived, and the cars started coming down the hill, bumper to bumper. Two dollars to get in the gate? No problem! Chaperons? They'll be here in a few minutes! Cars kept rolling in, and we began to suspect that this party was not just the football team. My friend Ann and I, who were collecting the entry fee at the gate, decided that we would keep them out by charging five dollars each. But they happily paid this, and went right on in. We asked someone where they were from, and they said, "Los Angeles"! That is when I really knew we were in deep trouble!

It seemed like everyone had brought a bottle. The cokes were only used for mixers. The huge party was getting wild and rowdy, and I knew that if I didn't handle this in some way, and my parents found out, we would never be able to have our own little nice parties again. I took the football captain aside and said, "Someone has called the police, and they are on their way!" I had emphasized "someone", so I would be off the hook! He said, in a booming voice, "Hey! You guys! The Fuzz is on the way!" The word passed like wild fire, "The Fuzz! The Fuzz!" and within minutes it was wall to wall traffic going back up that hill. In no time at all, the Cove was empty, except for my friends and me, and a huge mess.

We all sighed a big sigh of relief, and gladly set to, cleaning it up.After my girl friends left, I turned off all the lights and went on up to the house, where I found my parents quietly snoring with their daily night time nap, before going to bed!

We rented out The Cove for reunions, school dances, fraternity parties, church picnics, Greek festivals, and the annual Elk's Club dance and picnic. This was another way for us to afford our paradise.

The fraternity and sorority groups came down early in the morning, the day of their dance, loaded with flowers and palm fronds and fake leis, and tons of pineapples. They'd strewed these hither and thither until the Cove really looked like a movie about a South Seas island. Later on, a Hawaiian Band started playing, and all the guests, dressed in their sarongs and shorts and Hawaiian shirts, danced and sang and had a good ol' time. You know the reputation of fraternity parties!

The Greeks were wonderful, in their colorful costumes, dancing in large groups all over the Dance Floor. They cooked lamb over the barbeque pit, and brought fresh baked date pastries from home.

The local St. Stanislaus Catholic church held their annual picnic, where one year, over 5,000 people arrived. They visited a lot, and they danced and they usually ate a big fish fry. They had slot machines, and were able to gamble because the Cove was out of the city limits.

The Elks came and started the barbeque about four in the morning. They really knew how to cook barbeque. The food was *good*! The most interesting thing they did was to set up poker games. I had never seen any serious poker played before. I didn't see how they could possibly know what was in their hand, they held those cards so close to their chest!

And, then there was the Polynesian Society of Los Angeles, and their annual Luau. What a time I had with that! The Luau was held on Sunday, but on Friday evening, the Hawaiians, who were in charge of putting this benefit together, started arriving. They came with tons of food to chop, dice, and cook. Ukuleles played at all hours of the day and night. I went to bed at midnight, got up at four o'clock, and someone was still playing an ukulele.

71

They took me under their wing, especially Chief Pua Kealoha. He was big, strong, and funny. He laughed and told stories constantly. I had a six-stringed, koa wood, Martin ukulele, with bar frets, that a friend had given me. He told me he thought it was a concert Martin. Pua tried and tried to teach me how to play that ukulele. Finally he put it in my hands and said, "Bungy, dis one fine ukulele. You be sure you take dis all time where ever you go. Den, you fin' someone else to play it!" And then he said, "Les' go catch some lobsta', dey fine eating!"

And we would grab our face masks, snorkels and flippers, dive into the clear, sparkling Pacific, and catch some lobsters. When we'd caught enough lobsta', we'd swim back in and all the Hawaiians would stop whatever they were doing and we'd have a feast of really fresh broiled lobster over the barbeque pit, with ukuleles strumming, of course.

Pua taught me how to catch octopus and squid, too. He said all I had to do was to walk in the tide pools at low tide, and when I spotted a little dark hole, put my hand in to see if a squid grabbed it. If he did, I was supposed to yank it out, bite it between the eyes to kill it, and take it home to cook! This was a bit much for me, so he told me that if I could get hold of any copper sulphate, I could sprinkle that in front of the hole, and the squid would come out and try to push it away, and then I could grab it.

Daddy's shop was a hodge-podge of lots of unusual items. One day, I hunted around until, lo and behold, I found a paper bag with the words "copper sulphate" written on it in pencil! Oh! Joy! I grabbed a handful and went straightway to the tide pools, where I found this perfect hole, and dropped a bit of the sulphate right in front of it. Out came the squid or octopus, I never knew which, and I started to grab it, but it flashed before my eyes, "What in heaven's name will I do with it, when I catch it?" So, I just watched him until he once more retreated into his hole. I decided that I never could become a real Hawaiian.

Back to the Cove and the Polynesian Society's benefit luaus. On Saturday afternoon, more Polynesians from all the islands in the Pacific started arriving, Tahitians, Samoans, Tongans, Marquesans, and, of course, more Hawaiians. About four o'clock Sunday morning, the fires got started in the huge pits they had dug in the ground. Lava rocks were put on top of the blazing fire. When these started glowing red, and the wood had burned down, wet gunny sacks were put right on top of the rocks. As they started steaming, two huge pigs were lowered carefully into the pit. These were, in turn, loaded with chickens, lau laus, or fish wrapped in ti leaves, lots of sweet potatoes, and more. This was covered with more damp gunny sacks, and hot lava rocks were loaded on top of, and all around the pigs. About noon, the smell was so good coming out of that pit, it was hard to control the grumbling in my stomach.

The guests began to arrive early on Sunday, and entertainment started around noon, on the stage we had set up on the Dance Floor. All the famous Polynesian entertainers of that time volunteered to appear for this benefit each year. Chief Satini and his Hawaiian and Tahitian Review from the Seven Seas, on Hollywood Blvd. across from the Grauman's Chinese Theater, set the pace. Satini was the

Ba in her authentic Tahitian hula skirt, ready for the big Luau!

Ploynesian Society of Los Angeles with Luau pig ready to serve! circa 1950.

first Samoan to do the Knife Dance on the mainland. It wasn't until the late fifties that the Samoans started doing the now famous fire dances.

Then came Johnny Bright, whose brother, Andy, was so famous at the Moana Hotel, under the Banyan Tree in Waikiki. They both had this funny song called "The Bucking Horse Hula." They stepped into a cardboard horse and held it up with two suspenders that hung from their shoulders.

Hilo Hattie was always a crowd pleaser with her "Hilo Hattie does the Hilo Hop." Then she'd go into "The cockeyed mayor, or mare, of Kaunakakai," and the crowd would roar with laughter when she made that "that horse buck and fly, all over the Island of Molokai!"

Pua Kealoha, and all his gang from the Leilani Restaurant in Hollywood, played and sang and danced on and on through the day, and into the night. Probably every top Polynesian entertainer was there, so no wonder I looked forward to this fairytale day each year! And they all came to my living room and had tea! Sometimes, not during luau time, they just arrived for a day of swimming, diving, ukulele playing, with lots of singing of the old Hawaiian and Tahitian songs, and we all had fun.

The Dance Floor was also used for weddings. Peggy Slater, one of the most famous of women racing sailors, was a good friend of the family. She called one day, to say she was going to be married and asked if she could have the wedding at The Cove. She married with regularity, and we were happy to be a part of this one!

This time she was marrying a small, compact, handsome merchant seaman who was a radioman from a freighter. Peggy was six foot, with plenty of muscle and a bunch of red hair.

Peggy named all of her boats *Valentine*. *Valentine I, Valentine II,* and so forth. She decorated all of them in red and white, with hearts and flowers everywhere. A chrome-plated, cherub figurehead wrapped his wings lovingly around the red hull at the bow. Even the head had a heart-shaped seat. The frilly and femininely decorated boats formed an interesting contrast to a tough as nails Peggy.

Naturally, we used the Valentine theme for the wedding. We covered The Cove with masses of red and white flowers, and candles scattered everywhere for a delightfully festive and very romantic look.

The wedding went off without a hitch, and the reception ran late into the night. The next morning, the family gathered early to have breakfast outside by the Dance Floor, where we watched the sun shimmer and sparkle on the water, listening to the soft incoming waves at low tide punctuated by the occasional squawk of a gull.

Suddenly, a familiar red convertible (naturally it was red - all her cars were red) came flying up our dirt road and screeched to a halt, in a cloud of dust. Peggy got out, slammed the door and strode over to the table.

"Am I in time for breakfast?" she shouted in her usual reserved manner. "My darling husband got an emergency call and had to set to sea again this morning. I thought I'd join you so we can all wave at him as his ship passes by."

We all just sat there with our mouths dropping open. We found it hard to believe that the groom meant to sail away the day after the wedding. But we gamely put on our best smiles and jumped up as the freighter came into view on the horizon. We all waved goodbye frantically, hoping he saw us through his binoculars. Or, that it was even the right freighter.

"Goodbye, goodbye," we shouted, lining up along the shore. "Fair winds!" we called, hoping he could see us.

I think that marriage lasted about a month.

Peggy and her sailboats were racing machines and she had trophies all over her home to prove it. I had never raced before, only cruised, when Peggy called to say she needed another crew member for a big race coming up the next day. "Sure!" I said, thrilled that she had picked me! When I arrived at the marina, she told me to get into the forward hold, and my duty would be to "clear the jib." We motored out of the slip, hoisted our sails, and soon joined the other racers, about ten in all. The gun barked, and we were off. Everything was going well, until we came about, and she started screaming at me to clear the jib. I was going as fast as I could, but it wasn't fast enough for her. Pretty soon, I began to realize that no one was fast enough for her, and we all got on the wrong end of the stick that day! The Cove, and my life there, was a pretty easy going life, and to be found, all of a sudden, in this overly tense situation, completely cured me from ever wanting to race again! The next time she called (I must have done *something* right), I told Flo, who had answered the phone, "I'm not in! I'm not in!" in a whisper, hoping it wasn't echoing off the walls of the cellar.

Movie companies, looking for locations without having to go to the South Seas also filled our bank account. Johnny Wiessmuller, star of the *Tarzan* series of adventure films, shot a couple of his *Trader Hall* movies with us.

The studios rented The Cove for a couple of weeks at a time. Each day, big trucks arrived from Hollywood, loaded with costumes, camera equipment, caterers, sets and props. A couple of the trucks contained all kinds of trees in huge pots, along with piles of cut limbs and bushes. Quickly unloading the truck, the crew "planted" the greenery in an area of our beach, following the director's orders. After all the actors had run through the bushes and trees, had fights in them, or died dramatically in the middle of all that *jungle*, the set guy yelled, "OK, let's change 'em!"

A swarm of fellows scurried around switching every twig to a different arrangement, and suddenly we saw before us a completely different part of the jungle, all in the same place.

These low budget movies did the same thing with the extras. During the filming of a chase or fight with a lot of action, the extras, both good and bad guys, ran in and did their parts. The minute they got "killed" and the cameras had swung away from them, they jumped up, dashed off to the wardrobe trailer, put on a new outfit, and dashed back into the fight as another character.

Because there were so few of them, we got to know many of them well, and when we saw the movie in a real live theater, we had fun spotting our friends on the screen again, and again, and yet again!

Mama served tea constantly. She must have served a million gallons in her lifetime. It was not the actual beverage everyone loved so much as the whole ambiance of the tea. Mother did it up in the proper British manner, with trays of cakes and cookies and tiny sandwiches. I must have cut crusts off a thousand sandwiches in my lifetime. The crusts always went into the makings of delicious bread puddings.

The whole cast and production guys of these movies, were constantly up at the house having tea, it seemed. A couple of times, when the director yelled, "Action!" someone had to run up to the house to round up the missing crew.

At the other end of our half-circle bay in front of The Cove stood a big wooden pier about twenty feet high. When Johnny Weissmuller did his movies there, he always ended up diving off that pier. One day during the filming, Duke Kahanumoku, a good friend of Johnny's, came down to visit and they both dove off the pier. What an honor and thrill to see those two Olympic gold medal athletes swimming in *my* ocean.

Handsome Tab Hunter filmed *Return to Treasure Island* at The Cove and the surrounding bays. The producers needed a sailboat, so Ed Fabian, a well-known yachtsman, with his 42-foot *Resolute,* took the job. The director instructed him to sail back and forth along the coast. At the right moment, the heroine had to dive off the boat, swim to shore and clamber up the rocky beach into Tab Hunter's arms.

The day turned fine, the breezes wafted gently, but the radio contact between the boat and the director went kablooey. He went crazy trying to figure out what to do, shouting and waving his arms, and stomping up and down the beach! Ed had a twelve-foot dory, double ended and ideal for waves, so the director asked me if I wanted to earn twenty-five dollars a day, acting as the go-between. I had to row out to the *Resolute* in the dory, with directions from him, and then row back again and tell him the response. Of course, that meant rowing through waves, and landing on a rocky shore. My muscles got a thorough workout before the end of the week, but the treasure box in my drawer was overflowing with my daily twenty-five dollars! It was quite an adventure, and being part of show biz was loads of fun.

For *Return to Treasure Island,* our home became the Admiral Benbow Inn. The actors entered through our upturned rowboat front door.   The living room was the inside of the Inn, where a big fight took place. My half-barrel desk, where I did my homework, was right there when I saw the movie. We girls adored the blond and muscular Tab Hunter, and we went time and again to see the movie. It ended up a commercial flop, so we had to see it in a hurry.

Many other movie companies filmed, in part, at The Cove. Every once in a while I will catch an old movie on TV and suddenly see a flash of some corner of my old home, bringing back good memories.

Magazines also came out to our cove, all the way from Hollywood, with their models. Girls posed all over the beach, draping themselves over a boulder or a piece of driftwood, looking bored but glamorous.

The magazine, *American Home,* called, wanting to do an article on the beachcombing Hedleys. We invited some friends and planted intriguing jetsam all along the beach and started a big bonfire. The photographers had us jumping into tide pools, holding up beach finds, roasting hotdogs over the fire and watching the sunset.

Life Magazine came down and stayed the day, and on into the night, even though their work was done. We got out the old phonograph and they were soon waltzing away under the stars. I thought for sure they were going to stay the night.

Any day at The Cove held the potential for turning into the most marvelous adventure.

We were always having parties, and late at night, after one of these ended, and the soft breezes blew in off the ocean, Daddy would say, "Bungy, please run down and turn off the lights."

I made my way down The Cove, all alone. The swaying and creaking of the palms, and the clattering of their leaves, sounded like men whispering about nefarious plots of various and sundry capers.

I remember trying to figure out the better option:

#1. Turn the lights out on the way down the thousand feet, or,

#2. Run down all the way and start turning them off on the way back.

The electric wires for the ten or so lights ran from palm tree to palm tree. If I turned them off on the way down, I could hide in the dark, behind the big date palms, if someone came while I made my way back to the house. But if I ran down and started turning them off from the opposite end, I had the light to see for most of the trip back up to the house. I was only twelve years old, after all, and sometimes the mystery of the dark and strange sounds created by the wind in the palm fronds gave my active imagination too much to handle.

We had another concern with those lights. Daddy did the wiring himself using old indoor wiring he had scrounged up from somewhere. Basically it was a heavy copper wire wrapped in fabric. In the evening the wiring always got damp from the salt air of the ocean, with the palm trees dripping on it like mad. Since the cloth wire draped over the leaves, and the leaves were wet, I got an electric shock each time I pulled a switch. Naturally, I always ran around barefoot, which just added to the adventure. I steeled myself at each switch for that little buzz. When the palms started talking though, it did not take me long to pull that switch, get shocked, and run to the next.

About five years after we settled in, Daddy called the electric company wanting an explanation for our high electric bill. A fellow came down to do an inspection and could not speak for a few minutes after examining Daddy's wiring job.

"Uh, Mr. Hedley, you're going to have to rewire all of this. This is really dangerous wiring!" he said.

"I see," Daddy said. "Well, why don't you come on up to the house and my wife will fix us some tea and we'll discuss what we need to do."

Mother served tea and a few hours later the electric company man left, with Daddy promising to trim the palm leaves so they would no longer rest on the wires. The electric guy was sure nice!

Chapter 5

♪ *For it's starb'rd and lar'brd*
and jump to the lee –
Give me some time to blow the man down ... ♫

The day Dwight came into my life we had rented our beautiful paradise to the Polynesian Society for their annual *luau.* The Cove floated in a sea of flowers and *leis.* The brilliant colors and the sweet perfume of exotic plumeria, tiare Tahiti, and yellow ginger filled the air. Everybody was happily getting ready for the big day, greeting old acquaintances and making new friends. Two thousand happy "luau-ers" were dressed in colorful Aloha shirts and dresses. The sound of island music from guitars and ukuleles swelled throughout the afternoon. The big imu pits were beginning to send off their delicious smells of smoke cooked delicacies.

A perfect Southern California day, the sun shone brightly, sparkling off the water. We watched through binoculars as a sailboat let down its sails and threw out an anchor, just off shore. We saw it was Peggy Slater's *Valentine I.* Very shortly, a yellow rubber dinghy splashed into the sea. Three people paddled furiously the quarter mile toward us. A crowd rushed down to the beach to help them as they rowed in. Instead of a broad expanse of soft tropical sands, big rocks covered our beach. They were dark, sharp and slippery rocks, and very dangerous for anyone trying to come ashore.

It was high tide and the waves were pounding the rocks that day. We all got knocked down repeatedly and were completely soaked in our Polynesian finery, as we tried to help the visitors ashore. With all the slipping and sliding we ended up laughing and joking as we helped our unexpected guests, who also ended up as wet as we did.

Peggy introduced us to the great sailor, Dwight Long. "Dwight, this is Bungy," Peggy said, waving a negligent hand in my direction.

Tall and lean, Dwight had a square jaw and clear blue eyes that sparkled with good humor. A fan of wrinkles spread from his prominent brows to his cheekbones. His thick black hair swept back from a broad forehead. He smiled warmly with even white teeth. I liked him immediately.

"Bungy," he said, reaching down to help me up out of a bit of tide pool. "Now, that name's got bounce!"

All of us clambered up the rocky beach and on to dry land. "Dwight Long," I thought in amazement. This famous man who had sailed around the world, and had written a book called "Seven Seas on a Shoe String", which I had read, was walking on *my* beach. For me, it was the equivalent of a math major meeting Albert Einstein.

After a day of eating luau pig, watching the dances of Hawaii, Tahiti, and Samoa, and joining in all the merriment of the authentic Hawaiian luau, Peggy returned to her boat and sailed back to the 22nd Street yacht landing with her other crewman. But Dwight decided to spend the night! The next morning at breakfast, outside under the swaying palms of the Living Room, he asked, "Would anyone be interested in crewing for me on my sail boat, next Sunday?"

You MUST read DWIGHT LONG'S remarkable book—

"SAILING ALL SEAS"

IT WILL BE PUBLISHED BY HARPER & BROTHERS

American Ketch: "IDLE HOUR"
Five Year World Cruise
30,000 MILES COMPLETED

Left Seattle, September, 1934, sponsored by Mayor as a goodwill tour. Called in San Francisco, Los Angeles, Honolulu, Marquesas, Tahiti. At Bora Bora picked up Timi, a 15-year-old Tahitian boy who became my good man Friday.

Sailed six months in South Seas and then, en route to New Zealand, "IDLE HOUR" was dismasted in the forerunner of a hurricane. Accident occurred 1,200 miles from New Zealand. Took 25 days to limp in.

After extensive repairs, we crossed the Tasman Sea making for Sydney. Then we headed northward for the Great Barrier Reef, next to New Guinea, Bali, Singapore. In Colombo lost my Tahitian crew. Proceeded up Red Sea encountering slave trading bandits and Bedouin tribesmen and almost wrecked on uncharted reef. In Mediterranean sighted Italian bombers.

Were detained in Spanish waters as we had to detour around mine-infested areas. "IDLE HOUR," 32 feet long, 11 foot beam, 6 foot draft, 8 tons net; smallest craft ever to sail from America via the Pacific and Mediterranean to England.

On the last lap we were stopped by Insurgent gunboats and held captive over the Fourth of July. After arrival in New York "IDLE HOUR" was wrecked in the hurricane of September 21st. The remains are being removed by the Cruising Club of America.

Captain Dwight Long's advertising card for his book, "Sailing All Seas".
Published in England as "Seven Seas on a Shoe String".

Before anyone else spoke, I answered with an eager, "Yes!" Only twelve at the time, I guess I did not look like a likely hand, as he raised a skeptical eyebrow at my parents. Daddy assured him that I knew how to work hard. "And she's wanted to sail the seas from the minute she saw the ocean!"

From then on, for the next ten years, I regularly crewed on Dwight's thirty-two-foot Block Islander, *Island Belle.* I was always the youngest member of Dwight's crew. He patiently taught me all the rudiments of sailing as we went up and down the California coast, to the Channel Islands, out to Catalina and up to San Francisco.

Willing to do everything to learn to sail, I always got down to the dock early to get the boat ready. I swabbed the decks, polished the brass, took the covers off the sails, filled the water tanks and stocked up on ice. I loved this work! Indeed I rejoiced in it, because it allowed me to begin living my dream of sailing around the world.

I went aboard ready to "starb'rd this" and "port that" and "hoist the mains'l." However, even though he had sailed around the world for seven years, Dwight was not technical about sailing. He frequently had guests aboard who had never sailed before and he liked to put them to work. Sailing is not easy. It is fun, but not easy.

*Bungy, Ba and friends on their way to Catalina island
for weekend on Island Belle.*

And on any boat, it helps if everyone pitches in with the numerous duties. Most of his guests did not know a thing about sailing, so Dwight almost never used sailing jargon. "Pick up that rope over there and put it around this thing here," he said, or "pull on that rope until that white sail goes all the way up to the top of that pole!" Somehow, with finger pointing and pantomime, the job got done, and in the process, the guests all learned something about sailing, and always wanted to come back for more.

During the summers of those first years with Dwight, we sailed to Catalina nearly every weekend. The sea sparkled blue as sapphire when the sun shone, or, turned a deep dark gray with the rain. But most of the time, we had sunny days, perfect winds and deep blue seas.

In the olden days, Dwight called friends to find out who wasn't using their mooring buoy that particular weekend, and we'd sail into Avalon, the Capital of Catalina Island, find the buoy, grab the ring on the buoy with our boat hook, tie up to it, and jump in for a swim! Or, we traveled up the coast a bit, and threw out the anchor in one of the island's many coves for a few hours of snorkeling and fishing. In the evenings, we'd motor back down to Avalon, tie up to any empty mooring float, row ashore, and dance under the stars until midnight.

Sometimes, when we were just sailing around on a Sunday afternoon, we put a little excitement into our sail by throwing the life ring over the stern, jumping from the bow into the water, and waiting to catch the ring as the boat slid past. We'd grab it and hang on for dear life, as we bounded over the water behind the boat, like human skipping stones.

At sea, we enjoyed impromptu picnics and served tea at four o'clock every afternoon. Tea consisted of leftovers from lunch, plus a rich chocolate or coconut pineapple cake, washed down with mugs of steaming hot tea made over the pump-up primus stove in the galley.

Dwight acted like a tour guide, when we were sailing through the great Los Angeles Harbor, which is the largest manmade harbor in the world.

"Over there to the left of us," he explained, "is the federal prison on Terminal Island, sometimes called The Clubhouse. Look at that view they have!" He waved his arm to take in the whole of Los Angeles Harbor, and we all turn to take it in, too. "Makes you think crime does pay!" Dwight added sardonically.

He pointed out the big ships and told us where they came from. He always managed to throw in a few tidbits of local color. "Do you see that great big motor launch over there? That belonged to the actor Tyrone Power in the 1930s. They really had some wild parties on that one."

Or, "Over there, you'll see a Liberty Ship. One of the few left from World War II. The shipyards were building five of these ships a day by the end of the war. They were built to last only a few years, but this one is still going!"

Through Dwight, I met many of the great sailors of the time, like Alan Villiers, Irving Johnson, Harry Pidgeon, Omer Darr, Ed Fabian, and Thor Hyerdahl. Villiers had sailed around the world in square-riggers, and around the Horn many times. He also sailed England's gift to America, the *Mayflower* replica, all the way from England to the U.S., and then, back to England again. Dwight crewed on her return to England and I went down to the harbor to see them off. The crowds were waving and shouting, "Fair Winds!" The odd looking replica slowly backed away and out from the pier. Up went the sails, and she proudly headed out to sea, on her way back to merry old England, by way of the Panama Canal.

Irving Johnson and his wife, Exy, for years sailed the *Yankee,* a big 250-foot schooner, that went around the world every two years, with paying students. After he sold it, they built a smaller 52-foot sail boat, whose masts could be lowered. On this boat, he and Exy took paying passengers through the canals and rivers of Europe. What a life!

Pidgeon sailed around the world six times single-handedly. On his seventh voyage, when he was in his 70s, his new wife joined him. They built a 28-foot Seagoer, and started around the world. Unfortunately, they wrecked in the South Pacific and floated around clinging to debris from the boat until a passing freighter picked them up and delivered them safely to Hong Kong. Undaunted, they returned to San Pedro and built a 22-footer, hoping to sail once more.

They were moored down at 22nd Street Yacht Landing, and in the cold of winter, while I was gathering wood for the home fires, I also gathered wood for the Pidgeons. They had a little, teeney, wood stove onboard, and Mrs. Pidgeon cooked everything, from bread to cakes to soufflés, in that stove. I'd cut their wood into little

Captain Harry Pidgeon's Seagoer, launched and ready to sail around the world.

pieces, and when I'd bring them down a stack, they'd invite me into their little cabin. She was about four feet tall, and he was probably four and a half feet tall. They fit perfectly in their boat. I had to stoop over double, and make myself as small as possible, to even get in the cabin. She served tea and cake, and he talked about their adventures on the Seven Seas.

Dwight was always so interesting to be around because he knew so many people in the sailing world, and I never knew who was going to end up having tea aboard the *Island Belle*. Or maybe we would spend an evening of adventure talking on some other sailor's boat, in whichever harbor we had anchored at day's end. I never got enough of those wonderful sea tales that just poured out of these great men.

We were pulling out of our slip one day, and the gear on the motor slipped and we ran right into another boat that was docked close by. The owner came screaming up topside and Dwight apologized and handed him his business card, telling him to call and he would take care of any damage. The owner glanced down at the card, did a double-take, and said, "*You're* the Dwight Long who sailed around the world?" Dwight turned red from embarrassment.

When I was sixteen, Dwight and I had a sail organized to Catalina, with five or six of us on board. Just picnics on the sea, everyone brought something to eat or drink for these weekend sails. With my limited cooking skills, I decided to bring a pot of garbanzo beans cooked with chorizo sausage, onions, and a bit of tomato sauce. We enjoyed our dinner and dressed up to go dancing on the island at Avalon, which had only two places for entertainment in those days, besides the big ballroom that sat on the point of St. Catherine's Bay. Up at the Isthmus, Clark Gable had bankrolled a place called "Christian's Hut," which was very popular.

I put on my best skirt and a little off-the-shoulder top and thought I looked pretty fine. We all clambered noisily, but carefully, into the dinghy to row ashore. Dwight and I sat side-by-side in the stern. Suddenly, Dwight leaned across me and commenced to lose his dinner. Most of it went over the side, but some of it splattered disgustingly on me.

"It's those garbanzo beans!" he swore.

"Well, I don't think so!" I retorted.

"You know I can't eat too many spices!"

Nearly in tears, I carefully attempted to wipe the debris from my pretty skirt.

"Why did you have to lean over me to do that?" I cried. "You had the whole Pacific Ocean on your side, too, you know!"

Dwight looked at me, at his hand on my side of the dinghy, and then at the boat hull, and started to laugh.

"I'm sorry, Bungy! I leaned over your side so I wouldn't get anything on the hull! I now realize I do have the whole ocean, right here next to me!"

We soon cleaned up, and once more, headed in to Avalon, for our bit of fun and dancing.

Without really meaning to, I got a little sweet revenge, one spring. We took a group out to Catalina for Easter weekend, and naturally, I brought along a basketful of colorful Easter eggs, ready for a full-fledged hunt, on Easter Sunday morning. When everyone had gone to bed, after a typical late night ashore, I carefully hid dozens of the eggs all around the boat.

Since the partying the night before had included a large number of drinks for the older guests, no one displayed much enthusiasm as I went around that morning, yelling, "Get up! Get up! It's time for the Easter egg hunt!"

The reluctant sailors, most with pretty big hangovers, finally piled out of their bunks and staggered around the boat, searching for the eggs. I am amazed still, that they were such good sports! The uniqueness of having an Easter egg hunt on board a boat provided the guests with plenty to laugh about throughout the rest of the day.

About a week later, I got a call from Dwight.

"Bungy!" he yelled, "get down here to the boat RIGHT NOW, and find those eggs!"

Apparently the hunters missed a few of my brightly died eggs in the original search. Days later, the unmistakable sulfurous odor of rotting eggs permeated every corner of the boat.

"No more Easter egg hunts on board my boat, Bungy. Never again!" Dwight roared.

At eighteen, I found myself madly in love with Dwight. I shared so many of the same dreams and joys related to the sea with this very handsome and talented man. But, being eighteen, and having had no encouragement in this endeavor, I fell madly in love with someone else in six or eight months, of course, and went on with my life. Dwight never gave any indication that he felt anything for me other than a brotherly kind of affection. Since he was about twenty years older than I, at that time I thought he probably found my passing infatuation amusing.

I do not know how much closer we could have been. We had the best relationship, just like a loving brother and sister. Dwight knew that, like him, more than anything else, I longed to be out sailing on the sea.

At twenty-one, Dwight Long had bought and refitted the sailing ketch *Idle Hour* and sailed around the world, leaving Seattle in 1934. The trip made him one of the most famous blue water sailors in the world at that time. Sailing mates he picked up on his way west included a half-blind septuagenarian postman from Hawaii and a 300-pound English tea planter. Timi, a young Tahitian, joined him from Bora Bora all the way to Ceylon. Dwight detailed his adventures in his book, *Sailing All Seas on the Idle Hour.* He used his extraordinary filmmaking skills to produce a film, *Tanga Tika,* a story of life and love among the Tahitians.

Only 32-feet long with an 8-foot beam, the *Idle Hour* was the smallest craft ever to sail from America, via the Pacific and the Mediterranean, to England. On the way to New Zealand a storm dismasted the ship 1,200 miles out. It took Dwight 25 days to limp in to harbor.

Once refitted, he faced slave bandits and Bedouin tribesmen from Arabia and Africa as he continued his journey. He detoured around mine-infested waters in the Mediterranean. The Spaniards held him captive over the Fourth of July, suspecting him of attempting to assassinate Spanish dictator Francisco Franco. Six years and six days after he set sail from California, he arrived in New York, where President and Mrs. Franklin D. Roosevelt honored him with a meeting.

During World War II, Dwight served in Navy Capt. Edward Steichen's Pacific Naval Photographic Unit, assigned to the aircraft carrier *Yorktown II.* He spent the war years filming aircraft carrier warfare, and earned a Legion of Merit Award for his outstanding work. The footage he shot appeared in theater newsreels all over America, in the movie *Fighting Lady,* and, even today, in many modern films about the air/sea battles of World War II.

One summer, with a couple of extra guests, we sailed up to the Channel Islands, threw out our anchor in a secluded cove, and swam in pristine, deep blue waters. We hiked up into the dusty, dry hills, and along the few streams on the islands, sitting under the waterfalls, wearing crowns of woven, freshly picked ferns. We packed our lunches and ate high up, on the edge of lofty cliffs, overlooking the wide, sparkling Pacific.

One day, I decided to swim to a nearby 100-foot cliff and climb it. My whole life, it seems that I have always looked for the highest point. I had almost reached the top of the cliff, when all of a sudden, hundreds of sea gulls dive-bombed my head. They came at me from everywhere, screeching and screaming, battering me with their wings. I tried to beat them off with one hand as I clung to the rock face with the other. I had apparently trespassed on their nesting ground and they wanted me gone, *now*!

I climbed down as fast as I could, but it wasn't fast enough for those birds. When I got down about twenty feet above the ocean, I could not stand another minute of the battering, so I let go and dove into the sea. Alfred Hitchcock had it right in his classic movie, *The Birds*. That attack scared me for sure!

For our sails around these offshore islands, we always took masks and snorkel gear. The water stayed very clear out there and we could see every color and size of fish imaginable. We fished for our dinner right off the boat. Whatever the fish, we enjoyed the smoky flavor from it being cooked over a campfire, on the rocky beaches. After we were assured of our main course, we loaded the dinghy with potatoes for cooking in the coals, a big salad, and the fresh cleaned fish ready for baking on hot rocks. We finished with toasted marshmallows for dessert, using the Campfire marshmallows that came four to a little cardboard box. "Best Tasting! Best Tasting!" it said on the box. They do not make them that good anymore.

As the moon rose, and our eyes began to close, we reluctantly roused ourselves, loaded up the dinghy with our cooking gear, and rowed back out to the *Idle Hour,* through a gently lapping sea filled with moonlight. On these trips, we never ran into anyone else. We had the islands to ourselves. It was always hard to head back to Los Angeles Harbor and the real world!

Chapter 6

♪ *By the sea, by the sea, by the beautiful sea!* ♫

My friendship with the actor Raymond Burr began when I was fourteen, and knowing him has been a true adventure.

Flo and Mare graduated from the new Palos Verdes College near us, and their first jobs in the outside world were sets and costumes for the Players Ring Theater in Hollywood. One day they took me along. They told me to just sit in the auditorium and keep quiet while they worked. I do not know why they thought that telling me to keep quiet would work, since my second grade teacher had actually had to put tape across my lips to accomplish the same thing. She put it across Betsy's lips, too.

Raymond Burr stood in the middle of the circular stage, under the spotlights, directing Terry Kilburn, the star. I sat silently in the dark for what seemed like a long time. Finally, I turned to whoever sat next to me and we began to talk about what we saw on stage in what I believed to be hushed tones.

Suddenly, Ray looked right through the darkness, right into my eyes, and said in a stentorian voice, "Would you please shut up!"

Those eyes scared me so much I never opened my mouth for the next two hours. They certainly worked much more effectively than tape.

At the end of the play's run, my parents threw a big cast party at The Cove. Ray, of course, attended. I can still remember the wonderful party with lots of dancing and tons of food. With a lot of careful maneuvering, because of the crush of people, I managed to avoid him all evening. I did not want him to recognize the chatterbox from the rehearsal.

Not too many months after that, I found myself alone at our home when there came a strum of the zither. I flung open the door and there stood Raymond, his arms full of flowers. I froze. The afternoon at the theater flashed through my mind.

I stood there, paralyzed by those eyes. I finally managed to stutter, "Ahhh. No one's home."

He looked at me quizzically and finally rumbled, "Well, *you* are, aren't you?"

I backed into the entrance hall. "Yes. Yes. I guess so. Won't you please come in?" I was just able to get out.

We stood in the entry hall and looked at each other for a few moments. Finally he broke the silence. "I brought these flowers for your mother and they are getting pretty heavy. Do you happen to have any vases?" I finally saw that his arms were *full* of flowers. He never did anything half way.

Now, my mother loved flowers and she had plenty of vases of all sorts, but I could not find a single one that day. I hunted high and low, opening and closing cabinets, looking under seat cushions, everywhere. All the time he followed me with those awful eyes, as I grew more and more nervous. In desperation, I finally stepped into the kitchen, grabbed a big soup pot, plunked the flowers into it, added a bit of water and sighed in relief.

"I'm so sorry that no one is home," I stammered once again. He looked at me with a raised eyebrow and stayed for another ten or fifteen minutes, chatting politely to a young teenager turned to stone. He finally excused himself and drove back to Hollywood, no doubt wondering about my odd behavior.

He visited us often and this mixture of fear and awe continued for a while. I think The Cove was a good getaway from the movie industry for him.

Not only did Daddy build our house at The Cove topsy-turvy, but my creative parents turned on end the usual rules for family life. For example, the rules not only allowed kids to jump on the beds, they encouraged it!

We kids loved fighting and bouncing on beds, and I cannot remember Daddy getting mad at us even when we broke one, which we frequently did. I do remember sleeping on uneven beds, on mattresses on the floor, on beds propped up with books, and on beds held up with Mason jars. Daddy never had a problem *fixing* a bed.

When I was thirteen or fourteen, Daddy often looked around the dinner table after we finished eating and said, "Well, it looks like wrestling night tonight. Who will it be?"

And I always responded with an eager, "Me! Me!"

Mare usually shared my enthusiasm and waved her hand to volunteer.

He gave us five minutes to get into our costumes. Then, he struck the bottom of a pan with a spoon to ring the bell and shouted, "First Round!"

Mare and I jumped on a bed, circled around and then grabbed each other and started wrestling. Now, we did some fairly serious wrestling, with no consideration for the standards of proper feminine behavior of the time. Our rules stated that whoever threw the other off the bed three times won the match. The two of us throwing each other around definitely caused some wear and tear on the beds, but who cared? The Hedleys always had plenty of books and bottles lying around for the makeshift repairs.

The reason we put on costumes had to do with the fact that we knew the famous wrestler Gorgeous George, with his beautiful long golden curls, and his manager, Betty Wooky, who was a good friend of the family. They debuted the idea of all the colorful costuming for professional wrestling. He always entered to *Pomp and Circumstance,* so Ba put our record on and we danced around the room before jumping onto the wrestling "mat." Naturally, we had to copy his style.

One evening when everyone else had gone somewhere, Mare and I decided to have a wrestling match on our own. My parents' bed was the only one in the whole house declared off limits, so that, of course, was where we decided to hold the match. Prohibition added to the fun! Their bed was right next to a double set of long, narrow, horizontal windows.

We started the match and really got into it. Suddenly one of us threw the other off the bed, and right through the lower bedroom window! We still argue today about who did what to whom. After the crash of glass faded, we stood there in absolute silence. What should we do? Our parents tolerated bed breaking, but this was window breaking! We finally decided to take all the broken glass out of the window and throw it into the rocky tides where it would break up and be carried out to sea, or lay in the tide pools and be polished by the constant movement of the waves, until someone,

one fine day, was beachcombing. Then they'd say, "Look at this beautiful piece of glass! I think I'll take it home!" They'd stick it in their pocket and that would be the end of our broken window. We took all the glass out, threw it into the ocean, closed the curtains, pretended it had never happened, and went to bed.

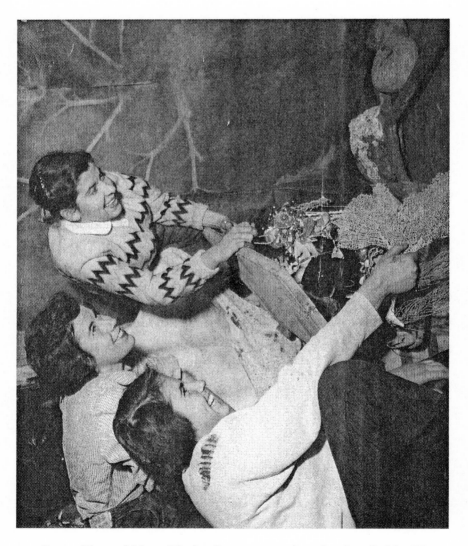

Bungy, Flo, and Mare, "finding" a treasurer chest, hand crafted by Eli Hedley.

The next morning Mother went out to wash windows. Mother loved washing windows so much that we girls did all the rest of the housework while she had fun with her favorite chore. Of course, we did live right on the ocean, a primo paradise place in which to wash windows.

As she started washing the long upper window, Mare and I stood inside warily watching her through the drawn curtains. Mother always hummed when she worked and we heard her melodic, *Hmmm, hmmm, hmmm. Ta da da da. Twas Friday morn when we set sail, and it was not far from land!*

She finished the upper window, and started on the lower. *The captain spied a pretty mermaid...* Her hand came through the curtain. The singing stopped!

She exclaimed, "Well, whatever happened here?"

Inside, Mare and I quaked in our tennis shoes.

Mother called, "Eli! Eli! Come quick! We don't have a window anymore!"

Daddy came along, and sizing up the situation, said, "You know, I have that beautiful door up at the shop that I have been wanting to use somewhere for a long time. If I turned it sideways it would fit right where this window was!"

It did fit perfectly, and since the replacement, a beautiful hand-carved mahogany door, looked so much better than the original window, no one ever asked how the window ended up broken. And Mare and I never volunteered to tell. But Daddy knew! He always knew!

My parents' friends, the Dick Elliots, our old Sunday School teachers, had no children of their own, so they loved us like we were theirs. He charmed us all with his funny and sweet personality. His wife gave us piles of ribbons for our braids, which I never liked because I thought it sissified to wear ribbons. But, never, ever, did I let her know I did not like them. Mother's rules insisted always on politeness and kindness.

One day, just before Halloween, this wonderful couple arrived with two huge boxes stuffed with old costumes that his film studio had decided to throw out, and which he had grabbed "before they bit the dust," he said. What a glorious feeling to have so many wonderful dress-up clothes just in time for all the spooky festivities.

The big night came, and Flo, always the Admiral-in-charge, allowed us into the box. We all got to pick out whatever costume we wanted: Indian, cowboy, fairy princess, ballet dancer. We excitedly donned our fabulous outfits and off we went to the nearest neighborhood to *trick or treat.* The first time around, we spotted the houses handing out the caramel apples and popcorn balls. Then, with bags bulging, we hurried home.

Quickly, we jumped out of those costumes, into new ones, and headed back out again. This time we hit only the houses with the best stuff! Daddy finally caught on to our devious plan after our third time out, but by that time we had already accumulated a palatial pile of goodies.

When we got a bit older, we continued to go *trick or treating,* only we challenged ourselves to achieve more originality with our gear. One year, Mare and I decided to go out for Halloween and see what trouble we could get into, and we got busy on our costumes. She dressed up as Charlie Chaplin, and never have I seen a better characterization. She had all his movements down to perfection. I decided to play Groucho Marx, complete with cigar and bent over walk.

The inspiration for adopting these two characters came from our transportation for the evening, an old 1928 Ford for which Daddy had paid twenty-five dollars, just to give us girls something to have fun with. The old battery did not work so we had to hand crank it to get it going. We painted it a cheerful bright red. Daddy taught me to drive in that Ford when I was fifteen.

Charlie and Groucho fit perfectly in that vintage car and we headed to the marina for some Halloween fun. It seemed like most of the owners of the many fine yachts moored there had decided to host a party. We strolled down the docks in character, doing our acts. We had lots of fun, made some new friends, and went to plenty of parties that night.

The next year, Mare and I, along with my girl friend, Frannie, decided to go out *trick or treating* together. Mare dressed as the short French artist, Toulouse-Lautrec. I decked myself out as a Christmas tree by spreading a blanket out on the floor and sewing green branches all over it. I decorated it with Christmas ornaments and silver icicles. I did not take the time to string popcorn and cranberries, but I did think of it. I wasn't much of a seamstress, so I dripped pine needles and bits of branches wherever I went that night. Frannie dressed as the *Spirit of Halloween*. She wore shorts, red rubber boots, a rain slicker, and an ice cream carton over her head with eyeholes.

We stopped by several restaurants and got candy, and pieces of pie and cake. Not a bad haul, but we finally got bored and we decided to go to the bars on the waterfront.

Young and naïve, we never considered the danger of going into San Pedro's rough waterfront at night. We hit a few bars and really got warmed up in our characters. The rowdy sailors, merchant seamen and longshoremen bought us peanuts and pickled eggs. The bartenders said to us, "Girls, I cain't tell how old you are, so you cain't have nothin' to drink, but you're welcome to stay a while!"

We had hit our stride, and had just entered one of the last bars when Frannie mumbled an incomprehensible, "Mmmm, hmmmmm!"

We just could not understand her under her ice cream carton. She kept repeating "Mmmm, hmmmmm." We still did not understand her. Finally, she pulled the carton off of her head and shouted, "Someone just pinched me, and I'm getting out of here!"

That did it! We all left in a hurry! I wonder if Frannie ever told her parents where we had gone. I know I never told mine!

What with Halloween, family plays, and wrestling, that box of costumes really got a workout through the year.

We had so many adventures at The Cove. When winter winds blew straight in, along with driving rain, we gathered around the woodstove in Mother and Daddy's bedroom while Daddy read to us, or we played tiddly-winks or checkers. Sometimes, Mare and Flo put on productions of plays they had made up. After all, we had the costumes for any production.

Before a laundromat came to San Pedro, I got to the do the laundry! Remember I told you that Daddy always made work fun? That is why I say, "I *got* to do the laundry!"

I'd drag out the two big galvanized washtubs, go down to the beach and bring up six tall flat rocks with plenty of holes in them. I'd set these in two triangles, and put the tubs on top of them. Getting the hose, I'd fill them with water. Back to the beach I'd go, and collect plenty of firewood, and set big fires going under each tub.

When the water was bubbling hot, I'd shave a bar of Castille hardwater soap in the washing tub, and throw the dirty laundry in. I'd take a big stick and start punching the clothes all around. When I thought they were clean enough, I'd lift them out with the stick and throw them into the rinse tub, punching them up and down again. When this was through, I'd take the stick, and lift the clothes out individually, and throw them across the clothes line, waiting for them to cool, before hanging them up properly.

If anything needed starching, I'd throw a bunch of powdered starch into a clean tub of water, stir, and hang the clothes on the line to dry. After they had dried, I would sprinkle each item with water, roll it up tight, put it into a towel, and wait an hour. After that they were ready to iron.

I often did the ironing at The Cove right on the beach. I stood with only a piece of colorful sarong wrapped around me, daydreaming that I was a real native on a lost island someplace in the tropics, facing the waves of the seas I one day hoped to sail. I sang Tahitian and Hawaiian songs at the top of my lungs as I was ironing away. Our secluded cove and our 2,000-foot driveway gave me ample warning of approaching visitors, so I had plenty of time to stop singing and slip into a pair of jeans or shorts before company arrived at the front door.

Daddy's shop stood just north of the house, and sat on a higher point, over-looking the ever-present ocean. He had a few electrical tools, like drills, a band saw, and a table saw, where, instead of using an ax, I sometimes cut the wood for our stoves. He had filled his shop with the most glorious junk! Every corner contained a treasure trove of stuff Daddy had picked up either on the beach, at marine salvage stores, on the docks, or who knows where else.

One day, I glanced up into the rafters, and spied a pair of honest-to-goodness snowshoes. The old fashioned kind made out of bent wood. The shoes had gut string lacings in the bottom. We girls got them down, and in our imaginations, proceeded to mush throughout the frozen wastelands of Alaska with Clark Gable and his trusty dog, Wolf, without ever leaving our little dirt road by the ocean.

The snowshoes gave Flo the great idea of skiing. We got a couple of old three-foot-long barrel staves and tacked some tin strips on top for straps, and on the bottom for speed. I scrabbled up the side of the cliff above the shop, fastened these skis on my feet with some stout string, yelled, "Geronimo!" and took off down the hill.

The cliff, covered with rocks, cactus and all kinds of debris, tilted almost straight down. Somehow I managed to survive this suicidal activity until the skis finally fell apart and Flo dragged me into other endeavors.

At Christmastime, we always had a tall, fresh tree with little candles stuck upright in abalone shells hanging on it. And we always had guests. Raymond Burr was my favorite. After we devoured delicious food and opened gobs of presents, we all settled in the living room with a bright fire crackling and real candles burning on the old-fashioned tree. He'd stretch out full on the floor and read us the Christmas story from the Bible, proceeding to excerpts from *A Christmas Carol.* With his rich expressive voice rolling out the words, he made us see the story so vividly.

On my sixteenth birthday arrived. We decided on a family dinner, just a nice, quiet time. Ray arrived unannounced with a yard-long sailboat made of flowers. All kinds of wonderful perfumes, luxurious bath salts and soaps and fragranced body powder lay hidden amongst the greenery.

Ba clowning around in a giant clam shell!

Chapter 7

♪ *South of the border, down Mexico way!* ♫

When circumnavigator and friend, Dwight Long, called to tell me he had gotten me a berth aboard the 42-foot ketch *Resolute*, I jumped at the opportunity. I could hardly believe my luck, beginning my career sailing the seven seas in a sail boat race to exotic Acapulco, Mexico. To top it off, I would sail in the company of those well-known and respected sailors, Ed and Dottie Fabian. One of the top old salts on the west coast, Ed worked as one of the most admired ships' pilots in the Los Angeles Harbor.

I tried to act cool about the news, however.

"I don't know," I teased Dwight. "I was going to enlist in the WAVES. Tomorrow was my sign-up date." I really had intended to sign up the very next day. It was the closest job I could think of, to be at least near the sea.

"I know," he answered with a laugh. "Your Dad told me. That's why I found you this berth. You wouldn't like the WAVES, Bungy. They hardly ever get to do any sailing!"

He was right about that. Not only did the WAVES not sail, but in the early 1950s women in the Navy did not serve on military boats of any kind. I would not have liked it.

In fact, at that time, very few civilian women ever even joined their husbands for a Sunday sail around the harbor. Men dominated the pastime and the sport. Peggy Slater, Dottie Fabian, Dottie Parks and I were just about the only females sailing out of Los Angeles Harbor in those days. Slater had earned some amazing solo and race-sailing achievements. Dottie Fabian sailed with Ed on the many charters they had for the *Resolute*. Parks had an excellent reputation for her yacht care and upkeep. Why, she even knew how to splice sixteen-strand wire.

Keeping these women in mind as exemplars, I did not intend to let the male domination of the sport of sailing keep me from going after my dream. I wanted to sail around the world. And, after all, I was not a total rookie. I did know how to splice, at least, three-strand rope!

This race turned out to be the very first of a three-decade series of annual sailing races from San Diego to Acapulco. Seven boats entered the competition that year for the 1,400-mile journey south. Today, the San Diego Yacht Club-sponsored race ends at Puerta Vallarta and forty or more boats may compete annually.

Of course, in the midst of the preparations and during the race, we did not even think about the fact that we were making sailing history.

To celebrate getting this job called for a special dinner with the family at The Cove, before the *Resolute* set sail. My family shared my excitement. We sat around the big table on the second floor dining room, candles flickering in the ships' wheel chandelier. I looked at the festive table and my loving family. My tall and lean Dad, with his thick gray hair in need of a trim, sat at the head of the table, dressed in his usual casual shirt and loose slacks. Mother took

42' Resolute becalmed in first San Diego/Acapulco Yacht Race, 1953.

the place of honor at the foot of the long table, petite and bright-eyed, reminding me of a happy sparrow. My older sisters, Flo and Mare, kept up a lively conversation, laughing and teasing all of us. Little sister Ba, with her long blond pigtails, looked on with big soulful eyes, already missing her big sis.

113

So there we were, around the long, memory-filled table, the night before I left for my first big ocean voyage. Daddy presented me with a wonderful knife and sheath handmade by a former school friend of mine.

"Bungy," Daddy said solemnly, "carry this knife with you to the far reaches of the seven seas. May you find your dream even more wonderful than you ever imagined. May you return to us happy and filled with your love of the sea!"

Well, that knife and sheath made a perfect and beautiful gift, except for one thing. I knew the real old sailors carried well-used and well-worn knives. I had to avoid the embarrassment of looking like a green rookie on the boat with my new knife. So, when I got a chance to slip away later, I took that gift outside, ground some dirt and salt water into the sheath, stomped on it a bit, washed it off and then happily stowed it away in my canvas sea bag.

Every sailor keeps his knife sharp and handy at all times, just in case he needs to cut down a sail or slice through a rope in a hurry. I carried that one with me for years.

Mother presented me with a small leather case that contained a travel-size Bible and Mary Baker Eddy's *Science and Health with Key to the Scriptures*. I carried these books with me on all of my adventures for the next thirty years. They provided me with encouragement, strength, and healing over and over again.

Early the next morning, Dwight delivered me to the boat in San Diego.

"Bungy, welcome aboard!" Capt. Ed Fabian called from the deck of *Resolute*, tied up to the dock along with the other six boats scheduled to race. She was well known to generations of Los Angeles Sea Scouts as well as Boy and Girl Scouts. Ed regularly took the young kids out to Catalina for exciting weekend educational excursions.

Ed had so much dominion. All the old salts had it. It could be seen and sensed in anyone who has come to terms with the sea. These experienced sailors exude a great calmness, an inner peace, which comes from having battled the strongest of elements, the weather, and won.

Alasdair Garrett, editor of the "Journal of the Royal Cruising Club," put it like this in the forward to K. Adlard Coles' *Heavy Weather Sailing:* "Indeed, the sea demands definite qualities in the seafarer – certain attitudes of mind and character. Humility, prudence and a recognition that there is no end to learning and to the acquisition of experience. Humility I put first, for who would dare be other than humble in the presence of two great elements, of sea and sky and all the uncertainties which they hold for us? Prudence comes second. It is the ingrained characteristic of the professional seaman-and I would define it as the ability to distinguish between the risk which can reasonably be accepted having regard to prevailing conditions and the risk which must be rejected as unacceptable."

I threw my sea bag on to the deck and jumped from the pier to the boat. Let me explain about that bag. My authentic bag, purchased at the Army-Navy Surplus Store, was a round heavy-duty canvas sack about three-feet tall with a stout drawstring cord running through a line of grommets at the top. It accompanied me on every journey. After a school friend joined the Navy, he came down to The Cove and showed me how to pack it properly.

First, I laid out the piece of clothing on a flat surface and smoothed it out as much as possible. Then, I very carefully folded it over until it was about a foot wide and rolled it up very tightly. Starting at the bottom, I lined the bag with these rolls. If I took the time to roll everything properly, I had practically wrinkle-free clothes when I pulled them out of the bag to wear.

Aside from work shorts, jeans and tee shirts, I always had to have a nice dress. For those special occasions, I had a three-quarter-length semi-formal made of some wonderful wrinkle free material. It had little velvet strips at the top with an overall floral design that never looked dirty. I just rolled that dress right up, shook it out when I needed it, and it never needed any extra attention. I also always found room for a pair of three-inch spike heels, too. A working girl has to have a little glamour, after all.

My light gear, like shorts and swimsuits, went on top of those seldom-used formal pieces. Then the heavier gear got packed on top of that, since the weather usually turned cold the first few days out. I liked having a sweater or jacket right on top of the bag.

Every boat I ever sailed on, I never got to unpack my sea bag. None of the boats had room to unpack it into anything aboard. I just literally lived out of that bag.

Most of the time, I wore a pair of shorts and a tee shirt to sleep in. That way, in case of a sail or rigging problem, within ten seconds I could be on deck.

I would be sailing with Ed and his wife, Dottie, along with their first child, five-year-old Lili. Dottie's parents from Nebraska joined us. The Nebraskans had never sailed before, but the Fabians were old hands.

Ed stood five-feet nine-inches tall, wiry with pure muscle from his life at sea. The sun had bleached his blond hair almost white. The kindest man I have ever known, he had a very gentle quality. I always said that Dwight taught me how to sail, but Ed taught me seamanship: splicing line, how to shoot a sextant and basic navigation. He really refined my sailing skills.

On the day of our race start, boats filled the whole harbor – both sail and power, big and little – coming to see us off with long deep blasts of their horns and the cheerful high-pitched tooting of their whistles. A fireboat shot a fountain of water up, up into the blue sky. After a powerboat towed each competitor away from the dock, we got our sails up and began to sail over to the start, an imaginary line between two big boats.

We sailed back and forth behind the line with everyone getting more and more tense as the start time drew nearer. We waited anxiously for the Commodore of the Coronado Yacht Club to fire the gun. The strategy involved getting as close to the line as possible without going over before the gun sounded. If a boat sailed over the line too soon, the judges made it turn around and get back into place behind the line to start again.

Finally, the gun fired with a bang, and off we went. Onward to adventure.

"Haul in on the jib!" Capt. Fabian shouted. "Tighten the main sheet! Let out the mizzen a hair!" We trimmed the sails one after another and headed out of the harbor with the other boats in the race.

Amazingly enough, this first day of the race turned out to be the last day that we saw any of them until fifteen days later, just before we reached the finish line in Acapulco.

The race rules required moving under sail alone, so the racing authorities sealed our motor before we left the harbor. A broken engine seal found at the end of the race disqualified the boat.

Our radio had about a 150-mile range, but we had none of the equipment that exists for navigating today. No autopilot. No hand-held, computerized satellite navigational system. In fact, our pre-electronics set-up made the trip seem very much like the old days of sailing with the big square-riggers. That suited me just fine.

We headed out into the mighty, blue Pacific. For a moment I stood on the deck and savored the magic of it all. From my earliest memories, I had dreamed of sailing. As a child, I always kept my room "ship shape and Bristol fashion," as the old sailors said, practicing for the time when I sailed aboard a ship to exotic and mysterious places. Now, here I stood, sailing the seven seas at last.

As we headed south to Mexico, dark clouds gathered, the wind picked up, and rain squalls were hitting us more frequently. "Bungy! Dottie!" Capt. Fabian shouted from the wheel, "Go forward and lower the jib to the third reef point. Then we'll do the same with the main. It looks like we're in for some rough weather! Look lively!"

The boat had begun pitching and rolling in the increasingly rough seas as Dottie and I carefully made our way forward along the wet, slippery deck, holding on to anything solid enough to help us. As she lowered the jib, I grabbed it and folded it into itself, both of us working as fast as we could against the rising wind. When

I managed to get to the third reef point, we tied the strings along the sail, leaving only a small triangle of the sail to steady the boat. Reefing the sail in allowed us to keep going at a good pace in the ever-increasing wind, but the shortened sail also made it easier to handle the boat. As we finished tying the reef points off, Ed shouted, "Look to the main! Haul it down to the second reef point!" No time for daydreaming in a race! Darker clouds scudded overhead as the temperature dropped and the wind picked up. A real blow was coming on fast.

Although our festive launch took place in the ever-present Southern California sunshine, the icy Pacific soon reminded us that we sailed in the middle of January. The sun hid behind a heavy bank of dark clouds and with a stiff wind blowing, it grew pretty cold. By nightfall, the rain started. It hit the surface of the sea with a sizzling sound. The groundswells came in solid and heavy, tossing *Resolute* with their irregular and unceasing passage. I had never experienced seasickness before, but I suddenly found myself hanging over the rail, fervently wanting to go below, climb into my bunk and pull the warm sleeping bag up over my miserable head.

I had on all my heavy weather clothes and wished for more as it continued to grow colder and wetter. I dressed in long underwear, a heavy wool sweater, a big warm parka from Army Navy surplus, thick wool socks, tennis shoes and a black wool watch cap pulled down over my ears.

By midnight all the fury of the storm surrounded us. The wind in the rigging made a tremendous noise. The advancing breakers hissed and danced in wild fury. The temperature hovered in the 40s.

The skipper ordered canvas up to protect the watch at the wheel from waves running three to six feet. We strung the 2-foot high, long canvas along the railing of the deck. While this kept the worst of the waves from hitting the helmsman, everyone still ended up freezing cold and wet by the end of his watch.

The waves rose like a living wall before us, then broke way up near the top. White spume spilled all over the boat. They came at us from all directions at once with a really choppy surface. Any gear below not firmly tied down rolled and skittered across the deck. Only a few hours before, we had the boat in spotless condition, with everything tied down and neatly stowed in its place.

Bungy at helm of Resolute in rough, cold weather!

My three-hour watch ended around midnight. After the captain took over the wheel, I made my way below, hanging on desperately to anything that came to hand. I was seasick, wet, cold and exhausted from trying to keep the boat headed in the direction of Acapulco.

I bunked up in the very front of the boat, called the fo'c'sle, the roughest place on any boat. We had stored a lot of the foodstuffs in an adjoining bunk, as well as on a shelf above my bed. At some time during the storm, a big bottle of vegetable oil had come loose and spilled all over my sleeping bag. Too worn out to do anything about it, I simply flipped the bag over and climbed in. As the trip progressed southward, the tropical sun heated up that tiny fo'c'sle and that oil grew more and more rancid and took on a life of its own, but that night, I simply did not care.

The weather stayed rough for days and my uncharacteristic seasickness continued unabated, no doubt made worse by trying to sleep in a miasma of stale oil. Below, the air grew stale and damp. The unending shaking of the boat grew exhausting.

However, when it comes to work, no one on board a sailboat has an option. Sick or well, everybody *has* to work. If each person does not take his or her turn at the wheel, someone else ends up having to do double duty. That gets old in a hurry, with exhaustion and anger building up quickly.

In the middle of the second night, the captain shouted, "All hands on deck!"

I threw on my parka and raced up the steps just behind Dottie into the wild night.

"We're going to put out a sea anchor," Capt. Fabian shouted. "Maybe that will settle us down a bit!"

"Bungy, you take the helm. Dottie, help me get the anchor out of the deck locker."

They staggered up amidships to the carryall wooden deck box and got out what looked like a giant canvas ice cream cone with a big hole in the bottom. Ed fastened one end of a rope to it and tossed it off into the ocean, and tied the other end to a cleat on the stern. It worked as a steadying drag on the boat.

Then, he got a couple of quarts of oil and poured them into a big canvas bag, tied a rope onto it and the other end of the rope onto a stay at the bow of Resolute, and tossed the bag into the churning sea. The oil leakage from the bag, formed a mini oil slick which did work to calm the waves a bit, at least until the oil ran out. The process demonstrated the truth of the phrase "pour oil over troubled waters" and explains why pouring a little olive oil into a pot of hot water keeps your spaghetti from boiling over.

Being at sea with such an experienced hand as Ed Fabian comforted me during this storm. I knew he had survived much worse during his sailing experiences.

As I stood on the storm-tossed deck of the *Resolute*, I longed desperately for one of Flo's wandering rafts, so I could just paddle it over to Baja and land. But, no matter how much I wanted to return to The Cove to see my beloved family, I had a responsibility to this boat and crew. The whole thing came down to an issue of loyalty. What was more important? If I jumped ship, swam ashore, and somehow managed to make my way back home through the deserts of Baja California, would they have enough people to sail the ship? The answer, of course, was no. My clear duty was to stay.

When my watch came again, I stumbled through the cabin to the wheel. The boat rolled and pitched madly up and down and back and forth, and I made my way aft hand-over-hand, grabbing on to walls and bunks and shelves and ropes. Occasionally, the boat rocked so badly I lost my footing and had to pick myself up off the deck.

Lili, which means "lovely flower" in Hawaiian, had the sweetest personality. She had an angelic smile and a head full of golden curls. She spent a lot of time in her own little bunk, with a net firmly fastened in front of it to keep her from falling out. She had absolutely no fear of the storm and played contentedly with her dolls and toys for hours on end.

As I staggered by on the way to my trick at the wheel, I heard this tiny little fairy-like voice say, "Peanut butter samich, please." Nothing else.

Well, I hauled myself around and made my way back to the galley where I braced myself with my legs stretched from bulkhead to oven. With careful coordination of my movements with the rocking of the boat, I managed to get out the peanut butter and slap some on a piece of bread. I did the same thing with the jelly. I had to try and get everything back where it belonged before the next big wave hit. I folded the bread over and staggered back to Lili's little bunk and handed her the sandwich through the top of the safety net.

She looked up from her dolls, reached out her little arm, grabbed the bread, took a tiny bite and said, "Thank you," with a great big smile.

Well, how could I not pay attention to this darling, good, little thing? She provided the highlight of my "commute" from bunk to helm, during that rough weather.

Storms, however, remain a fact of a sailor's life and all sailors always prepare themselves and the boat for them. During my sailing adventures, I experienced a lot of storms, some not so serious, others ferocious but quickly over, and a few that seemed to last a lifetime.

After three or four days of bad weather, the gray clouds finally turned into white clouds. The parkas and the heavy jackets came off. The sun came out. And with the sun, my attitude changed. After all, I finally found myself living the dream I had treasured for so long, sailing the seven seas.

At last, the deep blue sea sparkled. Overhead, the brilliant white sails pierced the magnificently clear sky. The gentle breeze caressed our skin like a soft piece of silk. For 360 degrees around *Resolute*, we saw nothing but ocean. With none of our competitors in sight, I sometimes forgot that we were in a race, but Capt. Fabian kept us mindful of our purpose and we hoisted as much sail as possible as we caught the winds that sent us flying over the waves southward. The sunrises and sunsets burst forth with color as God poured out his entire palette. The night sky was filled with stars so bright and so close, I reached up and tried to gather them into my hand.

We had many days of absolutely perfect sailing, averaging four to six knots. But as we got further south, sometimes the lack of wind left the boat totally becalmed.

On one of those days a 250-pound turtle came swimming by. Grabbing up a spare piece of rope, Capt. Fabian twirled it in a loop over his head, threw it in a perfect circle, just like a genuine cowboy, and lassoed the giant creature around his neck. "Yee haw!" he cried.

"OK, Bungy, get on the back of that turtle, and go for a ride!" Ed told me.

"Oh! I don't know, Captain," I replied.

"It'll be OK! Just step off the boat onto his back. You'll love it!"

I looked over the side of the boat at the impassive face of the sea giant. He paddled calmly along beside us. Occasionally, he blinked a solemn yellow eye. He did not look at all threatening. Still, I had my doubts about getting onto his back.

"Look," Capt. Fabian said, "Just get on his back and hold his neck up. If you keep his neck up he can't dive and you'll get a good ride out of it. If you lose your grip and he does dive, you just let go and swim to the boat!"

Well, for half an hour I tried to get my courage up to ride that turtle. It sounded so logical and everything, the way Ed explained about holding the turtle's neck up, but somehow, I just lacked the courage to do it. For years, I kicked myself for not going for the whole enchilada! I used this experience as an example my whole life to "go for it!"

If Flo had been there, she undoubtedly would have talked me into doing it. "After all, we *have* to ride the turtle," she might have said. And I would have done it!

An absolutely delightful woman, Dottie was a big dark haired lady who loved to cook and sing. I loved to eat and sing. Consequently, she and I got along swell.

Dottie started playing the guitar and singing in high school even though someone had once told her that she could not sing. She attended UCLA as an English major and took a job as an editor at a large paper in Mexico City after graduation. When she decided to head back to California, she got a job on a working schooner out of Acapulco. The boat, blown off course, developed a serious leak and ended up in Honolulu for repairs.

Dottie found a temporary job waitressing in a café. One day a friend came in and said, "Dottie, there's a handsome skipper on a schooner down in the harbor heading for Los Angeles via Alaska." Dottie dropped her menus, took off her apron and headed straight for the harbor, where she met the good-looking owner, whom she later married. The schooner was the *Resolute*.

Dottie got out her guitar in the evenings and we sang all the songs we knew under the star-filled southern sky. We sang an old sea chantey: "Come all ye young Laddies that follow the sea - Weigh ho! Blow the man down."

Since we were on our way to Mexico, we also sang a lot of Mexican tunes like *Cielito Lindo. Ay, yi yi yiiii!* It was so festive!

During one frustratingly still day, we lay becalmed. In the early sunrise, we saw a huge power cruiser getting closer and closer. We soon recognized the 85-foot Coast Guard cutter that accompanied the competitors throughout the race. Their job was to motor along the race itinerary and check on all the boats, standing available to anyone who got into trouble and needed help. Each racing boat called in its position two times a day to the cutter.

Even when becalmed, a boat always experiences plenty of motion, made evident by all the many and constant noises of the boat. The craft slaps through the swells, the rigging jingles and jangles. Even though the boat just sits there, not making any way or progress, a friendly and continuous tune plays through the stillness. I always preferred light storms to being becalmed, because the crew can do nothing to make the boat move forward in a calm. That sunny day, the *Resolute* lay still in the water as we stood on the deck, watching the big cutter as it came nearer and nearer.

The gleaming white Coast Guard vessel just kept heading right for us, making no sign of an impending turn to get around us.

"What the heck is he doing?" Capt. Fabian muttered, keeping an eye on the boat through binoculars. He tossed them aside as the cutter drew close enough for him to see every detail with the naked eye. The sound of the boat's motor grew louder and louder, the deep rumble rising above the normal boat sounds we had become accustomed to.

Ed picked up the megaphone and began to shout at the other vessel. "Ahoy, cutter. Ahoy!" We all stood anxiously at the rail watching its rapid approach. We saw no one standing on the deck and only a non-commissioned officer at the helm.

Suddenly, we observed a great deal of action on board the cutter. The captain and first officer flew up to the bridge and stared at *Resolute* with startled faces. It was clear to all of us, watching in growing panic from our boat, that no one had been in command! On all properly run ships, a protocol specifies who is on deck and in command. Apparently the captain thought the first officer was

127

on duty, and the first officer thought the captain was. When they realized no one was directing the helmsman, we heard the captain yell, "Full steam astern!" He was so close, we read his lips as he screamed the order.

The big cutter put on its brakes, or rather threw its engines in reverse, and almost squealed to a halt. The boat slewed to a stop within twenty feet of us. The huge wave that hit us in the bow, created by the sudden braking, tossed us up and down furiously for a bit, and we all grabbed something on deck to hold on to.

For the next few moments, it got really quiet there in the middle of the big blue ocean. We looked up at the Coast Guard captain's face and saw his clear embarrassment in his tight lips and red face. After a moment, he reached down and grabbed his megaphone.

Putting it up to his mouth, he called, "Ahoy, *Resolute*, what is your position?"

Capt. Fabian lowered his head and bit his lip to keep from laughing. After a pause, he raised his megaphone and replied, deadpan, "Exactly the same as yours, Captain." All of the sailors on both boats roared with laughter.

Finally, on the fifteenth day of the race, we sailed to within about 200 yards of the finish line in Acapulco along with the only other race boat we had seen during the whole trip. All day long we had just barely ghosted along, hugging the coast on practically no breeze at all. We watched our competitor coming in from a bit farther out to sea.

We saw them get a puff of breeze and moaned with dismay, as they moved closer to the finish. Then we got a whisper of wind in our sails and moved up a smidgeon, which I am sure, made them groan in despair.

The *Resolute* sailed somewhat closer to land, but both boats had the same distance to cover to get to the finish. This back and forth battle of sailing wits went on for two or three hours, with the finish line staying tantalizing close, yet unreachable. After days of sailing without seeing any competition, it seemed really strange to at last come up against another boat, only to move so slowly. Finally, our captain maneuvered us a bit closer to the shore where we picked up a slight wind from the land and we edged across the finish line, just ahead of them, finishing fifth out of seven. The first place winner had completed the trip in twelve days.

Boats filled the bay and crowds of people hooted and hollered to welcome us. Perhaps I should say they *"gritoed,"* the *grito* being what the Mexicans call their famous yell for independence. Into the middle of the bay we ghosted, and down went our anchor. Fifteen days at sea, and at last we had reached the end of our voyage. We celebrated our exciting finish by dancing on the deck.

Our celebration disappeared in a flurry of activity as the yacht club officials and immigration people came aboard to welcome us and check our papers.

"Welcome aboard, sir!" Capt. Fabian shouted.

"*Bienvenidos*!" called the yacht club official.

With all the paperwork formalities cleared, they introduced us to the host family assigned to entertain us during our stay. The race staff had appointed one Yacht Club member family for each boat and they planned parties for us all over Acapulco. After inviting us to dinner and dancing at the yacht club that evening, the officials motored back to the dock to allow us time to get ready. We quickly stowed our gear, swabbed down the decks, and got a semblance of order on board once more, before making our more personal preparations for the festivities.

As the sun began to set, I turned to Capt. Fabian and said, "The water looks so beautiful, I think I'll just go for a quick swim."

"OK," he replied. "Just don't swim too far from the boat."

I dove in to the clear blue water and naturally went about 100 yards from the boat, since I never had any real talent for following orders exactly.

Suddenly I heard what sounded like a giant's hand slapping the water. Slap. Slap. Slap. I looked around and here they came, a whole school of manta rays. These huge gray creatures can have a wingspan of over twenty feet and can weigh more that 3,000 pounds. Defying gravity, they threw themselves into the air and somersaulted over, landing on the surface of the bay with a loud thwack! Generally solitary creatures, dozens of rays seemed to fill the bay around me. Today, of course, we know rays are harmless, but in those days, they remained mysterious and very frightening.

Their passage completely cut me off from the boat. I looked back at the *Resolute* where I saw the skipper standing frozen on the deck, a rope half curled from his hand as he watched the rays flipping all around me.

In the midst of all the noise and splashing, I remained aware of the sunset just getting more and more magnificent, while faint sounds of mariachi music drifted out from the yacht club. The fifty or more rays kept right on their course, never even noticing the lone little human swimmer in their midst. On they went, out to sea and out of sight.

Trembling with both awe and fear, I headed back to the boat and climbed aboard with shaking legs. "Bungy!" Capt. Fabian yelled, shaking the piece of rope at me, "Don't you ever go swimming at sunset again!" That was the only time during the whole trip that I heard Ed lose his temper.

Many natives of the tropics advise against swimming at sunrise or at sunset, because the sharks appear then. And, as I learned in Acapulco, the manta rays also like to play at that time of day. But I always found it hard to resist starting or ending my day in the water.

The moon was rising over Acapulco Bay as we all lowered ourselves into the dingy. Capt. Fabian rowed us ashore to the welcoming dinner dance that was already in progress. We knew it was, because of all the merriment coming across the waters. We tied up to the dock, and with a bit of sea legs, wobbled up to the yacht club and were welcomed with open arms. And what arms they were! It was like all of Mexico welcomed us. We dined from a buffet that must have been fifty feet long. We danced to a mariachi band of violins, trumpets, marimbas, drums, and stand up basses. There was no lack of partners for me. I was counted among the heroines, who had made the long, adventurous voyage!

I danced several dances with a handsome First Lieutenant from our Coast Guard cutter that had tied up at the other end of the bay. As the evening drew to a close, he looked down at me and said, "Let's take a stroll out to see the bay." He stood tall and handsome in his uniform whites. We started the walk out to the end of the pier. It was all so romantic, just like in the movies.

The full moon shone down on us. A light tropical breeze blew in from the bay. A lively Latin beat poured out from the band up at the yacht club.

Considering the setting, he very naturally put his arms around me and started to kiss me. Now, even though I was eighteen, I was very inexperienced – what we called in those days, a late bloomer, so I shouted, "What are you *doing*?" and gave him a big shove. He teetered on the edge of the pier, his long arms windmilling wildly. Quickly, I grabbed his jacket and yanked him back. I had almost shoved him off the pier into Acapulco Bay. Not surprisingly, he never asked to see me again!

After a couple of weeks, all the festivities ended and the Fabians planned to sail *Resolute* back up the coast, hitting all the little unspoiled Mexican bays. They invited me to come "gunk holing" too, but by this time, homesickness had really gotten to me. My sister Flo planned to be married, and I wanted to get home as fast as possible. Unfortunately, I didn't have a great deal of money, so I decided to take second-class buses through Mexico to Texas and then head back to California from there.

I bought my ticket the next morning, bid a fond *adios* to the Fabians, and made my way to the bus station.

When the driver called out the Mexican equivalent of "all aboard!" I joined the other passengers pushing onto the bus. They included chickens, pigs, baskets of fruits and vegetables, and judging from the odor, a catch of fresh fish. Everyone laughed and had a good time, and pretty soon, I laughed along with them.

The hospitable Mexican people took such good care of me throughout the trip. I had purchased a brightly colored Mexican skirt and a white ruffled blouse and wore them for the journey. In Mexico at that time, women simply did not wear jeans or shorts.

In Tasco, the center of handmade Mexican silver jewelry, I wanted to tour the historic Catholic church on the square, but a vendor told me I needed to wear something on my head to go in. She handed me a woven hat shaped like an ice cream cone. All around the brim hung multi-colored fuzzy balls bobbing on short strings. When I offered to pay for it, she assured me that it would be all right for me to wear it into the church and bring it back afterwards. So, I went in with my little conical hat, the balls bouncing merrily with every step. I found it difficult to remain solemn in the sanctity of the magnificent old church in such attire. After returning the hat, giving my "*muchas gracious*," and receiving her "*Vaya con Dios*," I toured the silver market and the market square until time for my next bus to leave.

Near Mexico City, a nice young teacher got on the bus. He wore frayed but clean black pants and a well-worn but spotless white shirt. Teachers got paid very little in Mexico. He spoke some English. Since I spoke some Spanish, we enjoyed practicing with each other.

When we arrived in Mexico City, I learned that no bus left until the next day. My new friend offered to find me a nice inexpensive hotel. He introduced me to the desk clerk and to the manager and asked them to take care of me. The overnight stay cost me less than ten dollars. Everybody went out of their way to see that I had everything I needed.

That evening, he came for me and we strolled the streets and had delicious fresh taquitos from a street vendor. Later, we went to the movies, which proved an interesting experience. Everyone talked and laughed throughout the show and added sound effects to the action on the screen. They had obviously seen this movie many times before.

The next morning, the young man stopped by the hotel and escorted me to the bus station. I never saw him again, but I have never forgotten his kindness, so typical of the hospitable Mexicans.

From Mexico City, I traveled to Nuevo Laredo on the equivalent of a Greyhound bus, an improvement over the bus I had traveled on earlier. On board I met a bunch of students returning to the university in Monterey. Happy and loud, they just had a wonderful time. They made the trip seem short by teaching me some Mexican ranchera songs. I missed them when they got off because the bus suddenly grew rather quiet and dull, but I still remember a song they taught me called, "*Que lejos estoy.*" It told about being far away from the land of one's birth, written for those who had to go to the U.S. to work.

As I crossed the Mexican border into Laredo, Texas, and boarded a bus for California, I was ready for home and my sister's wedding at The Cove.

Chapter 8

♪ *Let me call you Sweetheart,* *I'm in love with you!* 🎵

Flo and her husband, Rusty, had gone to kindergarten together in Seminole, Oklahoma, before we moved out to California. He joined the Navy during the Korean War, and his mother told him to look us up when he came to the west coast. He came to dinner, and they clicked instantly. In fact, you couldn't have pried them apart with a crow bar. It was a forever thing.

They got married two days before Valentine's Day, so hearts and flowers once more made up the Dance Floor décor.

We adorned The Cove with what seemed like a million flowers and candles. It took us days to put candles all over the big rocks going up the side of the cliff around the fireplace in the outdoor Living Room. We had discovered that the local Catholic thrift shop had big boxes of used candles for sale, so we always had plenty. Four big steps led up to the living room from the dance floor, and the minister was to stand at the top of the stairs, with the wedding party at the bottom.

We invited a limited number of special friends and family for the wedding ceremony, and then lots of additional guests for the reception.

My family always did a lot of dithering. I do not know if they ever arrived on time for anything. The time wore on. The special wedding guests arrived. And waited. The flood of reception guests arrived. And waited.

And still no bride and groom.

Our house rambled along the western end of The Cove and the dance floor lay about 800 feet east of the house. I kept running back and forth, in my lovely semi-formal dress and high heels, to try to find out what was happening.

"Are you ready?" I called. "The guests are waiting!"

Someone in the house yelled, "Yes! Yes! We'll be right down."

I'd return to the reception to make a report and we'd all wait some more. Again, someone would say, "Go see what's happening!"

And back I would go, only to find that what was happening was exactly nothing.

We had put the pump organ in the middle of the dance floor for Amy Norworth, a dear old friend who had agreed to play the Wedding March.

A former Ziegfield Follies girl, she dressed like an exotic showgirl even into her 70s and 80s. When she sat down at the organ, she pulled her skirt way up above her knees, because the Ziegfield girls were known for their beautiful legs, and she still had them.

Amy was the wife of songwriter Jack Norworth, who was famous for "Shine on Harvest Moon," and "Take Me Out to the Ball Game." He was well loved in vaudeville. Just in case you've never heard it, this is the prelude to "Shine On Harvest Moon," which he always sang for us: "The night was mighty dark, and you could hardly see, for the moon refused to shine. A couple sitting underneath a willow tree, for love they pined. The little maid was kinda 'fraid of darkness, so she said, 'I guess I'll go!' The boy began to sigh, he looked up at the sky, and told the moon his little tale of woe ... 'Oh, shine on, shine on harvest moon ..."

Amy was a real character from Texas and she and Jack often invited us to their cute apartment in Laguna Beach for a bowl of the best and hottest chili we ever tasted. While we enjoyed this eye-watering meal, Amy played "Take Me Out to the Ball Game" on a huge organ, while their parrot sang along.

One sunny, summer day, we loaded her pedal organ on Dwight Long's sailboat and sailed up and down Newport Harbor for a Sunday afternoon. Amy played every song she knew, all the time pedaling furiously with both gorgeous legs pumping hard. The boats we passed yelled out their favorite songs, which she sang and played. She was cheered from one end of that harbor to the other. By the end of the day she said, "Whew! I feel like I have walked a thousand miles!"

Tonight, she was playing up a storm for our wedding guests, keeping them well entertained for quite some time. However, right before the ceremony, she got stage fright and practically fainted. We had to lead her to a chair and fan her for a bit!

Being a seasoned entertainer, Amy never got stage fright, so her little sinking spell caught us by surprise. We quickly grabbed another wedding guest, who fortunately knew the music, and seated him at the organ. Then, we continued to wait!

I made one last run up to the house all the way at the other end, just to see if the situation had changed.

Dashing into the hall, I met Flo coming out of Mother's room, laughing so hard she had to hold her sides.

"Mother decided that she had to have a mother-daughter talk," Flo moaned, wiping tears from her cheeks. "It was so funny. You wouldn't believe it!" She always refused to tell the rest of us just exactly what Mother had told her.

As I got back to the dance floor and the increasingly restless guests, our friend, the actor and director, Raymond Burr, decided someone needed to start directing and he and I went back up to the house.

Ray boomed in, and roared, "This wedding needs to get on the road...NOW!" When Ray used that commanding voice of his, coupled with flashing looks from his expressive eyes, everyone obeyed. The wedding "got on the road" immediately, with him at the helm.

The pump organ blared out the Wedding March. Here came dark-haired Mare, so pretty, in high heels and a full-skirted pink dress. With all the waiting, she grew so nervous that, instead of the usual stately march for bridesmaids, she nearly ran to the altar across the terrazzo dance floor. To this day, I can still hear her heels going click, click, click in a rapid staccato across that floor, in contrast to the slow and grandiose tones coming from the old organ.

Next came the groom and his dad, with the groom looking so handsome in his Navy uniform.

Finally the gorgeous bride entered the scene in her white gown. She just barely managed to compose herself following her meeting with Mother and managed to say, "I do," without laughing. The reception was a grand success, with plenty of tangos and waltzes. And the happy couple were off and running.

The Cove was not all fun! Surviving at The Cove demanded that everyone pitch in with the chores. And those chores were not always easy. Take our water system, for instance. Daddy located our well and its huge pump up the beach about 150 feet from the house, in a little shack right by the beach. The pump was huge, with a flywheel measuring two feet across. No telling where Daddy got it, but he hooked it up to electricity by running the old fashioned, cloth-covered electric wire from the house to the switch box.

Next, starting at the well, he ran old pipe up to about the middle of our 250-foot cliff behind the shop. With our help, he loaded up a huge old tin water tank into the back of the truck, took it to the top of the cliff, where we proceeded to lower it by rope, to about the middle of the cliff, to a convenient ledge. We came back down to the bottom of the cliff, scrambled up the side, and set the tank precariously on the side of the cliff, on that little ledge, using rocks and boards to get it straight, so it wouldn't tumble down the hill. From that tank, he ran pipes down to the house and through The Cove itself, using gravity to provide water to our paradise.

On the side of the tank he ran two one-inch by two-inch pieces of wood from bottom to top, about eight inches apart. He took a square piece of wood, gently slid this into the slot provided by the two "runners," and attached a long, thin piece of rope to it and ran this into the tank. The rope was connected to a huge piece of cork that floated on the water. In effect, the two outside pieces of wood acted like runners for the square of wood, which went up or down, depending on the water level in the tank, as the cork on the inside floated on the water, to help us see from a good distance away if the tank needed filling.

Each week, we girls took turns keeping the tank full. If we noticed the water level had fallen, all we had to do was push the big black button on the pump and it primed itself. With a *rumble, rumble, chunk, ka-chunk* the wheel began to turn, sending the well water up to the tank. But woe unto whoever forgot to check the gauge, or rather board, on the side, because if the tank ran empty we had to prime the pump in order to get it to work again. As we grew older and got busy with the outside world it seemed we girls regularly forgot to check.

To prime it, we had to remove a huge, heavy iron cap right beside the flywheel. We could hardly lift the heavy pipe wrench that we had to use for this job. After we removed the cap, we went to the old rock well, dropped a bucket on a rope into it, and pulled up a heavy bucket of water. You had to check the water in the bucket for scorpions, because the old well was loaded with them. As we lugged this bucket back to the pump house, some of the water always managed to slosh all over us. We set the bucket down and pushed the *on* button. The flywheel began to whirl. The sound was deafening. Immediately we dumped the bucket of water into the opening where we had removed the cap, and hoped that the water would prime the pump. We certainly knew very quickly if it did, because water pumped by this huge thumping machine gushed everywhere, especially all over the poor person who had forgotten to check the water level.

As the water was flooding all over us, we had to somehow get the cap back on and screw it down with the heavy wrench. You see, if we turned the pump off to screw the cap back on, the pump unprimed itself before we could get it tightened again.

I always felt great relief when the pump finally began pumping. Soon the house had plenty of water again, and everyone stopped yelling at whoever forgot to fill the tank. We had to remember only one more thing: to turn the pump off again once the tank filled.

I cannot remember how many times we all forgot that. One time, it ran over for such a long time (Mare probably got absorbed in starting a new painting in her grass shack studio), that it created a landslide. Some of the cliff slid down onto the shop, and moved the whole structure over two feet. It blocked the back door, which we never used again.

When our pump absolutely refused to work, no matter how we primed it, I grabbed my towel and Castile hard water soap, and dashed for the nearest tide pool, early in the morning, before school, and had a great time splashing around and getting clean. To me, this was the perfect bath.

I always felt like the whole ocean belonged just to me. After my walk home from school, I'd grab a peanut butter and jelly sandwich and either head up the beach to beachcomb, or jump in my swim suit and head out into my very own swimming pool, which just happened to be called the Pacific Ocean!

There was a kind of rock shelf that made it possible to walk out a bit before diving in. I had to dive shallow because the water was only two feet over the rocky bottom of the sea. Once clear of the obstacles, the ocean was infinite! Sometimes I just started swimming up and down the coast in front of the Cove. I'd swim about two miles without really getting tired, just blowing out the cobwebs of school. Other times, I'd take fins, mask and snorkel, and paddle around through the kelp beds just to see what I could see!

One sunny afternoon, I spotted what I thought was an empty rowboat about a quarter of a mile out to sea. Oh! Boy! A real prize! I jumped into the water and swam out as fast as I could. When I swam up to the rowboat, I saw that it was a purseiner skiff about fifteen feet long. At the stern, it was about eight feet across! These are the boats that were used to haul in the fishing nets of the great big fishing boats! How was I ever to get this prize home?

I pulled myself up and over the gunwales, and sat on one of the rowing seats, thinking of the big oars that were the fence back at The Cove. If I went back to get one I would probably lose my prize to the ocean currents. But, if I didn't, I'd end up at Cabrillo Beach! What to do!

I looked out at the horizon, and saw a small Chris Craft motorboat, and I waved and yelled. They came alongside and I asked for a tow down to the pier at the White Point end of the cove. They were really nice about it, and acted like it wasn't any problem! When we got to the pier, I tied my prize up, and jogged back to the house, where I told Daddy about my find. The sun was setting by that time, and he said that I would have to try and find the owner, since these boats were very expensive for the fishermen.

I woke up early the next morn, and headed down to view my prize. It wasn't there! It had vanished like a dream! I just hoped the fishermen who lost it had been looking for it, and had found it!

There was a Hawaiian lifeguard named Bill, at Cabrillo Beach, and he took a liking to my swimming. He said, "Bungy, you're a pretty good swimmer. You have a lot of stamina, but you aren't very fast. What say we train you, and you can start swimming in long distance races!" So, every day after school, all that winter, I went down to Cabrillo Beach and swam out to the light house at the end of the jetty and back. He entered me into a couple of five-mile ocean races, where I came in fifth out of about fifteen! Then he said, "You still have more stamina than speed, so let's start training you for swimming the Catalina Channel!" That was wonderful, until I found out I had to gain another ten pounds to help protect me from the cold waters of the thirty hour swim! I had just begun to think that boys had a little more fun to them than playing football! That was the end of my swimming career, but not my swimming.

The Army started taking an interest in the land they owned above The Cove. They opened up a practice firing range for all the new recruits. This was pretty dangerous because the bullets landed right in my ocean, right off The Cove! I'd be swimming along, and all of a sudden I'd hear little plonks here and there. These were the spent bullets landing on the water. Daddy contacted the Army,

Bungy, Mare, and Flo funning around in front yard at The Cove.

and soon we had a system. They put a pole at the top of the cliff, with a red flag on it. Whenever any of us wanted to go swimming, we'd look up first, to see if the flag was raised. If it was up, that meant that they were target practicing, and we'd better wait a bit to swim. There was only one problem with that. I'd be out swimming, having looked first to see that the flag was not flying. But the army never bothered looking to see if I were swimming, and would start firing practice while I was still in the water. When this happened, I'd swim the fastest I'd ever swum!

I soon found out that Raymond Burr had a great sense of humor. My sisters, friends, and I loved jumping into his World War II vintage

Jeep and going off down the road, singing and shouting gleefully, on our way to body surfing in Redondo. Huge waves tossed us up, down, and around. When we emerged from a particularly big wave, there stood Ray, water pouring off him, feet planted solidly in the sand, arms crossed, a big grin on his face and his eyes all crinkly with good humor and fun. Having withstood the wave's onslaught, with seaweed hanging from his ears, he looked as unshaken as a Hercules.

When we had swum to our heart's content, we jumped in the Jeep and headed to the fish market, on the wharf in the little village of Redondo Beach, where he carefully chose buckets full of fresh crabs, lobster, fish and whatever else caught his eye and we headed home. Arriving at The Cove, with a Strauss waltz coming from the Jeep's radio, he'd weave in and out through the palm trees, all of us laughing and singing and hanging on. Then we'd start up a big campfire on the beach as the sun set over a gold Pacific in front of us, and a full moon rose behind us over the towering cliff. He'd proceed to cook a huge pot of bouillabaisse on a hot rock beside the fire. After we'd all eaten our feast to the full, he'd stare into the fire, his eyes full of contentment, the tensions of Hollywood melting away, and we'd be happy for him.

One day, the news on the radio was exciting! A blind swimmer, Hawaiian King Bennie Nawahi, was swimming from Catalina to somewhere near our Cove. Two helpers were rowing a boat all the way along with him, which in itself was pretty good. They put a little bell on the side of the boat, so King Benny swam by the sound. Night came, and he was still out there.

The announcer said, excitedly, "We think maybe he's coming in to shore along the Point Fermin Wilder Edition coast line."

We dashed to the car, and raced down to where he might be coming in. We waited and waited. Lots of people came and went. All of a sudden Mare said, "There he is! There he is!" She ran down into the water to help him, but one of the boat guys said, "Don't touch him! He has to make it to high tide mark to make this swim official!" Mare said it was the hardest thing she ever did, watching him clamber over all those rocks, but she was right there at high tide mark to help him the rest of the way!

The rowers pulled up onto the beach, and after all the news people and everyone else had left, the boat was still there. Flo said, "I think we should come down early tomorrow to row it back to The Cove, and call them and let them know it is safe and where it is."

The next morning Flo, Mare and I went down below the park and the fourteen-foot row boat was still there. We shoved it out past the waves, jumped in, and started rowing. The currents and the winds were unusually strong and completely against us. We rowed and rowed. It took us eight hours to get that boat back to The Cove, which was only about three miles away! We were hungry, thirsty, tired, and triumphant!

A few years later, the radio was again the source of excitement. The most famous woman swimmer of our time, Florence Chadwick, was swimming our Catalina Channel. We raced down to a beach below Portuguese Bend. It was just at sunrise, when she came in, covered with motor grease to help seal in her body warmth. She was magnificent, and gave a yell of joy when she reached high tide mark! Our beaches were filled with excitement!

One time, in all their infinite wisdom, the Army decided to close the gate at the top of the hill. That was the only way into our home! They had put up a chain link fence ten feet high, with a padlock on it. After a few wrangles, Daddy and they came to a draw, so they gave us a key, and we hid it at the top under a rock. That didn't allow friends to come in, so they put a field telephone on the gate, and we put instructions for our friends to wind the handle in order to ring us all the way down below. Mother had them put our field telephone in the cellar so we had to listen carefully for the visitor's ring, especially if it were a date coming to pick us up! We'd tell them which rock the key was under.

Our mailbox stood right beside the gate, and was a small barrel on a post. Daddy always said to me, "How about going up and getting the mail? But, remember to look in the corners!" It took me a while to realize that the barrel had no corners!

The Mendez family lived on the cliff above us, on a farm. Their kids roughly matched our ages, and lots of times they either climbed down the big cliff to play, or we climbed up. Early on, my favorite play buddy was Chuy. We had lots of adventures together.

The Mendezes had a huge old workhorse named Chapo, and Mr. Mendez sent Chuy out on Chapo every day during the summer to herd their twelve cows out to the hills to eat. Sometimes I'd go with him. Early in the morning, Chuy and I climbed aboard Chapo's big, broad back. Chuy whistled and yelled at the cows until they started out from the corral, and off we went into the rolling California hills carrying a sack of peanut butter sandwiches, cookies, and an old mayonnaise jar filled with water. We found a huge peach tree out in the middle of nowhere, and as the cows were munching the grass, we ate barely ripe peaches to our heart's content.

We spent the day playing the kinds of games all children play on a hot summer day. About four o'clock we had to hurry to find Chapo and get aboard. He headed home at exactly the same time each day, and if we did not mount up before he decided to take off, he really didn't care whether he had a passenger or not. If we made it, he'd gallop off, and what a ride! We flew home! Instead of the cows in front being herded, all the cows were in hot pursuit behind. If we missed our four-legged bus, we had to hike over those hot, yellow, dusty hills, all the way back to the farm. That hike gave us a mighty big incentive not to dally.

During the summer, the farm's cultivated fields bloomed with acres and acres of stock, a wonderfully aromatic flower. In the evenings, the summer winds blew over the cliff and spilled that heavenly scent into The Cove.

Mr. Mendez drove like a bat out of h***! Every time Ba and I played at their house, our friends warned us when the time neared for him to come home. "Quick! Daddy's coming! Clear the driveway!" they yelled.

We all dashed around scrambling to get bikes and various toys out of the driveway because he just drove right over anything in the way. When Angela, the baby, was five or six, she was lying down in the middle of the road, with a coloring book, coloring away. She failed to hear her daddy coming, and he ran right over her.

We all just stood there, horrified. When the dust cleared, we saw that he had run right *over* her, not touching her at all. But the incident scared us thoroughly and we more diligently kept the driveway clear after that.

On full moon nights we kids used to start campfires and roast potatoes in the ashes. Those charcoal-scented potatoes tasted so good. We ended our supper with marshmallows and ghost stories and lots of scaring!

At the end of every summer, after running around barefoot all those months, the soles of our feet had grown tougher than cowhide, and we had a final contest the day before school started. We all got in a row and walked down to the bay on the other side of The Cove. Contestants had to walk straight, and not falter, even if that meant walking on glass, rusty cans, whatever. Whoever managed the challenge, and walked straight ahead and never said "Ow!" won. We had no prize, but we all fiercely joined in the competition. I can remember a lot of arguing about the finer points as someone insisted, "I didn't either step *over* that glass!" Or someone else swore, "No siree! That was not a yell out of me!"

Running around barefoot all summer let our feet spread out comfortably. One year, I did not start school on opening day because my feet had outgrown my one good pair of shoes. No one had thought to check before the big day if my old shoes still fit.

Something that was always a good fit was my parents and their friends. Mother and Daddy seemed to collect odd friends. One time, when we went camping up north, we passed a man hitchhiking through the pouring rain. Daddy pulled over and we all readjusted ourselves to let him get in the car. The fellow ended up staying with us for a year. He had just gotten out of prison and had no idea what to do with his life. He and I worked alongside each other, keeping The Cove clean and ready for fun.

Another friend was Franz Blas, a German artist down on his luck. He started teaching art and he asked Mother's permission for me to pose for his class. I sat in my jeans, plaid shirt and old straw hat with my hair in braids and my feet bare. He offered to pay me $15 an hour. Mother said I could not pose for pay, since Franz needed the money. At the end of each session, though, he handed me a box of 100 lollipops. To me, that seemed so much better than the $15!

One friend of the family came down for dinner and stayed two weeks. He had a radio program and wrote a column for the famous Farmer's Market in Hollywood. He just never wanted to leave. I think he wanted to become a beachcomber, too.

He and I liked to play jokes on each other. One evening, he and my parents planned to go out to dinner. I sneaked down to his car, pried off one of his hubcaps, put a handful of rocks inside and put the cover back on. When they got in the car and started moving down the road, they heard a horrible noise. *Clakety clack.* The car stopped, and started, and stopped, and started, and finally stopped and they all piled out, wondering what in the world had caused the problem. I just stood there laughing and then went over and fixed the wheel.

One of my favorite characters was Don Dickerman, The Pirate. He had moved to California from New York City, where he'd had several tropical night clubs and five wives. He now lived in Laguna Beach in a house he constructed around a real live tree! When you entered, you walked over a little wooden bridge. A stream ran under it, and the tree was a bower over it. His bath tub was in a little house at the end of a narrow path along his cliff. The view from his tub was such that one could open the door wide to the beautiful Pacific Ocean, and no one could see you! When no one was using the bath, he placed a beautiful, blond swim suit clad, store dummy in it!

Occasionally, down our dusty road, came a chauffeur driven limousine … it was Joseph Pratt, a famous industrial engineer and constructor. He loved The Cove, and I often wondered if it was the construction of the house that fascinated him. He was probably wondering why it didn't fall down.

I was a freshman in school when my Hawaiian friend, Pua, taught me how to weave palm hats, and whenever Daddy had decorating jobs at The Santa Monica Beach Club or The Coconut Grove in Los Angeles, I would go along to help, and after the huge ballrooms were looking like a tropical island, and the guests had started arriving, I got out my supply of palm fronds and started whittling them down to perfect lengths to tie into a circle, I'd jump into a colorful muumuu, put myself on a hand woven mat in a conspicuous corner of the big Luau, and start weaving and selling. Because the fronds were from the date palm they had a shorter leaf than the Hawaiian coconut palms so it was possible only to weave a half crown hat. It was easier and faster, but I could only charge $1.25 for them. But, as

Bungy Hedley weaving palm hats

Heart-of-the-Palm Weaving

By Bungy Hedley

Wearing palm hats may not be an unusual occupation for natives of Hawaii, Tahiti, or Samoa, but I believe it is for a seventeen-year-old girl who has just graduated from a Los Angeles High School.

Our home is in a grove of palms by the sea, between White Point and Portuguese Bend. It has the flavor of an island setting and our Polynesian friends say it reminds them of their homelands. Naturally we have learned a good many of their arts and crafts, one of which is weaving hats from the heart of the palm, which is a delicate green in color.

Some of my hats are with crowns, some without and as an added attraction I weave a little bird and place it atop a long slicer which I stick at the side of the hat.

I sell these to gift shops. Sometimes I'm invited to make and sell them at luaus, a popular form of entertainment in southern California in the summer.

A luau is a Hawaiian feast, where the pig is wrapped in ti leaves and burlap sacks and buried between red hot lava stones in the ground. It is completely covered with dirt and allowed to remain about three hours. With it are placed fish, chicken, and yams prepared in the same way. This delicious repast is served with long rice, poi, lomi lomi (raw salmon in lime juice and spices), and coconut pudding.

When I decide to weave palm hats as hats, I wear a sarong or a mu-mu, go barefooted, and surround my neck with lovely, fragrant ginger leis. To add atmosphere and stimulate sales. These hats are perfect to wear on the beach as they are light and cool, and at the same time keep the sun out of your eyes.

Bungy weaving palm hats to earn money to buy first boat.

the night wore on, and the guests got a bit jollier, they began tipping pretty well! The usual going rate of a real coconut hat, at this time, was $2.50!

This was how I financed the purchase of my first very own sailboat! The boat was handmade, all of eight feet long, and cost $100. It fit right into the back of our brand new woody, and I'd shove it in and head off to Cabrillo Beach, and on to the Seven Seas! One day I asked one of my girl friends, Mary, if she wanted to go sailing. She said that sounded like fun, but she wanted to know if the trip would be dangerous, because she had never learned to swim!

"Oh, no! I have a life jacket for you and we'll just be right off the beach and maybe a little way out, but we'll never even leave the harbor!" I assured her.

It turned cold that afternoon so we both had on warm jackets and jeans. We shoved off, and the four o'clock breeze came up briskly. The currents and winds were strong that day, and pushed us pretty far out into the shipping channels. All of a sudden, a big gust hit us, and over the boat went. I yelled at her, "Just hang on to the boat and don't worry!"

Well, luckily enough, it just happened that a 65-foot Coast Guard cutter was heading out to sea, on patrol, and spotted us. Over they came in their huge boat, making my little boat look like a toy. Leaning over the side, a sailor yelled down at us, "We'll put down the ladder and you can climb aboard!"

It is hard to climb up out of water, especially when wearing a lot of heavy, wet, clothing. We finally got my friend on board, by me pushing and them pulling. Then the sailors yelled, "OK! Now you!"

However, my boat was still upside down, with the mast stuck in the muck at the bottom of the harbor. I told them I did not want to leave my boat. I paddled around, clinging to the hull as they tried to convince me to climb aboard. They finally suggested that they throw me a line to tow the boat in.

"Look," I said, "if you tow it upside down the boat will break up."

I asked them to wait just a sec' while I dove under multiple times. Underwater, I unstepped the mast from the boat, and dragged it out of the mud, and up to the surface. I flipped my boat right side up and tossed the mast in. Those sailors expressed their unhappiness with me in colorful language every time I came up to the surface to take in big gulps of air. I certainly understood that they had more important things to do and wanted to be on their way, but they needed to understand how much I loved my boat.

After about twenty minutes in the freezing cold water I finally felt my boat was OK to tow and indicated I was ready to get brought up on the cutter. Since my clothes were a sodden mass by this time, including my heavy jacket, it took three guys to lift me out of the water. The suction of the water held me tight, and when that suction finally let loose, gallons of water poured all over their beautiful uniforms, all over the brass they had just finished polishing, and thoroughly soaked everything in sight on that gleaming vessel.

In the meantime, my gal friend was all nice and warm, down below, having a cup of coffee with the rest of the crew. My unhappy rescuers said to me, rather sharply I thought, "Here. Sit right here on the cabin roof and we'll bring you a cup of hot coffee!"

One year, Mary's dad, who was a commercial fisherman, let all of Mary's friends decorate the fishing boat he worked on so we could participate in the annual Fishermen's Fiesta. We had balloons and streamers hanging from the rigging, and danced and sang as the boat moved slowly in the parade. All the other fishing boats were decorated, too, to join the water parade through Los Angeles Harbor. The Harbor was crammed with all sorts of pleasure boats, coming to see this grand sight, everyone waving and hollering back and forth, flags waving and boat whistles tooting. The fishing boats paraded before the Catholic Archbishop, who blessed each boat as it chugged past.

San Pedro, the nearest town to The Cove, was unique in its beauty and its closeness with the sea. At that time, the majority of the people in San Pedro had Italian, Yugoslavian, Portuguese, or Greek roots and they almost all fished for a living. If they did not fish commercially, they worked as longshoremen or merchant marines. Many an old sea captain had retired to this village. Lots of descendants of the original settlers still live there, but not many of them fish for a living any more. Due to over-fishing and destruction of habitat, the fishing fleet has dwindled and the tuna canneries on Terminal Island have all closed.

Once a year, at Richard Henry Dana Junior High School, we were called to assembly to watch the Charles Laughton movie, *Two Years Before the Mast,* based on the book by Dana, the author and reason for the school's name. In his book, he made clear the appalling conditions under which the old-time square-rigger sailors worked. Sailors had no rights; they were like slaves, many times pressed into service. As a result of his experience, he led the fight to get seamen's rights. He became a true hero to all those who have ever plied the sea, since.

The school's copy of the movie was so old and well-used, we all hooted and hollered when the film broke, but by the time we got out of junior high we knew that movie by heart and understood the reason for San Pedro's prosperity.

Both the junior high and the high school were built as WPA projects during the Great Depression. Big double outside stairs lead up to the four huge doors in the junior high entrance. In the foyer, the floor tiles form a huge compass rose with all of its points. Mosaic tiled murals, depicting the discovery of Los Angeles Harbor by the Spanish, cover each wall. The display is just a fantastic artistic effort. It reflects the fact that the community just assumed that most of its children would grow up to follow the sea.

I had an English teacher who was very dramatic and wore lots of makeup, which was unusual for that time. She taught us Shakespeare. The only thing I can remember is the whole class cracking up when any of us were required to stand up and recite, "First the babe, mewling and puking in its mother's arms!" That was about as far as anyone got.

The highest honor in the last year of junior high was to become a Master Mariner. It took your grades, your teachers, and your fellow students to get you this. I think six were chosen. I am proud to say, I had the dark blue sweater with the Master Mariner emblem on the front. That is, until I was riding my brand new English racing bike which I had just gotten for Christmas. I started to make the turn in front of the school, and a car tried to get around me and didn't quite make it. My bicycle and I went sliding all over the road. It was so embarrassing! Right in front of the whole school. The man driving got out and helped me up. The only damage was a big hole in the sleeve of my beautiful sweater. I wanted to cry just because of my sweater, never mind anything else.

The very next day, I was riding home after school, passing a line of parked cars, when suddenly, right in front of me, a car door opened and I slammed right into it! I picked myself up, and the driver and I looked at each other, and he said, "Not you again!" Thank goodness that was the end of our acquaintance!

A bunch of us, all the way to twelfth grade, were into athletics, drama, putting on dances for assembles, and just having fun. Each year, the junior/senior water balloon fight happened. The word was passed. It was on such and such a night at Peck Park at nine sharp! My gal friends and I got our balloons and headed over to the park. You could hear all the yelling and screaming going on as we pulled up. We were late and started down the path to enter the fray, when we spotted police cars, without their lights, headed down the road, right towards us. We jumped into the bushes and hunkered down, really scared. Some police ran past us, and pretty soon we heard all this shouting and running, and we took off, jumped in the car, and sped home. Lots of parents had to reclaim their kids at the jailhouse that night. When I got home and Daddy asked me what I had been doing, I just said, "Oh, nothing much! Just bumming around with some friends."

Five of us girls ran around together at school: Mary, Ann, Shirley, Frannie and me. We had lots of other girl friends, and some boys, but we were the hard core that got ourselves into a few odd scrapes. None of us had much money, and all of us worked at odd jobs at one time or another. I had my ongoing job of keeping The Cove beautiful. Mary's whole family worked. She had a job at the hospital washing dishes, from the age of fourteen, every day after school, and got to keep $5.00 of her weekly paycheck. The rest went into the family funds. That was just the way it was for many families at that time.

Ann wanted to be a nurse, so she got a non-paying job as a trainee at the hospital, but because she was only fifteen she was put into Central Supply, and that didn't show her what nurses did. When she turned sixteen, she got a job at the local dime store, S.H. Kress's. All of us were in the very first drill team ever at this school, and we had worked really hard on the routines. We had a big football game to go to in Los Angeles, and were all excited. But Ann couldn't go because it was her first night at work! Jobs were really important, and her parents wouldn't let her skip out! We felt really bad! Shirley and Frannie both babysat, whenever they could, for their pocket change.

Our gym teachers all liked us, and they taught us lots of folk dances that we danced for the assemblies. Because I was so athletic, I got to lead the exercises at the beginning of each gym class.

In the locker room, four girls were assigned to two little dressing rooms with a shower in the middle. At the end of class, the two partners who shared a dressing room would dash like mad into the locker room from outdoor activities, slide under the locked door of the two others' dressing room, tie their clothes in knots and throw them into the running shower. We all had geometry class next, so whoever had not been fast enough had to undo their knotted, wet clothes and wear them to next period!

That got pretty tame, so we started bringing tomatoes to squash on the heads of unsuspecting ones passing by. That was pretty good, but not enough zing for the mess we had to clean up. So my partner in crime, Frannie, brought some raw eggs one day! We ran in and slid under the door, and stood hiding and waiting for the other two to show up. As they came up to the door, we leaped up and cracked our eggs on their heads! But, it was not our friends, it was the gym teacher! She laughed, but gave us a few demerits anyway!

Our geometry class was on the ground floor with great big windows that opened nearly to the outside gate of the school grounds! The bad boys (aren't there always those) waited until after roll call, and when the teacher was putting a problem on the blackboard, they'd sneak out the windows. They were always sitting in the back, hiding, and he never knew they left.

One day, Shirley and I decided to try our escape. We waited silently. "Shirley Cash?" "Here." "Bungy Hedley?" "Here." By this time we were biting our nails! Finally the teacher turned to the blackboard, and we got halfway over the windowsill when he turned back. "Whatever do you girls think you are doing?" We got sent to the girls' Vice Principal for that! But it seemed like all the officials in the school were so nice to us. Maybe because the stuff we did was just fun stuff and not mean stuff.

At seventeen, my tomboyish behavior made me something of a dud with the boys at school. All my friends began talking excitedly about the senior prom. I worried about what to do! No one had asked me. One evening, Raymond Burr was visiting. I had an idea. After a lot of procrastinating, I finally approached him, quaking.

"Now," I said, "I want to ask you something, but I want you to realize that you don't have to do it if you don't want to do it. My feelings won't be hurt if you say no, and I know how busy you are …"

When I finally stuttered to a stop, he looked at me for a long time and then said sternly, "What is it you want?"

I stammered, "Would you take me to my senior prom?"

He gave me another long look, then with deliberation, with arm and finger outstretched in that general direction, he commanded, "Go to your room! Stay there until you can figure out how a young lady properly asks someone to take them to their senior prom!"

What a horribly embarrassing moment! I slunk off to my room in despair, climbed my little ladder, and slumped down on my bunk, wondering what to do. After giving it some thought, I realized that he really planned to say yes! He just wanted to teach me a lesson in self-worth.

What to do? What to do? What would impress those big eyes?

I dashed into Mare's room and rummaged around in her costume box until I found a tight black sweater and skirt, very high heels, a beret, and for the final touch, a long cigarette holder. With this clenched between my teeth, I went slinking back into the living room. I flung myself into his lap, ran my fingers through his hair, and said, in my best exotic accent, "Monsieur, vould you pleez take me to my zenior prom?"

Eyes twinkling, he looked at me and said, "I would feel it the greatest honor to escort you to your senior prom!"

When the big day arrived, the telephone rang. "Bungy! Telephone. I think it's Ray," one of my sisters yelled.

I ran down the hall and dashed into the cellar. "Hello?" I said in my sweetest tone.

"This is your prom date calling," he said, "and I'd like to know what color your dress will be tonight." How exciting! He was not only going to show up to take me to my prom, but he was bringing me a real, live corsage to wear that matched my dress. I began to feel very special indeed!

He arrived for our date in his Jeep. This happened before his long-running *Perry Mason* TV series, and sometimes he had money and sometimes he didn't. I loved that rustic old Jeep, so I did not care, so long as I did not have to walk.

My date appeared at the door, so tall, so handsome, so absolutely gorgeous – in his tuxedo and black patent leather dancing shoes, bearing a huge purple orchid. I stood in awe of him and felt very nervous. He joked around and soon put me at ease.

I had not told anyone at school the identity of my date. We, or rather he, created quite a stir upon our arrival. The drama teacher immediately buttonholed him and started introducing him around, leaving me trailing along behind.

Ray let that go on for about five minutes, greeting everyone very cordially. Then he said, in his deep voice, "If you'll excuse me, I believe my date wants to dance."

And dance we did! We twirled and whirled around the dance floor, his eyes twinkling the whole time. He made me the hit of the evening. That night, my popularity at school shot up to 110 percent.

Lots of times, after I got home from school, I changed into jeans and a sweater, made myself a thick peanut butter and jelly sandwich, and hiked up the rocky beach a mile or two. I had a game I played with myself. I would see how far and how fast I could run over the rocks – rocks big and small, wet and dry, smooth and rough. The challenge ended when I fell. Then I picked myself up and, for a while, simply stood there looking out to sea. I do not remember my thoughts at that time, but something inside of me responded passionately to the call of far horizons, thundering waves and buffeting winds. I always liked it most when the winter rains blew in, carrying a salty spray from the waves constantly pounding into shore from the stormy sea.

I graduated, and because the Korean war was in full swing, my friends and I wanted to do something for the war effort. We discovered that there was a Los Angeles Harbor USO Group that gave dances every Thursday night. There were all these handsome guys, just our age, just dying to dance with us! And all in uniform!

It was a great sacrifice we were making, but we just jumped right in and started helping out with the organizing of swimming parties in the YMCA pool, where the USO was located, Cabrillo beach bonfire parties, and loads of dances in the big gymnasium! Our group had the most service men attending in all of California, except maybe, San Francisco! Mostly sailors, with a few soldiers thrown in.

We put on occasional sock hops that were always popular. At Christmas, we had a dance where we gals wore our formals. One time, we found a huge box of old ladies' hats in an alley, so we had a hat dance. We girls all made ours, and put the big box of hats at the door. The service boys got to select their chapeau for the evening as they came through the door! It was quite a success!

I got to the point where, if I danced with a guy once, and got his name and the name of his ship, then if I danced with him again within a few weeks, I could remember one or both! It was my war effort!

We gals all had favorites that we went out on double dates with, wrote to them when they went overseas, and met them at the docks when their ships came in. Mine was tall, had the sweetest smile, danced like a dream, and when he called to ask me out, would say with his darling southern accent, "Ah'd like to carry yew to the dance tonight!" Oh! Glorious! He wants to carry *me* to the dance tonight! And I promptly pictured myself in his arms, being carried into the dance!

He was having his birthday off the shores of Korea one time, and I decided to send him a cake. Not knowing how to bake, I cheated and bought an angel food cake, but actually made the icing. I wrapped it all up, and sent it to him on his ship. Pretty soon I received this nice letter saying how good it was and how they all liked it. When they got back, his best friend said, "Did he ever tell you about the cake?" It turned out that their mail came over the ocean on a wire pulley from another ship in the middle of the night. He was on watch in the radar room when the mail was delivered. The darkness of the room was only relieved by the red night light, and it was stormy to boot. He said, "Hey you guys, I got a birthday cake, I think!" So he proceeded to cut it up under the red light, and hand it out to the others. One of them said, "You know, this cake tastes kind of funny!" Someone lit a match. The cake was covered with mold! He got really upset with his buddy for having told me!! Wasn't he sweet!

Chapter 9

♪ I'm sitting on top of the world,
just rolling along, just singing my song! ♫

Daddy made our living from finding stuff on the beach, fashioning it into gorgeous items, and selling it all around Hollywood. We gathered driftwood and flotsam and jetsam from the coasts and bays of Mexico, up and down the shores of California, and to the wild and stormy beaches of Oregon. When Daddy decided we needed more driftwood to sell or make things from, we headed out on one of our many camping trips.

Mother handed out the safety pins, and we children got our blankets and sheets, and pinned them together to make sleeping bags. Then our cooking equipment, a heavy, black skillet, a coffee pot, and various other pots, pans, cups, and dishes went into a big wooden chuck box loaded onto the back of our pickup truck, and off we went.

I loved those trips, camping by the pounding blue Pacific Ocean. The minute we got to a beach that looked inviting, we shouted for joy!

Our first duty was to race to the water's edge, get down on hands and knees and dig a great big hole. Two of us staggered to the hole carrying a massive watermelon we had bought for fifty cents at a roadside stand earlier. We gently lowered it into the hole and covered it up with sand. As the ocean waves washed up and back over our treasure, the cold water did a great job of cooling down the watermelon.

Our second duty was to gather a big pile of driftwood, and light a campfire.

The third duty was to swim and play in the beautiful Pacific waters. Nice and warm when we were in Mexico, pretty cold in California, and sometimes freezing in Oregon.

Pretty soon, Daddy came along and always got us excited about finding the watermelon.

"Can anyone remember where we buried the watermelon?" he asked, getting up from a small hole he had dug in the beach. "I thought it was just right here, but I can't seem to find it."

That sent us scurrying all over the beach frantically looking for it. We dug here and dug there, until Daddy said, "Maybe this is the spot." And sure enough, he was right. I expect it was just a game he played with us, since we always found the watermelon, icy cold and sweet.

We set two long pieces of driftwood upright into holes in the sand and stretched a long piece of canvas across them for a windbreak. We'd gather around the warm fire, watching the sun slide into the sea, leaving reds, yellows, golds, and purples behind just for us. As it got dark, the stars came out, and we ate a delicious, smoke-filled repast. Mare scared us with ghost stores, and Daddy told us tales of the Wild West, because he was born and raised in Texas. My granddad went up the Chisholm Trail twice on cattle drives, when he was sixteen.

Flo, Mare, Daddy, Mother, and Bungy, beachcombing, or rather "working", from Mexico to Oregon.

Slowly, one by one, we crawled into our sleeping bags, looking up at the wide sky filled with stars, and a bright, full moon, sailing overhead. The sounds of the breakers rolling in from far lands lulled our tired minds until we slowly drifted off to sleep.

As we traveled, whenever we spotted berries, apples, pears or nuts along the roadside growing wild, Daddy screeched the truck to a stop, and we jumped out and picked as many as we could, always eating our fill as we harvested.

We shook big old nut trees, and gathered buckets full. In camp that night, we'd put the day's haul of those nuts on a big, flat rock and used a small rock to crack them. We picked out all the meat, ate some, and kept the rest ready for breakfast. We eagerly looked forward to morning when mother cooked pancakes loaded with the nuts and berries over the open campfire. The driftwood we had gathered the night before burned with bright blues and greens in the early morning sun, just topping the horizon.

I remember sitting around the campfire, warming myself after a swim, watching the sun slowly setting in all its glory, as I roasted hot dogs and marshmallows, before crawling into my sleeping bag. Sleep came while staring into the comforting campfire, which grew dimmer and smaller as the night wore on, but never quite went out because periodically someone crawled out of a warm sleeping bag and put some more logs on.

Awakening in the pre-dawn, pouring a cup of hot chocolate to warm my hands, I walked along the beach and watched the sunrise fill the sky. I remember the ever-present, delicious smell of the sea.

In those days, the beaches belonged to everyone. There were few fences and no rules. We always managed to find an isolated one that belonged completely to the seagulls and us alone. Occasionally, a few seals entertained us with their barking antics.

Sometimes, Daddy spotted a likely strip of beach and said, "Look! Doesn't that look like a great place to beachcomb?"

And we all looked, and Mother replied, "But Eli, see that big sign? It says "Private Property! It's even got a high fence around it!"

A fence never stopped Daddy, and we all jumped out and started scaling it. That is, everyone but Mother. When she attended college at William Woods in Missouri, she had the least athletic ability of her bunch of friends. When all the other girls went out the windows and across the roofs on illegal midnight forays, they had to haul Mother up, out, and down everywhere.

Since the passing of years had not improved Mother's climbing skills, half of us climbed back over the private beach fence and started pushing Mother up and over. The other half waited to receive her on the other side. Sometimes it took what seemed like an hour. But eventually, we all made it to the "perfect" beach, did our beachcombing, ate our picnic and had our swim. Then we hoisted and pushed her back over, and off we went, to find a legal beach to camp on for the night.

When we got back home, talking about what a good time we had had, we all exclaimed about how pretty the salts and minerals in the driftwood made our campfires, creating a rainbow of colors. After one such trip, Mother said, "You know, I think other people would like to have fires that pretty, too. Why don't we try making up some bundles of driftwood and see if we can sell them?"

We scouted along our beach for straightish pieces of wood, and before long, we had a nice collection, which we cut into about two foot lengths. I say "about" because the family never did anything exact! Daddy took a dozen or so, bundled them inside an artistic piece of old brown fishing net and tied it with a piece of wet kelp, which dried hard into the shape of a bow. He headed off to stores in Beverly Hills, peddling the driftwood packages. We ate many a can of beans off of those "Bundles of Beauty."

Later on, I saw that someone did the same thing commercially, selling little packages of granules of color for home fireplaces. This was definitely not as romantic as our driftwood. It seems like we

Hedleys regularly invented something, but we left it up to someone else to make a lot of money on the idea. It used to drive me crazy to know I lived in a family of artists more concerned with having the idea and creating one unique piece, rather than having an assembly line and making some real money. Whenever we hit on an item that sold pretty well, I always said, "Let's make 500 of them!" The rest of the family just looked at me like I was a creature from the Black Lagoon or something, and went on with whatever new idea they happened to be creating at that time. And there we'd be, broke again!

We camped all along the Pacific Coast to about mid-Oregon, and what beauty we enjoyed. We kids rode in the back of the pickup, with Mother's great big bear coat over us, all snuggled down, as we drove through the forests of giant sequoia and redwoods. We took in the cloud-sprinkled blue skies overhead, the smells of the earthy forests, the wild lupines and poppies in bloom, the scent of the ocean never far away. We even drove through that famous tree with the big hole in it, big enough for cars to drive through, which was a pretty scary adventure to a young kid in the back of a pickup.

One time we camped along the Russian River for a few days where we experienced the real novelty of swimming in fresh water. We caught fish and ate them along with potatoes we had buried in the coals of our campfire. We found lots and lots of pinecones, which, by the way, make really pretty fires, too, except for the sparks they throw out. This soon grew to be old hat since we found no beach combings! So, off we headed towards the coast, and new adventures.

At one Oregon beach, we rented a little cabin right on the edge of the sea. While we swam and did some beachcombing, an old guy drove up in a wagon pulled by a mule.

"Howdy," he said. "My name's Bob and my mule's name is Hazel."

Hazel looked us over and appeared to want to tip her old straw hat, but then thought better of it. Daddy offered Bob a cup of coffee, which he gladly took. During the course of their conversation, he told Daddy that we could drive our vehicle along the sand, right down by the water.

Well, we had never heard of actually being able to drive on a beach before, but since we always looked for new and interesting things to do, we all climbed in the pickup and drove down a little graveled driveway that ended with two long planks of wood. Bob explained that we needed to maneuver the truck just right, across the planks of wood that were placed right over the soft sand, in order to get onto the firm beach for driving.

Daddy eased the truck carefully up onto the planks as we gave excited directions from the back. Right in the middle the wheels slipped off the planks and into the sand. We did everything to get us out. We pushed and shoved, and heaved, but the truck was thoroughly stuck.

Pretty soon, old Bob, who had been standing off to the side, watching us, sauntered over, and offered, "Look's like you're not doin' so well. Hazel and I will pull you out for a dollar!" What a way that character had found to make a living. He had set the boards just about an inch off, so everyone who succumbed to the lure of an easy way to drive to the beach fell into the soft sand!

However, my family always had a way of turning every seemingly bad situation around, and soon Bob had become a friend. That night he appeared at our cabin with a homemade blackberry pie. Early the next morning he arrived with Hazel, and loaded us up in his old wagon. We sang and shouted our way down to a jetty made of enormous rocks that stuck right out into the wild, stormy Pacific. We all jumped out and he handed out bamboo fishing poles, with a string about twelve feet long that had a big hook, without a barb, tied to the end. We all looked at each other and said to ourselves, "What kind of fishing is this?"

Bob got a great big pick ax out of the wagon, and crawled down the rocks. There he proceeded to hack off bunches of mussels that fell into the ocean, to use as chum for the huge eighteen-inch long bass that we began hauling in, after putting more bits of mussels on our hooks. We did not even need a barbed hook, with the fish so close and numerous. You can guess what we had for dinner that night!

The next morning, we stuffed every inch of room in the pickup with our collected loot from the beach, and headed back down the coast to San Francisco. Once in the city, we stopped in front of a department store. Daddy went in and soon returned with the owner. After looking over our load, with lots of waving hands descriptions, they'd strike a deal. We'd unload our combings onto the sidewalk for him, and off we'd go, cash in hand, to get us a real live hamburger at a nearby café.

We worked that beach several years in a row after that. You see, our camping along the beaches *was* our work. We never took a vacation from beachcombing.

But, the hardest story of driftwood gathering happened in our own backyard.

A cove separates the two sections of Point Fermin Park in San Pedro, about three miles down from The Cove. For months Daddy had been eyeballing a bunch of "local" driftwood in this cove, while standing on the 250-foot cliff right above it. A steep, primitive path from the Wilder Addition of the park up above led down to the ocean, providing the only access to this site.

Daddy coveted that driftwood.

Early one summer morning, he said, "Boys! Get your jeans and tennis shoes on, we're going driftwood hunting!" That order confused us a bit because we usually went beachcombing barefoot and wore shorts.

My sisters and I climbed into the station wagon, and saw that Daddy had already loaded it down with ropes of every size and length, probably all the rope he had in his shop, and a great length of chain. Daddy hopped in the driver's seat with a gleam in his eye, shut the door, and off we went.

Shortly, we arrived at the destination and piled out of the car. We all lined up, looking over the cliff.

"There it is, Boys. See that pile of driftwood down there? That's what we're going to get," Daddy said. He said it as if he could taste that driftwood!

We inched closer to the edge of the cliff and looked down. Yes, indeed, far, far below us lay a large tangled mass of driftwood, looking from our vantage point like a pile of toothpicks.

We grew more confused. How in the world did he plan for us to get that wood up the cliff?

Soon he had us tying the ends of rope together and adding the chain, until he judged it just long enough to reach the bottom of the cliff. He tied one end to the rear bumper of the car. Then we all took up parts of the coiled rope and chain, and on his count of "one, two, three, throw!" we threw it out over the edge. That long length of irregular rope kept getting hung up on rocks and brush on the cliff, so we had to repeatedly jiggle and tug until the end finally hit bottom. We slung the remaining pieces of rope over our shoulders and slid and scrabbled our way down the so-called path.

"Wow! Look at this gorgeous piece," Flo cried when we all arrived safely on the beach. Indeed, we soon had to admit that some really beautiful pieces of wood had drifted into this nearly impossible to reach spot.

Under Daddy's direction, we quickly tied together all the pieces of rope we had brought down, and laid them out in parallel lines about two to three feet apart over the rocks. We began to gather and stack the best driftwood on top of the ropes at right angles to them. Some of these weathered tree limbs reached twelve to fifteen feet long. After we had gathered together a pretty good-sized stack, we firmly knotted all the ends of the ropes, drew the chain around the huge bundle, and tied it all off. We then had our bundle all tied and hooked on to the bumper of the car, way up on top of the cliff. Our package was ready to travel!

Flo and Ba made their way back up the steep path to the top and Flo climbed into the car. Ba stood near the edge of the cliff where she could see and hear Daddy, and pass on his directions to Flo.

"Forward! Stop! Back," she yelled, watching Daddy's signals from below. "Forward! Stop!" Time and again the pile got hung up on outcroppings of rocks and cactus. "Back up!" Daddy yelled. "Back up!" Ba seconded and Flo eased the car back toward the edge of the cliff as the bundle dropped slowly back toward us on the beach.

We went through this procedure several times until finally Daddy said, "Well, Boys, I guess we'll have to ride this driftwood to the top!"

Whoa! That sounded like lots of fun, just like riding a buckin' bronk in a rodeo! Flo lowered the big bundle down far enough for Mare, Daddy and me to get good handholds on it. Standing under the load, we braced our feet on the side of the cliff, and with Flo gently pulling with the car from up above, we walked the package all the way to the top, pushing out with our feet whenever it got caught up on something.

When we finally got up to the top, and the last pull brought the wood and us over the ridge, we tumbled down onto the grass and just lay there, panting and huffing, looking up at the sun and sky, totally exhausted.

After loading that wonderful wood all in and over the car, Daddy took us to the John's Creek Park Hamburger Stand across the road, and we ate the biggest hamburgers on the menu, excitedly reliving our adventure.

Daddy decided that the beaches to the south of us were calling, so we packed the station wagon with our sleeping bags and camping gear and headed out for Old Mexico and the fishing village of Guaymas.

If only we could have been transported there by magic carpet. Unfortunately, our route took us across the California and Arizona deserts, and through the border town of Nogales. We traveled in the heat of the summer, with no car air conditioning to ease the misery. It was hot! How we missed the cool Pacific breezes of our oceanfront home.

About midway through the desert, we came across a vast swimming pool fed by the irrigation ditches that criss-crossed the desert. A large fountain in the middle of the pool gushed crystal clear, cool water constantly. The owner told us that the water in the Olympic-sized pool changed every five minutes. A palm-thatched restaurant, probably called "The Oasis," overlooked the pool. As soon as we stopped, we jumped into our bathing suits and hit that delicious water. Splashing each other with joy, we sang endless choruses of the old Sons of the Pioneers song:

All day I face the barren waste

without the taste of water,

cool, clear, water ...

We swam and dove and played for an hour or more. Then we piled back into the car, sopping wet to help keep us as cool as possible in that dry 100-plus degree heat. I have tried many times to find this oasis, but it has just vanished, like a mirage!

We finally arrived in Guaymas. At that time, the little coastal town had no tourist facilities at all. It was just a sleepy, dusty fishing village. However, a lack of amenities never bothered the Hedleys. Daddy met a family that lived in a little grass hut, out on a point, with a big palm thatched pavilion next door. There we camped, right at the water's edge, with Guaymas Bay at our feet. We swam and beachcombed, and Daddy dickered with the locals for lots of items for his decorating.

The day before we started back home, the local fishermen caught a 200-pound sea turtle. They actually swam it up to the shore, killed it, took it out of the shell, and cut out turtle steaks. They threw everything else into a huge black pot over a fire, and proceeded to make tons of turtle soup, which we all had to eat, for the sake of politeness, no matter how awful it looked or tasted! Now, of course, these magnificent creatures are an endangered species. Too bad they weren't at that time.

Daddy bought the empty, uncured shell of the turtle from the fishermen, and we loaded up the next morning to make the long, hot drive home. All the shells we had collected, and the Mexican artifacts and crafts we had bought, went into, on top of, and under everything, including us, in the station wagon.

Much thought was given as to where to put the uncured, and by this time slightly smelly, turtle shell. Daddy finally tied it to one of the front fenders, and we girls argued all the way back to The Cove about who had to sit on that side. Daddy had this story he used to tell us about these wonderful, polite girls named the Williams sisters. They never argued with each other, were always polite and helpful, and were pillars of their schools. For years I thought there really were Williams sisters! I used to really want to be like them, and I'd even stop arguing. Daddy had a great way of disciplining us.

With no air conditioning in the car, we traveled with all the windows down through the blazing hot desert, that turtle shell getting riper and riper. It became a kind of awful, stinking presence in the car that no one could get away from! I wonder how many times Daddy thought about tossing the thing on that long trip home, just to stop the complaining. We stopped periodically to get a cold soda. Orange Crush saved me. To this day, one sip of an Orange Crush and I smell that uncured turtle shell again.

The best beachcombing ever, happened on a stormy day, when Mare went up the beach for a hike. She came running back down screaming, "Help me! Help me! There's a pelican up the beach who can't fly!"

Flo and I dropped everything and ran back up the beach with her. Here sat a pitiful picture. A bedraggled pelican, who, when we approached, would flap his wings, and squawk, and go nowhere. We planned our rescue carefully. Flo and I grabbed him around the body, enfolding the wings, and Mare clamped his huge beak together so he couldn't get at us. We struggled back to the house and wondered what to do with him. How could we help him?

We built a huge cage out of fishnet that we hung from the corner of the house, and put him in it. Then, we jumped in the car and dashed down to a live bait shop near where the fishing boat fleet was, and got him a bucket of fresh fish.

Daddy beachcombing at Trade Winds Cove.

Mother decided he looked as wise as Abraham Lincoln, so from then on he was Abraham. He wouldn't let us get anywhere near him, and we threw the fish over the net walls of the cage. He'd catch and eat them all. After a few days, when we could see that Abraham was stronger, Daddy said to us, "Now, Boys! You know you don't want to keep a wild thing cooped up. He belongs free, and so you just have to let him go!"

We carefully took down the net all around him and said, "OK, Abraham! You are free! We'll miss you!"

He looked at us a long time, tried flapping his wings and realized he still couldn't fly. So he just kind of waddled around. He found the overturned barrel that sat in the yard outside Mother and Daddy's bedroom window, and claimed it as his own perch. Every night, when we gathered in this room, he pecked at the window, for all the world, acting like he wanted to come in, too.

Each day, after school, we'd go down to the bait shop and get him his bucket of fish. He became tamer and tamer, and from then on, would be watching for our return! He began following us around everywhere.

It took him very little time to realize that we all went into the front door, so he began trying to follow us. It would be a real battle to get in the door without him. One day, one of us was not so quick, and he got in. Immediately he didn't like it, and started flapping his big, long wings. The entry hall shelves were loaded with bric-a-brac, and his wings started sweeping those delicate items off the shelves, all the time, Abraham squawking away. We were finally able to capture him and put him outside. He never tried that again, and was happy with his barrel perch.

He was getting stronger all the time, and could fly about three feet off the ground. He'd fly to meet the car each day, and coast along right beside us, knowing his treat was in the car.

We ate our noonday meal outside lots of times, and one day some nuns drove up and asked if they could picnic down by the Dance Floor. We said, "Certainly," and thought nothing more about it, until we heard shouts and screams. We looked down through the palm trees and saw that the nuns, who had been playing softball, were all pushed back against the cliff. Daddy told me to run down and see what was the matter.

I ran down, and Abraham had all of them against the cliff, pecking their long black robes, and squawking to beat the band. I was able to grab him, apologize to the nuns, and lug him back up to the house. The nuns gathered their things together and left in a hurry.

One morning he spotted a bunch of his fellow pelicans, floating in the ocean right off The Cove. He looked at them a long time, and suddenly took off from shore, as graceful as anything. He flew out to them, and settled on the water floating alongside them.

When friends came to visit, who knew about Abraham, they'd ask where he was. We'd step to the beach, clap our hands, and call "Abraham!" And up from the middle of a group of pelicans, he would rise and fly in, landing right at our feet. He always came back to us when the rest of his buddies took off for unknown places.

As summer wore on, he kept getting stronger and flying off for a day or two, to return as if he'd never been gone. Finally, he was gone for two months and we thought that was the last of our friend, but one day, here he came, and landed right in front of the house. We all rushed out and greeted him warmly. Daddy spied a fishhook in one of his wings, and got it out. Abraham stayed another day, and took off, and we never saw him again! And that was truly a great beachcombing find!

Chapter 10

♪ *Sailing, sailing, over the bounding Main!* ♫

A world famous sailboat-racing event is the Trans Pacific Yacht Race, which is run every other 4th of July from California to Hawaii. This is a major sailing event and something like 500 boats enter each race.

Year after year, I crewed for Dwight on this special day, just to see the race begin. With various and assorted guests, we'd start out early in the morning, motoring down from our Terminal Island slip to the mouth of the harbor. We'd put our sails up, and join the thousands of water craft of every make and kind, coming in from every port up and down the west coast. We were all there to give these brave mariners a big sendoff to Hawaii, an average of two weeks away. This stretch of water is daunting to many a would-be around the world sailor. It must be the sense of isolation that one feels after a teeming Los Angeles!

The Island Belle was all spic and span. The galley was loaded with goodies for the beautiful and exciting day sail. We tacked back and forth, along with what seemed like a million other boats.

This year, the big four-masted sailing ships, called the Tall Ships, had come to show off their magnificence to the world, and had anchored in Los Angeles harbor for this event. These magnificent old ships had been reclaimed from boat junkyards and now represented the pride of their nations. Sailors in their crisp white uniforms, some of them 100 feet off the decks below, lined their rope footholds, ready to loosen the great square s'ls as the first boom of the cannon shot sounded, to start the race.

"BOOM!" and they were off! More sailors leaped to the sides, scrambled up the rope ladders on the three masts, ran out onto the rope slings under the booms of the square sails, and all together, unloosened the tie-downs of those huge sails. The big canvas sails were hauled up by sailors down on the deck far below, and out they popped. "Bam! Bam! Bam! Bam!" they sounded, as the wind caught the canvas and forced the sails out. It made the hair stand up on the back of my neck to watch as they preceded the racing yachts out of the harbor, on their way to Hawaii.

BUT ... that was two years ago, and for this year's race I was on going to be on one of those 500 sailboats, heading for Hawaii and paradise!

I'd been haunting the docks, doing the odd job on this boat and that, like sanding and varnishing and scraping off barnacles from the bottoms of boats when they hauled into dry dock, always looking for another boat going anywhere. One day, I heard that Kyle Pratt planned to sail his 106-foot schooner, *Dwyn Wynn,* in the Trans Pac race, and was looking for a crew!

The year before this, Kyle had been leisurely sailing along the Mexican coast, visiting little bays here and there (this is called gunk holing), in his 52' sailing sloop. Upon arriving in Acapulco, he had received a message telling him his mother was not doing well. He had left the boat anchored in the harbor while he flew home to see her. A friend called to let him know that the president of Mexico had impounded Kyle's yacht and commandeered it for his own use. This happens quite often all over the world. Despite the devastating loss,

Kyle had pulled himself up by his bootstraps, acquired the *Dwyn Wynn,* and was setting sail on another voyage as soon as he could.

With good recommendations from my previous sails, I signed the articles, got my sea bag together, and hopped aboard, joining eighteen others, anxiously anticipating the voyage of a lifetime. Unfortunately, a few days before the race was to leave, something happened to the motor and we had to get a new one. When the engine arrived, it was huge and the mechanics used a block and tackle to maneuver it carefully into the hold. With the motor installed and operational, we finally waved goodbye to our friends and family on the dock ... three days after the official start of the race.

We ran into two or three days of the usual California coastal ground swell, with light rain and clouds, but soon found the sun and the sea turned from slate gray to deep blue. Off and running to the beautiful islands of Hawaii, we set all sail as soon as we hit the trade winds and did everything we could to make up for lost time.

I found the *Dwyn Wynn* a magnificent, comfortable boat to sail on. Besides being 106-feet long, the boat had a fifteen-foot beam. Try walking that off in your back yard to get an idea of her spaciousness. Because of her size, we had some luxuries that many smaller boats lack. There was a freezer stuffed brimful with all kinds of wonderful meat cuts, which made for a refreshing change from the usual dried, canned and powdered food generally available on smaller boats making long voyages.

We even had plenty of fresh water to drink and salt water for showers. Of course, on-board showers could be a bit hazardous. You had to get your clothes off in an itsy bitsy room, brace yourself from falling over as the boat rolled, and as soon as you turned the water off, quickly towel the salt off your body and out of your hair. As the weather warmed, we dipped buckets on ropes into the crystal clear blue of the Pacific, and sloshed it all over ourselves, and others, using my handy dandy Joy soap for shampooing and soaping down. It was the best for cutting the salt water and for grease on dishes. I "never left home without it!"

Keeping clothes clean was always a problem at sea, until I found that if I took a long rope and tied a really good knot to my jeans and shirts with one end (I didn't want to lose my wardrobe), tied the other to a stanchion, and threw the clothes overboard, they'd be clean in a half hour! Of course there was a bit of a problem. I dried them in the hot sun, put them on, and at sundown, when the night air became cooler and more humid, the salt absorbed the moisture, so the jeans were always damp.

Every sunset and sunrise I climbed the mast to the crosstrees, sitting with one leg on one side of the mast and one on the other, my arms wrapped around it. From a hundred feet up I had a 360° view all to myself. While sailing along, the top of the mast arcs into a huge circle, probably ten to fifteen feet around. The tall mast goes backward and forward and sideways as well, constantly in motion. Once we hit the trade winds, we moved along at nine to ten knots. That speed provided quite a ride up there for the Queen of the Universe, as I liked to think of myself, as I clung high above the deck enjoying the view. I spent my most wonderful times on any of the larger boats I crewed on, perched high up on the crosstrees. I loved the chance just to get up there all by myself with horizons far and wide.

I often watched when dark clouds started to pile up and I could see rain coming down in black sheets. The question would be, "is this coming right at us, or will it veer?" One never knew until it got closer, and then, watch out! The squall would hit in all its magnificent fury, which can last only a few minutes, or a half hour. And just as suddenly as it came upon us, it would pass and the moon would shine once more, or the sun would break through. The reef points would be shaken out, the sails hauled up, and the boat would once more tool along in peaceful bliss!

Some nights, as I took my trick at the helm, I heard the dolphins softly puffing as they leaped and played beside the boat. Seeing these amazing animals up close for the first time was the thrill of a lifetime. They seemed to delight in giving me the gift of their presence. They played for fifteen minutes or half an hour, and then, just as suddenly as they had appeared, they disappeared, and the soft sound of the sea washing against the boat's hull reigned over the night again.

About eight days out from California, our freezer broke. Unfortunately, we did not realize it immediately and all that gorgeous meat went bad. We had to chuck it all overboard. The sharks happily followed us for a couple of days.

To solve our meatless situation, we put some trolling lines out and within a few hours caught fourteen two-foot long albacore tuna.

"Someone teach me how to clean them," I begged, always eager to learn something new.

Well, someone did and I ended up cleaning thirteen of those big fish. Believe me, I never forgot how to clean a fish after that.

Food is really important at sea. A sailor burns up a lot of energy with all the counter movements he takes to balance against the constant movement of the boat. I know I always felt starved. The cook on the *Dwyn Wynn* was a pastry baker and didn't know much about regular cooking. In fact, he was a worse cook even than me, which made him very bad indeed.

THE CHRISTIAN SCIENCE MONITOR

Youth Section

"We caught mahi mahi using a white rag."

Bungy with two of fourteen albacore caught with white rag lures, on Dwyn Wynn voyage.

He boiled all of the nice, fresh albacore with a bunch of cabbage we'd been keeping in the cooler. Our newly repaired freezer was suddenly filled with boiled fish! We had boiled albacore and cabbage for every main meal. When the cabbage played out, we had the tuna with beans. We had boiled albacore with spaghetti, and boiled albacore with rice.

We found a whole case of catsup in the stores and we all started using catsup by the cupful. We also had peanut butter, and someone suggested we try that. When a person gets really hungry, he can find all kinds of surprising combinations that do not taste half bad. That is probably why, in the old days of sail, sailors happily ate maggoty beef and weevil-filled biscuits.

One day, the cook made a magnificent gelatin salad. We all yelled, "It's Jell-O," thrilled to have something new and delicious on the menu, until we discovered that it, too, had boiled albacore in it. We just poured on the catsup and spread on the peanut butter and wolfed down that salad before it melted in the heat of the tropics.

The crew aboard the *Dwyn Wynn* worked well together because the captain knew what to do. Kyle kept us busy painting, varnishing, sanding and cleaning. He knew that an idle crew in a cramped space like a sailboat was able to get into trouble in a hurry. A busy, hard-working crew stayed too tired to cause major problems.

The decks on this beautiful boat were solid teak. Two or three times we scrubbed these decks on our knees with holystones and a special product that made the wood bright white. At sea, an amazing amount of cleaning is always needed. I do not know where the dirt comes from, with no land in sight. But there is a lot of it.

189

We saw pods of whales and schools of dolphins on our trip to the islands. While they swam alongside, I sang Frederick W. Faber's old, old hymn, "There's a wideness in God's mercy like the wideness of the sea; there's a kindness in God's justice, which is more than liberty."

Ratlines were ladders made out of small rungs of wood attached to the stays or wires that held up the masts. To climb them, you grabbed a wire on each side of the ladder, and begin your ascent, making sure to place your feet close to the wire stays, never in the middle, just in case the rungs would break. Now, the boat is always in motion, moving from side to side, or up and down from bow to stern. When the boat takes a roll and leaves you hanging out over the ocean, you hang on for dear life. When it rolls back the other way, you run up as many rungs as it is safe.

When you reach the top, you can sit on the crosstrees, like you are sitting on a bench, and hang on tight!

One fine evening, just at sunset, I climbed the ratlines up to the top and was contemplating the sunset and the universe when I saw a green flash! This is a phenomenon that happens just as the sun slips over the horizon in the evening, when clouds, sea, and sun, are just right. The flash is so quick, you hardly think you have seen it, and it is very rare. For years I had been trying to see this wonder. I was thrilled!

As we neared the Island of Oahu, we sailed along the coast, past famous Diamond Head, looking as exotic as the pictures on post cards, and on into Honolulu Harbor and Pier 6, right under the famous Aloha Tower. We had to tie up to the commercial docks everywhere we sailed, because we were too big for the small yacht harbors.

We had barely finished tying up to the dock and were finishing with Immigration, Hawaii being a Territory at that time, when the Coast Guard and the feds boarded us.

"We've had a report that illegal gambling has been taking place aboard this ship," the frozen-faced federal agent said to the captain. He handed Kyle a document. "We have a search warrant."

And with that announcement, a squad of officers fanned out across the boat, searching for an illegal slot machine. The one we had aboard had proved quite popular with everyone during the voyage, but apparently some disgruntled crew member decided to rat on the skipper. The feds even had divers splashing into the harbor waters, searching beneath and around the boat.

I have no idea what happened to that machine, but those officers never found it. I cannot imagine how the crew managed to scuttle it in time. They had to do it right under my nose! I was certainly glad the captain did not get into trouble, since the penalty for transporting a gambling apparatus across state lines was prison time. The Pacific Ocean makes for a mighty wide state line.

In a couple of days we cleaned up the boat thoroughly and then had time to enjoy acting like tourists. Dwight Long had given me a great fourteen-foot hollow koa wood surfboard. Actually a sailboard, but lacking the sailing equipment, the heavy board took two or three people to carry it and it was almost impossible to turn around in the water. We borrowed a pickup on a few afternoons and hauled it down to famous Waikiki Beach, where we all took turns

Aloha Airlines post card of Hawaiian islands, where Dwyn Wynn sailed after trip of 2500 miles and 19 days.

learning how to surf. The boys did better than I did because of their greater strength. Dwight told me that the famous director, Preston Sturgess, had bought it from the famous Duke Kahanamoku.

Pua Kealoha, my Hawaiian friend from The Cove, earned a gold medal in the 4x200 meter free style relay, and a silver medal in the 100 meter free style in the 1920s Olympics. He was one of the original *Waikiki Beach Boys* along with Chick Daniels and Joe Minor. He had told me how he and Duke Kahanamoku, the most famous Hawaiian Olympic gold medal swimmer ever, started out as coin divers.

One day, across the bay, I spotted a dozen or more boys diving into the harbor when one of the big President Lines came in to port. The tourists lined the deck, waiting to pass through immigration, throwing coins out, as far out as possible into the bay to create a race of swimmers, churning the water. These coin divers were the best swimmers in the islands, but they were tough. I watched for a while, until I could stand it no more, and dove overboard and swam across the bay.

The regular coin divers swam all around, catching silver coins right and left. I just swam up and joined them. I spotted a quarter floating down and I leaped up out of the water and grabbed it. As I hit the surface and went under, one of the divers whacked the bottom of my hand. It flew open and he grabbed that quarter that popped out so quickly, I almost questioned if I had ever held it in my hand. I eventually managed to snag a dime, which I held on to proudly as I swam back to the Dwyn Wynn.

"You are lucky to have survived without getting into some serious trouble," Pua told me back at The Cove, after I had gotten home. "Certain families tightly control the coin diving concession. They don't allow anyone else to participate in this dangerous activity. After all, it's their livelihood."

Of the nineteen aboard the *Dwyn Wynn*, some were paying guests. When they got off, a crew of six or seven of us remained to keep the ship up. The captain got a charter to sail through the islands, and about twenty-five people came aboard. We had people sleeping everywhere. In our bunks, on the decks, in the main salon.

The wonderful thing about the charter was that the crew got to go along with the customers when they did their sightseeing, and we joined them for dinner and dancing every evening. It was a dirty job, but someone had to do it!

With our guests aboard, we worked our way northwest to the most distant island of Kauai where we took one of Captain Walter Smith's small touring boats up the Wailua River. The flora and fauna was so rich and varied, and smelled so exotic that you felt as if you were stepping back in time to when Captain Cook came ashore for the first time. The captain and crew of our tour boat played their ukuleles and sang old Hawaiian songs, and told us the history of the Islands. We reached the beautiful fern grotto that had huge stalactites and gigantic ferns hanging and growing all over the place. The perfect acoustics of the grotto are famous and two of the crew sang the Hawaiian Wedding Song, "Ke Kale Ne Au." Their voices rang out so clear and true, above the sound of a waterfall flowing from the top of the cliff to the floor of the cove. For the couple of days we were there, we swam in the cold streams and waterfalls, and sunned on the golden beaches of this most gorgeous island.

But then, it was time to gather our guests together and head on down to the Big Island of Hawaii.

As the *Dwyn Wynn* approached The Big Island, we sailed along tall black cliffs, dotted with waterfalls cascading into the deep blue of the sea. Hilo had a commercial harbor with a dock big enough for us. We started our brand new beautiful engine, lowered and tied down the sails, and slipped slowly into Hilo Bay. No one else wanted the wheel at that time because the entire crew lined the rail, staring hungrily at the little town of Hilo, so I said I'd be happy to take the helm, grabbed it, and brought that big boat right in to the pier without a single scratch. After we tied off and got all the guests ashore, and the boat ship shape, a bunch of us crew went ashore to do all the touristy things.

At that time, Hilo was a quaint, old-fashioned town. Buses, called *sampans*, which held maybe eight people, rattled all over the place. They had no windows, just a top, and all the seats were just right there in the open. Canvas shades rolled down if it started raining, which it frequently did in Hilo.

We wanted to go out to the sugar cane fields and up into the hills, so we hired a *sampan* and had the driver take us to Kilauea volcano. Several years later, when I had a chance to return, this area looked completely different. A tidal wave, volcanic eruptions and lava flows, and a million more people, worked mighty changes in just a few decades.

After a couple of days of sightseeing, we waved *aloha* to our new friends, hauled in the lines, started the engine and put her into reverse. The boat did not budge. We shifted into forward. The boat still did not move.

Apparently, sand had filtered into the bay on the tides, and settled all around the boat while we remained tied up to the dock. We were stuck.

Finally, Capt. Pratt had an idea. Ten of us lined up on the dock side of the boat while the rest climbed out to the end of the long main boom and straddled it to hang on. We pushed the boom out to the sea side of the *Dwyn Wynn*. Then the group of ten ran over to the sea side and rocked the boat. We did this back and forth several times, with the engine groaning in reverse. The boat did not budge. We shifted into forward. The boat still did not move. We reversed once more, until, with a big shudder we pulled free.

"Hurrah!" we all cheered, and waved *aloha,* again, as we sailed out of Hilo and headed around the Island to the District of Kona, where we anchored offshore from the village of Kailua.

While there, we kept a watch at all times, just in case the ground swells and offshore winds decided to pick up. If this happened, it would be possible that the anchor wouldn't hold us, and off we'd go, either to wreck on shore, or drift merrily out to sea. We used our longboats to row the guests from the boat to the village. This was real authenticity for them. They had arrived in paradise! But we had to work hard at those oars.

After a few days of visiting The Parker Ranch, famous for their *paniolos* (Hawaiian cowboys), touring a coffee plantation, and visiting the King Kamehameha Hotel with their wonderful collection of outrigger canoes, Hawaiian royalty capes, and other Hawaiian history, we were ready to weigh anchor and wave good by to the friendliest people on earth! With the sails full, and the sea sparkling, and the deck beneath my bare feet, what more could I ask for?

We stopped at Lahaina on the island of Maui, where we pulled up to the little stone breakwater there. Back when King Kamehameha conquered all the islands and consolidated them, he made Lahaina the capital of Hawaii. One of the ports where the whalers stopped, it had all the flavor of the islands, plus the whaling past.

We went into the famous old Pioneer Inn that had seven rooms and two baths. The inn looked pretty old and battered. It had a large 100-year-old bar where all the whalers used to congregate. It even had a resident ghost, an old fellow who sat in a rocker on the second floor veranda. He never spoke, just rocked back and forth and looked out to sea. He was supposedly the grandfather of one of the local characters, Haines Freeland.

We found the best place to eat down on the waterfront. A little wooden shack made of big planks, sat on beams that went out over the ocean. Broad cracks in the tiny dance floor let the dancers see the waves breaking on the rocks underneath as they swayed to tunes playing in a big old jukebox. The little café had a small bar, and their really good fish dinners proved popular with the locals as well as customers from the yachts passing through.

Off we sailed past Lanai, and on to Molokai, The Pineapple Island, probably the most mysterious of all the islands. It is believed that the very first native settlers of the Islands came to Molokai first, from sailing thousands of miles in their outrigger canoes.

We pulled up to the commercial dock, which was loaded with huge stacks of pineapples, waiting for the inter-island barges to pick up this sweet cargo, and carry it to the Dole factory in Honolulu. Those barges and a few Matson freighters handled all the inter-island traffic, both freight and passenger. A couple of big Hawaiian stevedores strolled over to help us tie up.

"Could we buy some of these pineapples?" we asked.

They just laughed, "Take as many as you want. We got plenty!"

Gleefully, we got three or four pineapples apiece and sat on the dock, hacking and slicing those huge pineapples with our sheaf knives. We ate the juicy fruit until we could eat no more. They were so good, or *ono*, as the Hawaiians say.

During this stop on Molokai, we had a problem with one of the heads, or toilets. Today, all heads onboard boats operate chemically, but in those days, the flush was a hand pump that emptied the contents right into the ocean. Users had to remember to put a limited amount of paper in it. Notorious for clogging up, boat heads were truly awful to work on at sea.

When we discovered that one of ours had clogged, the skipper told me to dive down from the dock and find the outlet. "Take the dock hose with you, Bungy," the captain explained. "Put it in the outlet and hold the hose hard against it, and let it run to the count of three. We'll see if we can unstop it backwards. I've tried everything to unstick it from this end. If this doesn't work, we'll have to tear the whole thing apart."

As I swam to the edge of the hull with the dock hose in hand, he stuck his head out of the head's large porthole and shouted, "Remember! Count to three!"

I dove down and found my way to the outlet. I spotted it easily because it had a long piece of toilet paper hanging out from it. I stuffed the hose in and counted, "1. 2. 3." I pulled the hose out and popped to the surface.

"No good! Try again," the skipper shouted from the porthole. "Count to five this time."

Down again. 1. 2. 3. 4. 5.

Up I came, coughing salt water.

"Still no good. Try again!"

Well, enough of this whole thing! I dove once more and this time I left the hose in the outlet to the count of ten. I came up to the top, and looked up. The skipper had his head hanging out of the porthole, with the most disgusting stuff dripping off his ears and the top of his head.

"I told you five!" he roared. He was not happy with me, but at least he did not have to tear the head apart!

Finishing the tour, we sailed back to Honolulu and Pier 6. I stayed another couple of weeks while Kyle looked for more tours, but no such luck. I started hounding the docks at Ala Wai Yacht Harbor, looking for a boat needing a crew, to hitch a ride home.

Chapter 11

♪ *Jada! Jada! Jada-jada-jing-jing-jang!* ♫

A pier head jump occurs when one job of crewing on a sailboat ends, as you tie up at the dock, and a sailor finds a last-minute job on another boat. My hitch on the Dwyn Wynn ended in Hawaii and I was growing desperately homesick for The Cove 2,500 miles away. Not having the $99 for a bone-rattling fourteen-hour flight home on one of the prop planes of the day, I went along the docks looking for a "pier head jump."

Many crews from the sailboats that had entered the Trans Pac Race had to fly home to get back to their regular jobs and I figured at least some of the boats would need crews to help them sail back to the Mainland. Unfortunately, because the *Dwyn Wynn* had spent some time touring the islands, most of the boats had already sailed for home. The job prospects were limited. After only a few inquiries, however, I did find one opportunity.

I located the famous racing yawl, *Jada,* stepped up to the stern and yelled, "Anyone aboard?"

Captain Bill Sturgess, Sr. stuck his head out of the cabin, and said, "What can I do for you?"

"I heard you were headed back to California tomorrow, and might need another crew member. I just got off two months on the *Dwyn Wynn.*"

He looked me up and down and said those dreaded words, "Do you cook?"

Having just finished a few weeks of partial galley duty, more like fending for yourself, on the *Dwyn Wynn,* and being very accomplished with peanut butter sandwiches, pancakes and garbanzo beans at home, I nodded in the affirmative, mumbling a noncommittal "ummm, hmmm," while looking in every direction but his.

I had instantly fallen in love with the *Jada*, a 62-foot long, 7-foot beam racing yawl. A pure speed machine, she cut through the water like a hot knife through butter. I certainly could not let a little problem like not knowing how to gourmet cook keep me from sailing with Sturgess, well-known up and down the west coast for his racing abilities and many victories.

I felt a thrill of excitement run through me as I admired the *Jada*'s sleek lines with the 100-foot mast soaring into the blue sky.

Capt. Sturgess said, "Well! Come aboard. You're hired!" He motioned down below, where I tossed my sea bag, stuffed with all my worldly possessions, onto an empty bunk. I was ready to sail.

"Bungy, let's get down to the local store and get our supplies," he said, later that day. "I really want to head for home tomorrow."

We went to a big supermarket and stocked up on canned, dried and powdered food of all sorts. The skipper had a long, long list and we kept filling more and more shopping carts.

The sheer quantity of it all stunned me. I felt confident about handling the canned goods. I certainly knew how to open a few cans, heat up the contents and serve. But in addition, those carts bulged with sacks of beans, rice (which I had never cooked) and potatoes (which I could bake very well in a campfire), bags of flour and sugar, and hefty containers of shortening. I began to think I should confess the limitations of my cooking skills, especially when the captain asked my opinion about some of the supplies.

I had no idea how to actually cook. But I did know I needed to get home. So I kept my mouth shut.

At the meat counter Capt. Sturgess purchased a couple of huge lamb roasts.

"Ah, this will be perfect. Sometimes at the beginning of a trip things are a little rough. Stomachs can be a little nervous. You can cook these up and then everyone can just slice it up cold for sandwiches."

"Oh, sure," I said, enthusiastically. "That's a great idea!"

I knew how to make sandwiches. Figuring how to get the lamb cooked in the first place was what was going to do me in.

We finally came to the end of his shopping list and headed back to the *Jada*. We loaded everything aboard and the captain left me to store it all.

"You'll know where you want to put everything," he said, waving a cheery goodbye as he headed topside and down the dock.

Well, maybe I did not know how cook, but I did know about storing things aboard ship. Space is at a premium and food is very important. Fifteen hundred miles from shore, the cook has no supermarket to run to for some missing ingredient. That makes it vitally important to make out a complete inventory of all the stores at the beginning of any voyage. Boats posted inventory lists on storage bins and in and under bunks all through the ship. Some of the bigger boats had storerooms, but that convenience almost never existed for boats of *Jada's* size. I packed dried goods and canned goods into every little nook and cranny. As we sailed, anything used got crossed off the list immediately, so everyone on board knew exactly what remained.

The minute a boat disconnects, rolls up, and stows away the dock hose, preserving fresh water becomes a must. Everyone, from then on, bathes in salt water, washes clothes in salt water, and cleans the boat with salt water. On *Jada* we had ½ cup of fresh water for brushing our teeth, and two cups of water daily for drinking.

Our fresh water consisted of a fifty-gallon tank, and some extra five-gallon jugs tied to the mast on deck. That would have done us well for the fifteen to twenty days expectation of the trip, but as the trip grew longer, we started cutting back on our consumption. Because of my complete inventories, we were able to carefully ration our food stores as we lay becalmed for over a week.

Once I had everything but the lamb tucked away, I leaned against the counter in the galley and stared at those big hunks of raw meat bulging out of the tiny sink. Was that pile of meat growing larger as I stood there? What in the world was I to do with it? Boil it? Fry it? Put it in the oven? The other five people on board surely expected something delicious.

Inspiration struck as I remembered that my old friend, Jack, a wonderful ship's cook, had signed on another boat down the way. I gave those chunks of lamb a gentle pat and headed down the docks, searching for him.

I had no luck at all locating my expert until finally a friend I ran into said he thought Jack had just taken a job aboard a luxurious sailboat tied up just a couple of boats along. I made my way down the pier until I came alongside that beauty, all agleam with shining brass and polished decks.

"Ahoy, aboard!" I called to a woman resting on a recliner beneath an awning on the deck of this gorgeous yacht. "Is Jack aboard?"

Jack, a former ad exec, had found Madison Avenue too all consuming, and had left to cook in Alaska gold mining camps and then in lumber camps in Washington and Oregon, before he found the sea. Then he started going from yacht to yacht. He had a little trouble with the drink, as they say, but he certainly knew his way around a galley.

The yacht's owner sat up from her lounge chair and pushed her huge sunglasses back into her blond hair.

"Oh, no, dear, I'm afraid he isn't here at the moment."

I began to get discouraged. "Oh, boy, am I in big trouble," I moaned.

She leaned forward with interest.

"Why don't you come aboard and tell me about it? Maybe Jack will get back soon."

In my old cut-off jeans, a well-worn tee shirt and a pair of frayed tennis shoes, I tramped up the gangway uneasily. I shortly found myself seated next to this utterly elegant and gorgeous creature. Her long scarlet nails perfectly matched her full painted lips. Her white halter-top and shorts emphasized the even tan of her long legs.

"All right," she said, encouragingly. "What's the problem?"

Practically in tears, I explained to her about the lamb.

"I don't have a clue as to what to do with these roasts. Should I boil them or bake them, or fry them or what?"

"Oh, lamb roast? That's my favorite dish," she said.

She then gave me the simplest recipe for preparing them and wished me well.

I headed back to the boat where I cooked that lamb according to her instructions and it turned out perfectly. I just never knew where I might find a good Samaritan.

The *Jada* set sail for California the next day and for the first three days out the entire crew lived off of oatmeal and cold lamb roast sandwiches.

The rest of my cooking can only be characterized as *ugh!* I had no imagination when it came to food. I searched through the on-board cookbook, looking for something different, but simple, to cook. Scalloped potatoes looked relatively easy and we had all the necessary ingredients on hand.

There was a fifty-pound sack of potatoes tied to a stanchion on deck. Every day I had to cull through them to remove the bad ones. We had plenty of powdered milk, margarine, salt and pepper. I was ready!

I sliced the potatoes thinly into the pan, seasoned them generously, put pats of margarine all over the top and mixed up a batch of

Brochure of Jada when she went commercial several years after Bungy's trip.

★ Price of $25.00 includes 3-hr Harbor Cruise - Call 234-4383 or 233-4949 for reservations.

★ Tour: Includes ½-day City Tour of San Diego, Round Trip Transportation from your hotel & 3-hr Cruise $32.50. Contact 427-8630, El Paseo Tours, Inc.

★ 62 foot classic Stephens yawl, built in 1938 of the finest teak and mohogany with polished brass fittings.

★ U.S. Coast Guard certified to carry 28-30 passengers for day-sailing, 6 passengers for overnight sails.

★ Experienced, licensed captains will guide you to those points of interest you choose.

★ Uniformed crew members are selected for personality as well as seamanship.

★ Cocktails and snacks are included on all sails; of course, other refreshments can be arranged to suit your personal taste.

★ You'll cruise under sail around beautiful San Diego Harbor in the gentle, constant breezes; or join us for whale-watching during the California Gray Whale migration season.

Seaport Cruises Inc.

803 West Harbor Drive, Suite I
San Diego Seaport Village
San Diego, California 92101

Back side of Jada Brochure.

powdered milk with water and poured it over the potatoes. "Oh, this is great!" I thought, "I can make something really good for the crew."

I carefully propped the pan straight in the perpetually leaning oven. On a fast moving sailboat, the boat goes forward and backward and sideways as it progresses. An unchanging wind tilts the boat mainly one way for long periods, but still, there is always movement of some kind. A cook has to make allowances for that movement.

Well, I got those potatoes in the oven and they began cooking. "Hmmm!" I thought. "What goes well with potatoes ... canned chicken? canned roast beef? or, my favorite, fried Spam?"

Suddenly, the boat hit a couple of combers and the waves pitched us all kinds of ways. Before long the unmistakable scent of something burning wafted from the oven. I opened the door and saw an almost empty baking pan, with a lumpy coating of burnt milk and potatoes smoking gently all over the sides of the oven.

I worked for half an hour scraping it all off. However, I found the potatoes well cooked, so I piled them onto a plate and we had them for dinner, along with some canned chicken. Not too bad!

Perhaps sailing cooks invented the three-second rule: the one that says if food falls on the floor, it is still edible if it is picked up within three seconds. The realities of cooking on board a fast moving sailboat meant that quite a bit of food at one point or another touched the deck. Everybody on board knew that, but hunger kept them from thinking about it too much.

I really hated the cooking, trying to find something that the crew would not complain about. While no one ever criticized my cooking outright, about eight days out I decided something had to be done. I proposed a deal with a sixteen-year-old crewman who hated to take watches.

"Oh, man," he whined every day, "I have to get up in the middle of the night again!"

"Look," I said to him, "you hate to take watches and I love them. How do you feel about cooking?"

"I love to cook!" he said.

"All right! Why don't we go to the captain and propose that we switch duties?"

He agreed to the idea. Not surprisingly, so did the captain, who said, "That's the best idea I've ever heard."

So from then on, I took the boy's watches and we had a good cook on board. I have often wondered if he ended up as one of the great chefs, but perhaps his cooking only seemed exquisite in comparison to mine.

Sailing to Hawaii, a boat picks up the trade winds almost immediately and they practically push the boat to landfall. On the way back, sailing goes against the winds. Our proposed fifteen-day journey ran to twenty-eight days, not only because of contrary winds, but because we also ran into a lot of calm.

One night, as we lay becalmed, Capt. Sturgess put a spotlight down near the water. It bounced off the phosphorescence in the sea. Some of it looked like those pieces of paper with little dots of candy on them, only the candy was brilliant lights. Others looked like fist-size blobs of iridescence, and around and through all this, swam different kind and sizes of fish, that were also attracted to our spot light. Thousands of sea creatures swam up through the light. We stared entranced at the most superb of nature movies. The calm went on for five or six days. And every night we got out the spotlight for an hour or so in the theater of the great Pacific.

On the *Jada*, there were four other crewmen. But, because we had only three bunks, we operated under the *hot bunk* system. When I came off my watch, I woke up my replacement and rolled into his warm bunk and he went to the wheel. This system is used all the time on smaller boats. We all *hot bunked*, except the captain, who had his own bunk. The captain is always on duty.

I did not always sleep in a bunk. Sometimes, I stretched out in the nice, big cockpit. Its thick cushions made it quite comfortable. Many a night I slept out under the stars, with moonlight making it hard to sleep because the night was so bright. "Somebody! Turn off the moon!"

One evening, the trade winds were fair, with occasional tropical squalls we could see on the horizon. The moon was full and white. We were all on deck, talking and laughing. Suddenly the crew went silent. We stood transfixed. We were seeing one of nature's wonders, a full circle rainbow, with all its bands of colors. This was caused by the rain squall and the brilliant moon, colliding at exactly the right time for our viewing.

When I finally switched duties with my young crew mate, who took over the cooking, I really had fun with my new watch mate, Bill, an old Scotsman of sixty or more. A short little guy with a big moustache, his ever-twinkling eyes reflected a spirit of fun. He had sailed a lot throughout the islands, and in fact had sailed all over the world for years. From midnight to four every morning, we shared the dogwatch.

Bill played a really good ukulele and he strummed away while I steered the boat and we sang old songs, from Mexican ranchero tunes, to folk songs, to South Sea melodies and sea chanteys, every song in the world that either of us knew.

Early one morning, around three o'clock, I stood at the wheel and Bill came on deck with his ukulele and began to play. The wind had died down and we rode gently through some pretty big swells. I kept the boat headed into them so we just moved up and down, avoiding the sideways rocking. We had both mains'l and jib up, but with no wind to help, I had to really work the wheel back and forth, trying to keep us head on into that constant roll of swells.

The mast soared about a hundred feet above the deck with the crosstree running at right angles to it about eight feet below the top. The crosstree holds the stays, or shrouds, that keep the mast up.

We sang under the full moon of a gorgeous tropical night. I struggled with working that wheel all the time, trying my best to keep the bow headed into the swells. The rigging creaked and groaned and the sails flipped and flapped loudly.

"Let's sing the 'Hawaiian Wedding Song'," Bill suggested. "Do you know it?"

"Oh! Sure! It's one of my favorites!" I said enthusiastically.

So we began singing that hauntingly beautiful two-part harmony.

"*Eia au ke kali nei*," I sang. "*Aia la I hea ku'u aloha*. (Here I am waiting, where is my beloved.)"

211

"*Eia au ke huli nei*," Bill returned. "*A loa'a 'oe e ka ipo, maha ka 'i'ini a ka pu 'uwai*. (I've searched for you, now that I've found you, calm the desire of my heart.)"

I got really caught up in my part and completely forgot the wheel. Suddenly a big swell came out of the middle of nowhere, rolling towards us. It loomed over us thirty feet high, it seemed! It looked absolutely gigantic in the light of the moon, like a shimmering silver wall bearing down on us. Because I had lost my concentration during the song, the boat had turned just enough that the wall of water hit us sideways and rolled us so far over that the crosstrees at the top of the mast touched the water on the port side. Then the boat came back the other way like some crazy pendulum and the crosstrees dipped in the water on the starboard side. For a few minutes, we rocked crazily back and forth, hanging on for dear life, until we got back to some semblance of normal.

Everybody below flew out of their bunks, books jumped off the shelves, pots and pans crashed in the galley.

Capt. Sturgess came screaming up from below.

"What's wrong? What the heck happened! Did we hit something?"

His hair stood up on end and his eyes flashed with fury or with panic.

Bill and I managed to stutter out an explanation. "We were only singing the 'Hawaiian Wedding Song'…"

Sturgess stood there on deck breathing heavily. He grabbed the ukulele from Bill and for a moment I thought he intended to throw it overboard. Finally, he growled and shook it at us and stomped back down the ladder. We never saw the ukulele again and neither of us ever had the nerve to ask for it.

I tried the captain's patience another time during this journey, involving an unauthorized swim. Many people collected the hand-blown glass fish floats that rode the Pacific currents all the way from Japan. My sisters and I had often found them washed up on the beach, still tied to bits of net, while beachcombing at The Cove. The blue ones were fairly common, the green ones more rare. Red ones were very, very rare and very valuable. We collected four or five of the blue and green floats with a scoop net as we sailed along on the *Jada*. One day, when I finished up a chore on deck, I saw a red ball lazily floating along on the flat, calm sea about fifty feet away.

"Red float! Red float!" I yelled, diving into the sea to retrieve the rare treasure. Thoroughly excited, I never even considered the danger. I swam out and grabbed the float and turned back to the boat. By that time the wind had picked up slightly and *Jada* had already sailed a considerable distance from me. Luckily for me, the watch had seen what happened and lowered the sail instantly while I swam like mad back to the boat.

Capt. Sturgess leaned over the side, grabbed my outstretched hand, and yanked me back on board.

"We're about 1,500 miles from anything but water, water, water, Bungy!" the captain yelled when I got back on board. "What were you thinking?"

Well, the truth was, before I dove in, I had thought only of retrieving a rare and valuable red fish float which I actually now had in my possession. Once a beachcomber's daughter, always a beachcomber's daughter!

A good captain always has a healthy concern for safety aboard sailboats. We did safety drills. Life rings hung aft in case anyone got swept overboard. All of us carried a knife in a sheath to cut the lines rapidly if we got tangled in the rigging or if a sail should split and come loose, flapping dangerously in a brisk breeze.

Sailors constantly face dangers from both the sea and the weather. Only a fool acts carelessly. It had been very careless of me to jump overboard. Had a good wind picked up at the moment I dove in, the boat would have been long gone. The ocean is a big, big place, and one human being can be mighty hard to spot in its vastness. Strangely enough, I never felt fear while at sea, no matter how bad the conditions, and in storms it can get pretty tough.

Jada's Capt. Sturgess was a wonderful sailor, well known for his racing skills. Part of his success undoubtedly came from his uncanny ability to focus on what needed doing and doing it right then. The crew did not always see that as a plus. He really had a one-track mind.

When he saw a line that needed attention, or a sail that needed hauling in a bit he just could not see anything else. He headed right to the problem and woe to anyone or anything in his way. Whenever a crew member saw Sturgess get that glint in his eye, he had better get out of the way.

Once, he stepped on a book I was reading, while I was reading it. I sat in the cockpit on a cushion with my book opened on the deck in front of me. Sturgess, sitting on the other side, suddenly announced, "That line needs tightening." He got up and marched right across the deck, tromping on my book as he went. He never even noticed.

Had *I* been a bit smaller, I have no doubt that **he** would have stepped on *me*. He often stuck his foot in buckets on deck, while his eyes focused up in the sails.

We arrived in Santa Barbara, California, after twenty-seven days at sea. All that brilliant green! Green trees, palm trees swaying, flowers everywhere! Land, oh land! And then, the irony. None of us could go ashore because of the immigration regulations in place then, before Hawaii became a state. We were supposed to check in at the immigration dock in Los Angeles Harbor.

We had run out of fruits, vegetables, milk or anything fresh weeks before. The skipper sent a kid he spotted on the dock to the store for supplies. Soon we had a big bowl of fresh fruit - pears, apples, bananas, oranges, and grapes - sitting in the cockpit. We all gathered around, gobbling up that juicy goodness and drinking big glasses of ice cold milk. Suddenly, the captain decided he needed to do something about the sails immediately, and stepped right in that bowl of fruit! He just squished the pears and the apples and kept on going. The entire crew had learned during the voyage to pick up things in front of him, but in our relaxed state near journey's end, we completely missed this one.

That same day, we sailed down the California coast from Santa Barbara to Los Angeles Harbor and found the immigration dock the next morning. The immigration officers and the agriculture inspectors came along and checked us over. We had to eat or throw overboard the remainder of the fresh fruit we had purchased in Santa Barbara. By that time, only two oranges and maybe a banana remained that no one had room for.

215

Since The Cove lay only about a half hour away from the immigration dock, I called Daddy to come pick me up. Until he arrived, I worked with the rest of the crew cleaning up, and putting equipment and gear into proper storage. When Daddy came aboard, Capt. Sturgess held a little ceremony for me at which he concluded, "Bungy, there is no doubt, you make a better seaman than a cook!" I considered that a great compliment.

Chapter 12

♪ *Far lands are calling, calling to me! Ahe! Ahe!* ♫

Nat Gozzano, a lean and handsome set painter for the movie studios, had purchased the *California*, a 63-foot three-masted barquentine, and had begun looking for a crew to sail around the world. He had a berth at the 22ⁿᵈ St. Yacht Landing, my stomping grounds.

I joined the crew and once again, I would be the only female on board and I would have more sailing experience than anyone else. In fact, I was the only person on board with *any* deep-sea sailing experience.

That was quite often the case on the boats on which I crewed. Since I was a girl, however, all the men just assumed that I knew nothing of value. I always had to be very careful with the guys and their macho attitudes. Trying to get these fellows to do what I knew needed doing took a lot of ingenuity. My technique for dealing with male egos was like dancing around the May pole, or walking on egg shells. Basically, I had to tell them what to do in such a way that they did not know I had told them. They had to think the whole thing was their idea!

The *California* was the dream of a guy who lived up the coast near San Francisco. Most barquentines are great big boats, but the designer had scaled down the plans to sixty-three feet and built it himself. Unfortunately, he never got to sail it.

The boat had three masts. The sails were all gaff-headed with booms on top and bottom. That gave them more sail space, but made them about five times harder to set and to work than a regular tri-shaped mainsail. Added to the foremast were a couple of square sails and a *fisherman* to be used way up high on the mast in really light winds. It was a very romantic looking boat, but was hard to sail.

Of the other crew members, there was Chuck, a California abalone diver. He volunteered to navigate, and spent hours going through navigation books and charts, practicing and shooting his sextant to learn the skills needed to get us around the world. We could always find him sighting the sun or the moon, or an attractive woman, with his sextant in hand. Nowadays, computers and satellites handle the navigation, probably more accurately and certainly easier, but not nearly as romantic looking.

Chuck worked with a commercial diving company. He took me to their office, which was a little shack at the end of the pier, one day. The fellows that worked there dressed me up in one of those old-time diving suits, just like Jules Vern's *20,000 Leagues Under the Sea!*. It took awhile to put on the canvas suit, buckle on all the weights and slip my feet into the bulky boots that weighed about eighty pounds. I finally donned the big brass helmet with its round thick glass window in the front and they clamped it down onto the suit. Chuck and his buddies helped me clomp across the pier, turn around carefully and slip down the iron ladder attached to the side of the pier, finally sliding into the waters of Los Angeles Harbor.

GLOBE-GIRDLING GAZE—The crew of the schooner California take a look at far horizons as they start a two-year trip around the world. Crew members are (left to right) Dick Cas-sarino, cartoonist; Arthur Stebbings, salesman; Charles W. Lewis Jr., diver; Lady Weldon (Bunge) Hedley, and Capt. Nat Gozzano, studio artist. (News-Pilot Photo)

Four Men, Girl, Start World Tour on 63-Foot Schooner

Crew members on bow sprit of Barquentine California, ready to sail around the world.

CAST OFF—A well-wisher casts off the last line holding the schooner California to its California Yacht Anchorage dock as the vessel starts a two-year trip around the world.

California casting off for Hawaii.

The second I hit the water, they turned the air tank on and the suit began to fill with pressurized air. I felt free as a bird until I realized I'd better start controlling my air before I started floating out to sea. I pressed a little gadget with my chin and it allowed air to escape into the water. Less air and I sank, more air and I rose. A simple system, but a little scary.

The dark, grungy, green harbor water made it difficult to see anything. I stayed down about five minutes and never got more than ten feet from the pier, but my imagination filled the dingy bay with images of ghostly sunken ships spilling out golden treasure off deserted tropical islands.

Another crew member was a very handsome young man who had worked as a Disney Studio cartoonist. He had an unimpaired sense of self-esteem, but knew nothing about sailing. He just had an adventurous urge in his soul and he thought a circumnavigation of the globe might satisfy that desire.

The third crewman planned to take bags of coffee beans to the Marquesas Islands to start a plantation. Little did he know that those islands already had a very special and delicious coffee, but no one to work the plantations. The natives simply did not have to work for a living; they just plucked everything they needed from a tree, or the ground, or the sea.

For months, we five worked very hard getting the *California* ready to sail. It was in such bad shape that it seemed like everything needed replacing or refinishing. We sanded and we painted. We varnished and we caulked.

221

The old diesel engine needed lots of work. Just when the captain was sure he had it running, it would backfire. Bang! A huge cloud of black soot blew all over everything and everybody. Then we had to scrub down the whole boat again. What a mess!

One week, we pulled up all the floor boards down below, to get to the iron ribs that ran about a yard apart, the whole 63-foot length of the boat. The ribs marched down the sides of the boat, curving down from the deck to the keel. We wire brushed and painted every one with a rust preventative paint. Now, that was work!

Nat had been able to make enough money to retire from set painting. He had dreamed of buying a boat and sailing around the world for years, and now his dream was coming true. His parents came from Italy, and he could really cook Italian! Many evenings he stirred up a typical Italian dinner for all of us. His chicken and pasta was unforgettable. A friendly, hospitable man, he often invited my family, Dwight, and others aboard for a savory repast.

We kept setting a date to sail and kept putting it back. Every time we got something on the boat fixed, we found something else that needed work. It took us almost six months to get ready to embark.

As a kind of shakedown cruise, we took a tour group, the employees of some big company, for a charter. With about thirty people aboard, we sailed to Catalina, twenty-two miles away.

Three days earlier we had painted the deck and, unfortunately, it had not completely dried when we began the tour. We ended up with paint tracked everywhere. The guests tromped it all around, gouging out the paint with their street shoes. Those shoes are always a real no-no on deck, but we had forgotten to ask them to wear tennis shoes.

The weather turned out fair with a rolling swell. A lot of the passengers got seasick. But we spotted plenty of sharks, seagulls and other sea life, and that kept most of them happy.

We reached Catalina and sailed into St. Catharine's Bay to anchor. This bay has huge swells and bad currents, so boats have to put out two anchors, one off the port bow and one off the starboard bow, leaving the stern free to drift back and forth a bit.

All the charter people went ashore for dinner and dancing. We used our dinghy or they hired a shore boat for a dollar or two that taxied people back and forth to their boats.

Late that night we finally had the partygoers all back on board and sleeping. I drifted asleep myself, in a sleeping bag on deck, for a short time before my watch came up. Suddenly I woke up, sensing something wrong about the boat's behavior.

"Oh, my gosh," I thought, "What's happening?"

I jumped up and found that the coffee entrepreneur, who had the watch, had nodded off. Both of our bow anchors were dragging.

A flotilla of other boats filled the bay that evening. The waters of the inlet had turned rough and some of the other boats were dragging anchors, too. The bay was a mess. We had just missed one boat and were nearing another. The tide and the wind pushed the *California* sideways with both anchors dragging out.

The bowsprit pointed out into the ocean, but between that open water and us floated one of those old fashioned 1920s yachts with a long strip of windows running the length of the boat. My heart jackhammered in my chest as I saw that, like the lance of a jouster, our bowsprit aimed to shatter every window as we slid alongside.

I yelled, "Get up, get up! The anchor's dragging!"

Chuck came flying up on deck and he and I jumped out onto the bowsprit. Nat flew down into the engine room to start the big old diesel. As we closed with the other boat we fended it off as the *California* slid inexorably toward it. We both pushed with all our might, our arms braced against the older boat. I finally jumped up on to the other boat and ran down its deck just managing to hold the *California* off with all my muscles straining, sweat pouring down my face.

On our deck, Chuck strained against the force of the boats, too. I ran fifty feet along the deck, pushing frantically, as we both yelled at each other, "Push! Push!" Finally, as the stern came around, and we cleared the last fragile window, I jumped back on the *California.*

We bent over wearily, trying to catch our breath, trembling from exhaustion. Nat had the engine running by that time. We got the anchors up, motored off to a safer spot and reset the anchors. Our guests were still all sleeping just like babes in the woods.

The next day, we motored up to what is called The Isthmus, in the middle of the island. The guests got to snorkel, fish, hike and swim for a good time. However, we had to work really hard trying to keep them all happy. We had no radios, no TV. The facilities for entertainment on board were pretty primitive. We heard lots of complaints, "There's nothing to do." Some of them enjoyed the scenery and just the opportunity to relax, but many of them said, "Let me get off of here. Sailing is so boring."

Sunday afternoon, we sailed back to our berth at the 22nd St. Yacht Landing and thankfully bid our guests good-bye and got back to the work of getting the *California* ready so we could begin our sail around the world.

One hot afternoon, we worked at wire brushing all the rusty rigging. Then we put on a coat of silver rust preventative paint. To do this, we dipped a rag into the paint, squeezed it out and wrapped it around the wire and pulled. We hooked one of the sail's uphaul lines to the bosun's chair pulley. Chuck mounted the chair and we pulled him eighty-five feet up to the top of the mast. This lucky fellow got to paint going down all those wires, while someone not so lucky, like me, slowly lowered the chair from down below.

Humphrey Bogart's boat, *Santana*, floated just across the dock from us. While we were painting the rigging, the wind picked up and pretty soon one of my Norwegian friends, who worked as Bogart's skipper, came flying across the dock.

"Vat are you doing!" he screamed. "Stop dat! Stop dat dis minute!"

He shouted furiously, waving his arms. No doubt he cursed us in Norwegian, but I could not be sure, since, thankfully, I did not understand that language.

He stomped on board and let us know in many colorful phrases that the wind had blown spatters of our silver paint all over the white, sparkling teak decks of the *Santana*, which was always kept in absolutely tip-top shape.

Well, the mess appalled us as much as it did the skipper. All of us dropped everything and got paint thinner and rags and, starting at the bow, got every speck of that silver paint off his yacht.

One Sunday, the *Santana* arrived in the late afternoon, after a weekend at Catalina, and I saw Bogart getting ready to get off. I grabbed my camera and jumped off the *California*.

As he was about to walk past our boat I begged, "Can I please take your picture, Mr. Bogart? Please?"

He got a disgusted look on his face and I knew he was thinking something like, "Here, I come down to the one place where I don't have to worry about autograph seekers, and I get hounded anyway."

"Oh, please, Mr. Bogart. Just one!"

Finally, he said in his gruffest Bogart voice, "Well, OK, go ahead, kid."

"OK," I said, "Smile!"

When I clicked my little trick camera, it sprayed water right in his face. The most shocked look stopped him dead. Then he gave this great big laugh, put his arm around me and gave me a hug and went off chuckling down the dock. Too bad I did not get a picture of that!

The work on the *California* continued and we always had one more thing, one more thing. We still had not gotten everything properly stowed away when Capt. Gozzano finally said, "We're leaving Saturday. We'll sail to Catalina and we get the boat ready for sea there."

Well, of course, all of our family and friends came to see us off. We had a big celebration, with horns tooting and plenty of cheering and whistles. Finally, the captain shouted, "Let loose the lines!" We untied the bow and stern lines that were holding us to the dock...and we were on our way to sail around the world.

Twenty-two miles later, we anchored once again at Catalina, but very shortly went on to Santa Cruz Island where we spent about a week giving the boat the final touches to make us seaworthy.

Since I was the only one of the crew who had been to sea before, I asked them, "What kind of watches are we setting?"

"What do you mean, Bungy?" they asked.

"Well," I explained, "Everybody has to take their turn at the wheel. We need to set up a schedule."

"Well, whoever wants to steer, can steer," someone said with a nonchalant wave of the hand.

"No. No. No," I said. "We have to take turns and set regular watches. Someone has to be responsible for the sailing of the boat every single hour of the day and night. It doesn't just sail itself, you know!"

Well, this started a big argument. Because they lacked sailing experience, the crew failed to see the need for setting watches. They simply did not realize how very hard life at sea can be. There is no free ride. The crew works all the time. Sailors who are not manning the wheel must take care of the boat. Otherwise, it will start falling apart without constant maintenance. And every sailor on board must take watches, no matter how tired. Life on board can get really sticky. People start complaining, "It's unfair. He's not doing his share."

Girl Signs as Boat Crewman

Schooner to Sail Around World on Pleasure Mission

SAN PEDRO—A desire to span the world in a sailboat, held by Lady Weldon Hedley, 19, may soon become a reality. The San Pedro High School graduate, better known as Bungy to her friends, has signed on as a member of the five-man crew of the 63-foot schooner California, expected to set sail within the next week or so.

"The pleasure journey will cover the entire world," assures Skipper Nat Gonzano. "There might have been some doubt before Bungy joined the cruise, but there isn't now. That girl's determined."

May Have to Work

Gonzano admitted that it might be necessary to stop off at some ports to work awhile before the journey is completed. The crew expects to draw quite a bit of its food out of the sea.

In the group are also competent boat repairmen who might be able to hire out their services in some of the world's ports.

Miss Hedley, who will be the only woman aboard the boat, is no novice in marine activity. She has participated in the Acapulco races, riding atop a 75-foot mast part of the way. She also owns a sailing dinghy.

Bungy Beautifies Boat

To speed up preparations for the trip she has been painting

of the **SOUTHERN COMMUNITIES**

4 Part VII–L–SUN., JULY 25, 1954   Los Angeles Times

GETTING AHEAD—Where feminine interests are rare, Lady Weldon (Bungy) Hedley, San Pedro, is determined to soar. With a background of years handling small boats, she has signed on as a crewman on a 63-foot schooner soon to sail around the world. *Times photo*

Bungy resting on main boom of California.

Sailing etiquette requires a sailor to always report to his duty station at least five minutes early in order to relieve the one on duty. Rough weather turns three or four hours at the helm to sheer exhaustion. Showing up late for a watch can start a serious fight.

On any boat, the crew lacks the luxury of having the outside world as a buffer. The sailor's world is a really small space. In the case of *California*, it was a space sixty-three feet long and about thirteen feet wide. Most modern manufactured homes have more room than that. Living in such close proximity makes it vital that everyone in that space gets along.

No matter what I said, the crew kept refusing to do the watches.

"OK," I finally said, "I've not yet unpacked my sea bag. I'll just go get it, and I'd appreciate it if one of you will run me in to Avalon in the dinghy. I'll catch a boat or a sea plane home because I am not going on this boat if we don't set watches." I tried to communicate just how serious an issue this was to me.

They finally agreed to set watches of three hours on, nine hours off. The skipper did not take regular watches since, generally speaking, the skipper on any boat is always on call.

Having established a watch schedule for the crew of the *California*, I asked the next burning question on my mind. "What about cooking?" I asked.

"You're the woman. You're doing the cooking," the men responded in unison, looking at me as if I had lost my ability to think clearly. The mindset of that era, which believed that males and females had very distinct roles, once again came to the surface.

"Oh, no," I said. "I will take turns, but I am not doing all the cooking."

My words shocked them since they just assumed that the woman, whose "place," at that time, was in the kitchen, would cook all the meals. Well, they had never tasted any of my culinary efforts, and I certainly did not plan to sail all the way around the world eating my own less-than-adequate meals. After a great deal of lively discussion, we finally agreed to rotate around, with each crewman taking a day in the galley.

By the end of our journey, having eaten my cooking a number of times, the skipper recognized my limited skills by saying, "Bungy is the only person I ever knew who could cook every meal by opening three cans."

After a week of really hard work without the distractions of family and friends, the skipper deemed the *California* ready to set sail. After months of preparation, we finally set off in typical weather, putting up with a cold, wet drizzle the first few days.

Unfortunately, our would-be coffee planter found that he hated sailing and we had not even cleared the harbor before he got seasick and took to his bunk. That left four of us to sail this really hard-to-sail boat.

Before we had sailed many days, the skipper found a lot of our food stores missing. It did not take him long to figure out that the coffee planter had recovered from his seasickness. He apparently was getting up late every night and helping himself to the food while claiming to be too ill to work during the day!

"Here's the way it is," Nat finally told him. "You don't work, you don't eat!"

Nat put him at the helm for the night watch and he ran that boat every which way. He just refused to pay attention and we suspected he did it on purpose. He frequently let the boat turn around and get itself in irons, with the boat not moving and the sails just shaking back and forth. Then we all had to jump up from our bunks in the middle of the night and work the sails and the boat until we had fixed his mischief. That meant we all lost sleep due to his incompetence and irresponsibility.

Basically, we ended up having to have someone supervise him all the time, so he turned out to be more work than help, really.

The skipper eventually put him on morning and afternoon watches when more of us were up and about anyway, to keep an eye on him, but he still failed to do the job right. He finally started paying some attention, but he stubbornly refused to do anything more than two hours at a stretch.

We all suffered through this little rebellion, which negatively affected the crew's morale. The cold, wet, overcast weather did not improve the mood of the boat, but before long, we got to the trades, that broad band of tropical winds circling the globe north and south of the equator. Once a boat gets there the sails very rarely need resetting. Sailing there is the best sailing in the world. Those soft, warm winds constantly caress the skin. And even the most recalcitrant boat with the worst hands just skims along like a happy child.

Once again, I volunteered to take the dogwatch from midnight to three. That gave me the freedom to climb the mast and enjoy my sunsets and sunrises, my three-hundred-sixty-degree view and that awesome feeling of owning the universe.

One night the skipper and I worked on some chores on deck with the cartoonist at the helm. Around midnight, because of a slight shift in the winds, Nat ordered us to come about. Nat had to figure out how to sail the *California* because it had what sailors call a "bastard" rigging. In other words, it had a unique design, not a true barquentine design.

In order to turn about, we had to back wind the jib. That meant that we had to take the jib all the way in front of the last wire or forestay holding the mast up, then pulling it manually toward the wind, putting pressure on the bow so it would swing around. It was supposed to the work this way. I was to run out to the end of the bowsprit, gathering the sail as I went. Then I'd throw the canvas around the front stay, while the skipper hauled in on it on the opposite side. If it worked, we could back wind it on the proper side. The back winded sail hauled the bow of the boat around turning us about and setting us sailing on the new tack, or direction. The jib was a big sail, ten to fifteen feet tall at least, and in the shape of a long triangle.

Nat said he would handle the sheets, the lines that took the sail in and out on the deck and made the sail looser or tighter. The cartoonist manned the helm. My job was to run out on the bowsprit, sticking out in front of the boat like a tree limb. Since the boat moves quite a bit up and down and back and forth, we had a safety basket underneath the bowsprit. If I fell, I would most likely end up in the basket instead of the sea.

As I got ready to make my run out to the end of the bowsprit, I yelled back the length of the boat, "Bring her up into the wind!"

That meant for him to bring the front of the boat up to point right into the wind. That way, the sail just flapped back and forth with no wind holding it taut. That took all the pressure off the sail so that

I could more easily gather it up. When the sails are tautly full and pulling the boat, no one can manhandle them.

He threw the helm over all the way and did not bring the wheel back to the center. Basically, for this maneuver to work, the helmsman cannot just throw it all the way over, and then bring it all the way back. The movement has to be done a little at a time. When he got it into the wind, the boat just kept on going, because he had turned too far.

I had gathered the sail up and started up the bowsprit, but instead of the boat staying pointed into the wind, it just kept on going. When the boat got to that certain point, the full wind just grabbed that jib, popped it out of my arms and smacked me into the safety basket and nearly overboard. I desperately hung on to a piece of the sail and scrambled to get back up on the bowsprit.

Again, I screamed down at him sixty-three feet, "Haul it into the wind!" hanging on for dear life as I swung out over the ocean once more.

And once again, he threw the helm over, and the boat did exactly the same thing on the other side. Clinging like an abalone to a rock, I screamed at him again, fearing that at any moment I would get tossed overboard and lost forever.

Somehow, in the midst of all the clamor and very real danger, I noticed the magnificence of this wild night, with a beautiful moon overhead. As I clung to the sail, swinging madly back and forth, I saw the waves and the white caps on the water below me as clearly as if the sun shone on a cloudless day.

"Haul it into the wind!" I yelled again.

But he had had enough.

Throwing up his arms in disgust, he let go of the wheel and yelled back up at me, "I ain't takin' orders from no girl!"

Then he left the helm, stomped off and, and disappeared below, heading for his bunk.

That left the captain and me to operate the boat.

For a moment we stared at each other, jaws agape.

"Grab the wheel!" Nat screamed as he lowered the jib in a flurry.

I raced off the bowsprit and down the length of the boat and soon got it back under control as I grabbed the wheel. Nat came back to the wheel shaking his head in frustration.

"What do we do now?" I asked.

"Well, the two of us can't manage coming about by ourselves," he said. "Just keep on the way we are for the rest of the night." Leaving me on watch at the wheel, Nat made his way below, where I hoped he had a few words with Dick for abandoning his post. By morning, we found we had gotten off course only a little bit, so it did not matter that much in the long run.

Setting the squaresail up on the fore mast gave me the most pleasure and fun while crewing on the *California*. The squaresails, huge squares of heavy canvas, made the boat into a barquentine. More than anything else, it made me feel like I worked aboard one of the old square-riggers that sailed around the Horn in the old days.

To set the top square sail, two of us had to climb up the ratlines that ran up at an angle, joining the mast high above the deck. The ratlines formed a ladder of little ropes tied between two shrouds, or stays, that held up the mast. Once at the top, we stepped out onto a heavy rope that ran underneath the top boom, one of us on either side of the mast.

The big sail was furled and rolled up onto the spar and tied all along the length of it with short canvas strips to prevent it from getting loose. We had to step out there on the rope, hanging onto the sail and the spar as the thick rope beneath our bare feet sagged and swayed with our weight.

Once we got started, we had to move quickly out to the edge of the spar. We had to pull those little looped ties as fast as possible, because if we did not, the sail filled with air and popped up before we were ready. That could throw a sailor right off his foothold. It was a long way down to the deck or the ocean below.

The second that sail filled, we grabbed hold of that boom tightly because it shook the whole mast. I just loved the excitement of doing that job. It made me feel like I was a character in all those sailing stories I had read.

In a heavy blow, we had to lower that square sail really fast, too. Ropes and pulleys from the deck lowered it, but we had to climb up there and gather the sail up into itself. As we pulled it in, we quickly rolled it up on the spar. We had a bunch of the canvas tie strips stuck into our belt loops and our mouths. As we rolled it up, we reached around with a tie and pulled it around the canvas and the spar and tied it down. It took a lot of effort and teamwork to get that big sail in, especially when the wind blew stiffly.

Back in the 1950's, remember, we sailed with no modern navigational aids. Like sailors of old, we used the stars and the sun to determine our position. Approaching Hawaii on the *California*, we ran into a five to six day period of low-lying, solid overcast. Our navigator failed to get a sighting of sun or stars morning, noon or night. Without this sighting, we had no way to compute our latitude or longitude.

We attempted to keep track of the miles with a taffrail log, but the very first day, a shark ate it. That left us with dead reckoning, basically guessing how fast the boat traveled. Dead reckoning takes into consideration the kinds of currents the boat is running through, how fast the winds are pushing it, and how a storm might have affected our speed and direction.

To estimate how fast the boat moved, we took a little piece of wood, threw it overboard, and counted, one Mississippi, two Mississippi, as it moved from the bow of the boat to the stern. Then we could figure out how many feet it traveled in however many seconds. We all got pretty good at reckoning without a stop watch. In fact, I tried it many years later while sailing on an out-rigger canoe, and was pleased to see that I could still figure my speed with chunks of orange peel.

We got to the point where we expected to sight the Hawaiian Islands, but although we looked hard for three days, we simply failed to find them. These islands form a little speck in a big, big ocean. Look for them on a globe to get a better idea of the challenge facing us in that overcast weather. Or, picture a large piece of paper with some dirt on it, and you're looking for a pencil dot in the middle of it all.

Capt. Gozzano got us started on a search grid, using our compass to tell us our direction. We sailed about five hours north, turned and sailed five hours east, then five hours south, and then west, making big squares. We all began to get a bit worried. After all, the next landfall was the Philippines, thousands of miles to the west.

One morning at the wheel, I thought, "If God is omniscient, doesn't that mean He knows everything, and so He must know exactly where we are?" Psalm 139 came to mind, "If I take the wings of the morning and dwell in the uttermost parts of the sea; even there shall Thy hand lead me, and Thy right hand shall hold me."

Convinced then of my safety in God's hands, I happened to look back over my shoulder at that moment and saw a tiny pinpoint of land through a brief break in the clouds. I saw just enough to know I was not looking at more clouds. It turned out to be the big island of Hawaii. We *had* been heading for the Philippines!

Excitement filled the crew as we brought the *California* about, and headed for land. As we approached the islands, from something like fifty miles out, the scent of the pineapples and sugarcane surrounded us. The tropic breezes brought to our noses a different kind of ambrosia after the days at sea. We all stood on deck taking deep breaths of the most luscious, earthy smell imaginable.

It got late as we neared the islands, so we stayed outside the bay at Hilo and just sailed back and forth until dawn came. As the sun rose magnificently, turning the sky and sea pink and gold, we lowered sail and chugged into Hilo Harbor under the power of our diesel one-lunger going *pochita, pochita, pochita.*

Since I happened to have the wheel, I got to bring the big sail boat into the commercial dock where the freighters come in. I eased the 63-foot *California* right up to that pier. As the others congratulated me on my expert handling of the boat, I breathed a sigh of relief that the dock still stood undamaged and this huge boat sat at rest where it was supposed to without any marks on it.

All of us thought of Hawaii as such an exotic place in those days. The huge tourist impact had not yet happened. As we strolled the few blocks into quaint downtown Hilo, it seemed so foreign, and tantalizingly strange. Flowers bloomed everywhere, especially orchids of every shape and color. The frequent rain so typical of Hilo fell gently as the locals strolled about under their ever-present umbrellas.

Capt. Nat Gozzano and Bungy after arriving in Hawaii.
Trip of 23 days, 2500 miles.

We enjoyed touring the sugar cane factory where they gave us samples of five or six grades of sugar. We had fun experimenting with every one of them on cereals and in coffee and tea.

After a few days we sailed to the other side of the Big Island and anchored off the little village of Kailua. In wonderful contrast to Hilo, the Kona side of Hawaii was quite dry and hot. Bougainvillea thrived in the heat, splashing the town with its hot pinks, golds, reds and whites. The huge volcanic mountains that divide the island gave too much rain to one side and not enough to the other. The scarcity of water on the Kona side had taught the locals to carefully conserve. If we wanted water with our meal in a local cafe, we had to bring our own.

Kailua was only a little village at that time, about three blocks long, with none of the big hotels it has now. We enjoyed several meals at the historic Kona Inn. The Inn's swimming pool was filled with salt water from the bay, and moved up and down with the movement of the sea. At high tide, magnificent waves broke and splashed right into the pool.

Allan Hale Jr., who played the Skipper on the long-running TV series *Gilligan's Island*, was making a movie there. After we watched a shooting, we all got to meet him and he invited us to join him for dinner at the Kona Inn. A very funny guy, he kept us laughing for hours.

We went snorkeling at Hoonaunau Bay, which has since become a state nature preserve. We swam with every fish imaginable, along with one-hundred-fifty-pound turtles. The clear and warm water, only about four to five feet deep at most, with a beautiful reef that keeps the sharks out, made swimming there so deliciously pleasant and easy.

We met locals who took us here and there, and invited us to their home up by Kilauea Volcano for dinner one evening. The old Hawaiian homes were all wood, with large lanais (verandas), going around the whole house. They had lots of windows that were always open. No one had air conditioning. It wasn't needed. The tropical breezes blew most of the time, and everyone moved just a little slower, just like in the southern states.

We were taken up to the northern end of Hawaii, to Kohala, where big mountains and valleys abounded. We got permission from the camp headquarters of a 6,000 acre ranch to do some hiking. We climbed over their fence, shooed away wild cattle, and hiked up to a 1,000 foot waterfall that was cascading down the high cliffs and into the sea beyond.

Soon, we set out to sea once more, and headed up to the island of Oahu and the Ala Wai Yacht Harbor. For a couple of weeks, we toured Honolulu and swam and surfed off Waikiki. We snorkeled at Hanauma Bay. Way up in some canyon filled with banana trees with ripe bunches hanging off them, we fished in a cold trout stream. The owner of this piece of paradise took our fish and cooked it over an open fire. We sat on rough hewn logs and ate with our fingers. The proprietor had been in World War II, and had come here after the war was over, and claimed homestead!

I had read a lot of Hawaiian history and, while visiting the famous cut through the high valleys called the Pali, I thought of the wildness of those ancient Hawaiian warriors. King Kamehameha held his last battle there, and so many men were thrown off the high cliffs. The winds were so strong up there, I had to lean nearly in half to move at all.

Lots of crews on boats, planning a circumnavigation, only got as far as Hawaii. That first long stretch into the Pacific brought home the true depth of the challenge of circumnavigation: the dangers, the isolation, and the physical exhaustion. The sail to the islands convinced them that they had sailed far enough; the rest of the world did not need to be seen, at least not from the deck of a sailboat. As a consequence, lots of seagoing sailboats were put up for sale at the yacht harbors in Hawaii.

During those relaxing days, the crew talked about the trip and their dream of sailing around the world. Before long, it became clear that the physical challenges and personality conflicts we had faced on our journey, so far, had convinced all of us that we no longer wanted to sail around the world together, or for some, not at all.

Home drew me strongly, so I took a bus out to the huge Quonsett hut that was the airport at that time. I had a few minutes before boarding, and made my way up the old wooden stairs to the second floor cafe, which was a bare board platform about half way to the ceiling. There, I had my last bowl of saimin, before boarding the plane for the mainland.

While we had prepared the *California* to sail around the world for all those months, back on the mainland, Nat had often visited The Cove. At first, I thought he came because he enjoyed my parent's hospitality, but after awhile it became clear that he had strong feelings for my sister, Mare. He followed me home from Hawaii, after a few weeks, and the two of them announced that they loved each other dearly, and set off to Las Vegas to be married. They had to marry in a hurry, because he had to return to the *California,* and he wanted her to go with him! For several years, they made their home aboard the barquentine at Ala Wai Yacht Basin, where their first daughter, Cala, was born. Get it? Cala, for California!

The *California* never sailed around the world, and Nat eventually sold it. It served as a dinner cruise boat off Diamond Head for a while. I got to go on several of their cruises, which were very different from our voyage. They had installed a new, nearly silent, diesel engine. The mains'l went up for looks only, since the engine did all the work. Still later, I heard it had sold again and did dinner cruising out of San Diego. Eventually, the *California* went aground and broke up in a storm off the California coast.

California full rigged with square sails.

Chapter 13

♪ *There's no business like show business!* ♫

Each time I got home from a sailboat adventure, I immediately went down to the docks, job hunting. Soon I found a doctor who had a motor sailer, looking for a captain. A motor sailer usually has just one smaller mainsail, a jib, which is the sail in front, and a powerful motor. The motor does most of the work, with the sails up just to steady the boat. It offers some flexibility in that the motor can be shut down in order to also have a nice peaceful, slow sail, too.

The doctor hired me. During the week I did maintenance on his boat, scraping, painting and cleaning. He brought guests down on weekends and I ran them over to Catalina and then acted as steward and served meals and drinks. He did all the cooking, since he liked to cook. That was certainly a good thing from my point of view. At only 42 feet it was not a very big boat, but still had lots of room on deck.

On our first trip, after we had cleared the San Pedro lighthouse and were headed to Catalina, we put it on autopilot. The owner said to me, "Go forward and keep an eye out."

So I stretched out on the sunny deck with my head propped up on one arm. I lazily watched the horizon, because a sailor never knows when another boat, a piece of driftwood, or maybe even an iceberg, will come along. When I realized the boat had begun a slow turn to the left, I whipped up and started back. The doctor stood at the helm, laughing.

"I was just testing to see if you were asleep or not!" he said, waving me back. After that he trusted me completely with the boat.

The deal worked out well for me because I got to live aboard during the week while I kept up with the cleaning and varnishing. He taught me how to maintain the engine, too.

We anchored at the 22nd St. Yacht Landing in San Pedro. A lot of wealthy people kept their boats there, but a lot of really interesting characters lived along there, too. This yacht harbor lay closest to the main harbor entrance, which made it easy in, easy out for the moored boats.

Other docks and landings in the area lay tucked in among the factories and commercial areas along the inner harbor. One yacht landing I recall sat next to a coconut oil, or copra, factory. When the wind blew right, it really stunk. Coconut oil smells great rubbed thinly on a suntanned body, but believe me, it turns into a very unpleasant odor in the hot sun by the millions of gallons.

In all those other yacht harbors, boat owners had to wash down their boats almost every day to get the soot and grime off. We had no problem with this at the 22nd St. site because the prevailing sea breezes blew the pollution inland!

Two elderly Norwegian sea captains there had sailed around the Horn on the big old sailing schooners in their early teens. These real characters both captained yachts at the Landing, one of them on Bogart's *Santana*. About seventy at the time, they generously took me under their wing and treated me like their treasured granddaughter or niece.

"No, that boat's no good," they told me when I asked their advice about a possible job.

"Yes, you can work for this person. Is OK," they said, if I found something they approved of.

Together, they taught me a lot of the lore of the sea, telling with heavy accents their stories of sailing through the roughest waters of the world and living through it.

When they found out I worked for the doctor, they expressed their dismay. "No, no, no. You cannot work with this doctor," they said, solemnly shaking their heads.

"Why not?" I asked.

During a long pause the two old sailors looked at each other and then back at me.

Finally, one said, "Bungy, have you ever noticed that all of his guests are women?"

"Yeah, but so what?" I replied.

I was still so young and naïve. I just showed up every day and did my job, not really aware of anything going on between the doctor and his guests. After the Norwegians alerted me to the possibility, I finally recognized all the hanky panky going on and handed in my notice. However, I must say that the man never made a pass at me. I didn't know whether to be complimented or insulted!

Through sailing I met many wonderful, fascinating people.

For instance, John Ford, the director, had a huge, gorgeous schooner called *Aaroner* berthed at the end of the slip at Ala Wai

Yacht Basin, where all Hawaii-bound boats eventually ended up. One time I met the actor Sterling Hayden on board. Not long after that, he failed to get custody of his children, so he sailed his boat, *Wanderer*, to San Francisco, took his children out for a day sail, and sailed off with them to Tahiti!

Of course, the little local sailing jobs just provided a way to bide my time until something bigger and more exotic came along.

My older sisters went on several USO shows with Ray during the Korean War, from Greenland to the Philippines to Japan to South Korea. Each time I asked permission to go, and he always replied, "No! You're too young!"

I kept asking, however, and finally the time came when he agreed take me along. The tour covered the military bases throughout the western states. The shows aimed to make the troops laugh, and leave them a little less homesick than they had been before we arrived.

Ray worked out a comedy routine with me, since I cannot sing and I did not look fantastically glamorous like the Hollywood starlets that were in the show. Each performance, I delivered my lines as the straight man pretty well and we got some good laughs. Actually, Ray got the laughs! We were doing two to five shows daily.

One night we performed in a ballpark, in front of over 2,000 GIs, all sitting down and looking up at us with a sea of upturned faces. Ray said his lines and I promptly went blank.

His eyes caught me again. It was always the eyes, and as I stood there trying to remember my line, I wondered what I had done wrong to deserve the look he gave me, when actually it was probably just his regular look.

Absolutely nothing came to mind. He just stood there, looking down at me and waiting. He looked out at the audience and shrugged, still saying nothing. He looked back at me and waited some more. Just by standing there, he let the audience know I had forgotten my lines, and got those soldiers to laughing and laughing.

After what seemed like hours to me, but probably took less than two minutes, he said in his reverberating voice, "Wellll?" The audience howled even more.

Thankfully, his voice broke the spell and I finally remembered my lines and we went on with the skit.

Another time the actor who was supposed to throw a shaving cream pie into Ray's face for the finale fell ill, so I had to perform this most important part.

Ray took me aside and looked at me very sternly with those eyes.

"Remember, this is the finale, and after the pie is thrown I must give the closing speech, so *do not throw it hard. Do not get it in my eyes!*" he warned me.

The finale came, and with caution lights whirring inside my head, I tossed the pie very gently. So gently, that it popped right back off his face, leaving not a trace on him! The whole pie, still in its plate, landed upright on the floor.

I looked at him with my mouth agape in disbelief, then looked down at the pie. Quickly, I stooped down, grabbed the pie again and this time, threw it much harder. So much harder that the cream smashed into his face, his eyes, his hair, and down his suit.

Theatrically, he slowly wiped gobs of cream from his eyes so that he could see, bent majestically to retrieve the pie plate, and started collecting all the shaving cream from his face, his chest, a nearby table and the floor. He very meticulously repacked it all in the pie plate, all the time looking balefully back and forth from me to the audience with those magnetic eyes.

The GIs laughed so hard they could hardly stay upright, while I quaked in fear.

When he got the pie all back together, he strolled menacingly up to me, took the back of my head in his big left hand, and proceeded to smash the pie in my face, booming with that big voice of his, "I told you, *do not throw it hard!"*

It was the best finale we ever had.

My favorite times came when he invited me to spend a few days or a week at his home for a vacation. He had a vegetable garden, ducks, chickens, funny little dogs and a burro.

One night he and I sat alone in his house, seated at opposite ends of the long kitchen table, reading. An old-fashioned school clock with a huge pendulum hung on the wall. The only sound was the tick, tick, tock of that old clock. After an hour or so had passed with neither of us saying anything, I became very aware of that clock tick-tocking. I started getting a little nervous, because Mother had trained me from early on to "always entertain your guests." I felt more and more guilty that I was only entertaining myself by reading.

I began to think that my lack of sociability might be considered rude, so after another half hour of trying to figure out a way to break this awkward silence, I cleared my throat and said something like, "It has certainly been a lovely day, hasn't it?"

He put down his book, looked hard down that long table that seated fourteen comfortably, and said, "I thought you were the one person in this world I didn't have to talk to." We understood each other better after that – in companionable silence.

One afternoon I listened to the grunion report on the radio and ran to find someone. "The grunion are running!" I shouted to Mare, who was busy painting another Renoir on the front door. "Call Ray! He wanted to come with us!"

"OK, right away, I'm practically through!"

I got buckets, beach blankets, towels and a gunny sack all ready to throw into his old Jeep upon his arrival.

Grunions come in on the ocean waves to lay their eggs in the sand. Coming from who knows where, and returning the same way. The powers that be can tell us when they are supposed to come, but lots of times the little eight-inch-long fish never show up, so grunion hunting is iffy.

Ray came screeching in from Hollywood after dark. We loaded up all the gear, including a picnic for the long wait, and took off for Cabrillo Beach.

The beach was loaded with "other hunters." There were so many other fires that we were glad we had brought our own driftwood. It got later and later and all except two other campfires had left. About 1:00 a.m. a wave came in and silver shapes started jumping around in the sand. The bright moon shining on the wet sand made them visible. "Grunions! Grunions!" we shouted, Ray loudest of all. Every time a wave came up, thousands of these little fish were left to lay their eggs until the next wave. We filled the buckets, took off our jackets and filled those, too. As suddenly as the grunion appeared, they disappeared. Exhausted, we built up our fire, gutted a dozen or so grunions, and put them on the hot rocks right beside the flames. Mmmm, mmmm, they were good!

The next day, Mother invited a bunch of friends and we fried up the rest of the grunions for a rare feast.

I began paying regular visits to lots of the docks spread throughout the harbor, looking for another sailing berth on a yacht, any yacht. Like the sailor in John Masefield's poem, I just had to "go down to the sea again."

Chapter 14

♪ '*Twas Friday morn when we set sail ... !* ♫

Once again, my old friend Dwight Long came to my rescue. He called one fine day and said, "Pack your sea bag for a long voyage. I'm going to do my best to get you aboard a boat on its way to the South Pacific!"

I flew to my bedroom, got out my trusty sea bag, rolled up my sailing gear, and carefully stowed it into my sea bag. Amidst my foul weather gear, swim suits, shorts, and a sweater, I also carefully rolled up my handy, dandy, never-wrinkle semi-formal, packed my set of books, and my sheaf knife and I was ready to go!

Dwight and I sailed down to Newport Beach and just as it got dark, *The Island Belle* nudged into the steel hull of the gaff-headed sailing schooner, *Te Vega*. Dwight yelled, "Ahoy, there! Anyone on deck?"

The night watch leaned over the rail and peered down through the wispy fog. "Oh, Capt. Long! Come on aboard. Capt. Darr's waiting for you in the main saloon."

We tied off to the nearby pier and clambered aboard the 134-foot beauty. I stood on the deck and stared up at the tallest masts I had ever seen. I could not have touched my fingers together if I had thrown my arms around the main mast and hugged it.

"The main mast was lost in a storm and they have just replaced it," Dwight explained.

All through the ship, last minute preparations continued for departure the next day, for a nearly three month cruise of the islands of French Oceania. "Tahiti, here I come," I breathed silently to myself. My long-held dream of sailing to these fabled islands appeared on the verge of coming true.

I followed Dwight down into the main saloon. As I stepped through the door, I stopped and gaped. It looked like the setting for an adventurous Errol Flynn pirate movie.

Te Vega Brochure: luring passengers to set sail for Tahiti.

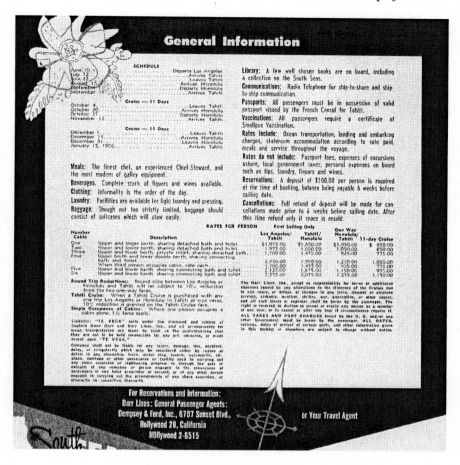

Inside of Te Vega Brochure.

Te Vega stretched fifteen feet across and the main saloon went all the way from starb'd to port. To the left (or port) sat a long, elegant upholstered sofa. It looked pretty upscale to me, compared to our faded 1940s rattan couch back at The Cove. Over-stuffed lounge chairs were bolted firmly to the floor. On one wall hung a bookcase with bars across the front to keep all the books in place while the boat was under way. In front of the sofa stood a highly polished mahogany coffee table.

On the starb'd (right) side hung the passengers' dining table on gimbals, which allowed the surface to remain flat, keeping the dishes from slipping and sliding all over the place.

Gimbals are tracks under the table, having curved arms that move freely back and forth. They have adjustable stops so the table can be stopped at the right angle to the boat. Once a boat reaches the tropics, the trade winds blow so steadily that the boat heels over in one direction or the other, with very little variation for days. At that time, the table is fixed in place at the proper angle. Although the diners sit on a tilted deck, the table, and all the dinnerware and food on it, stay level. This certainly helps with eating, and clean-up, too.

Capt. Omer Darr rose from a comfortable leather lounge chair, behind his polished desk, both bolted to the deck, and came forward with his hand outstretched. Above medium height and blond, he had that sense of dominion all the good blue water sailors have. During World War II he had sailed through the South Pacific, charting bays, islands and currents, compiling all the information needed by the Navy for transportation and battles. I later learned that he had great patience and was very willing to teach others everything he knew about sailing.

The two old friends greeted each other warmly. Dwight waved in my direction.

"Here's your new mess cook I promised to bring along."

Darr looked astonished. "But this is a girl, and in a crew of sixteen men. I don't know. It's impossible!"

I held my breath as my long-time friend and sailing mentor spoke about my sailing abilities, my good sportsmanship and my hard workmanship.

Captains Darr and Long debated the wisdom of giving me a job good-naturedly, until my friend Dwight finally overcame Darr's apprehension. He made a final push.

"I have never even thought of a girl working on a boat before," he cried. "Where will she sleep? No, no, my friend, it is impossible. Think of the trouble she could get into with the crew! Some of these guys are pretty rough!"

"Surely you have a space somewhere aboard this big boat for one tiny girl to bunk in," Dwight replied. "I can assure you that she will do the work of several men. And as for causing trouble, I've known her for a long time, and her family, too. She's not going to be a problem."

Darr finally waved me over to his desk, where I signed the articles of the sailing ship *Te Vega*, bound from Newport Beach, California, for a three-month cruise of the South Seas. My pay was $100 a month, and, being the mess cook – all I could eat. That sounded like a pretty good deal to me!

Before the journey ended, I would see the Marquesas, Taumotus, Tahiti, Moorea, Raiatea and Bora Bora, before sailing on up to the Hawaiian Islands and home. I had read of these islands in Nordolf and Hall's *Mutiny on the Bounty* trilogy, in books on sailing canoes, guided across vast unknown oceans by the reflection of the stars in the water held in half a coconut shell; and in the numerous autobiographies of round-the-world sailors.

255

For years, I had crammed my head and my heart with the mystique of the South Seas and now, at last, I had my dream within my grasp. The dream lost none of its glory because I had signed the articles as mess cook, the lowliest swabbie in the crew.

Jack, the cook, and I had been "along the dock" friends for ages. He was the cook I had searched for in vain when I had all that raw lamb to deal with on *Jada*.

My job on *Te Vega* included washing dishes three times a day for twenty-four people; scrubbing the pots and pans; swabbing the galley deck twice a day; serving the crew and the officers; and keeping an account of the stores. I was to cull through the huge sacks of potatoes, boxes of lettuce and cabbage, bags of oranges and crates of apples that were stored in one of the longboats, every day, looking for the rotten ones and chucking them overboard. Anything else pertaining to food also fell to me. I was on my way to paradise and never gave this busy work schedule a second thought.

Capt. Darr had a great deal of concern about my sleeping accommodations. Certainly he would not allow me to sleep in the fo'c'sle with the sixteen male crew members. Finally, he assigned me to a bunk in one of the ship's richly appointed staterooms that was empty. This was right next door to his private quarters.

The accommodations for the captain and his elegant wife were even more luxurious than the finest staterooms on board. Highly polished wood gleamed from every wall. Instead of bunks, they had a big bed, covered with a richly tapestried sea-blue spread. Above the bed, a compass hung on the ceiling, so he knew the moment he woke up if the boat was sailing on the right heading. Built-in drawers and cabinets filled every nook and cranny. A large mirror on one wall reflected the opulence of that stateroom.

Sometimes, when the moon and stars beckoned me, I took my sleeping bag and a pillow, and slept in one of the longboats on deck. If it rained, I slipped under the longboat for shelter. I always had to figure out how to prop myself in to keep from rolling all over as the boat moved with the motion of the wind and sea. In light winds, I also liked to sleep in the woven rope safety basket under the bowsprit, with a piece of waterproof canvas under me to keep me dry, when the boat took an unusually deep plunge and the sea waves tossed their spray too high. I threw my sleeping bag on top of the canvas, curled up in it, and, with just the stars and the moon and the porpoises for company, I really did own the universe!

Because of the luxury of the accommodations, I might have felt like Cinderella in the castle, except for the fact that my cabin doubled as a storeroom. The first part of the journey, I had to crawl over boxes of dry stores, cases of beer, and sacks of onions and other vegetables, just to reach the upper bunk, the only clear spot in the room.

As the stores dwindled, or were stored away properly, bags of dirty laundry started taking their place. I definitely preferred the boxes and sacks to the bags of smelly laundry. The stores blocked access to the nice built-in drawers, but I lived very well out of my sea bag. That is, as long as I did not confuse it with a sack of dirty laundry.

We set sail from Newport Harbor at ten o'clock on the morning of June 10, 1955. A huge crowd waved us farewell. My mother, as usual, cried, but I did not shed a drop. I felt too much excitement for tears. A fleet of other boats sailed out of the harbor with us, horns tooting joyfully, their crews shouting, "*Aloha*! *Aloha*! Fair winds!"

Capt. Darr planned for our journey to be the first in a series of luxury cruises for the well-heeled tourist who wanted a taste of real adventure under sail. We carried six guests that first voyage. Architects, lawyers and businessmen, all lacking any sailing experience, made up the crew. Maybe they had no experience, but their enthusiasm was unbounded. They sailed with the same dream as I, to taste the beguiling South Sea islands, which had called to them, like it called to me all these years.

Before we got out of sight of land, my duties called. Immediately the cook and I began stowing, straightening and cleaning. The stove, an old commercial diesel behemoth, always had a miasma of oily smoke about it. I loved it when Jack told me to go on deck and peel a million potatoes. Just to get into that fresh salt air was worth the peeling of those potatoes.

Off the California coast, a ground swell began, and the weather turned overcast with low clouds and drizzle. I had sailed the California-Hawaii run several times and occasionally had succumbed to seasickness, until I got my sea legs. This time was no different. We cooked and served dinner to a dozen people; washed the dishes and pots; emptied the garbage over the side; brewed a fifty-cup pot of coffee for the night watch; laid out a bunch of hard tack, peanut butter and jelly on the table for the crews on their watches; and mopped the entire deck, before I was able to scramble up the iron ladder that ran above the engine room, race over to the leeward side and heave!

I managed to keep up with my duties only because a good many others on board suffered from the same condition, so there was not very much demand for food. Despite the *mal de mer*, however, my hours on duty remained unchanged, from 6 a.m. to 9 p.m. with an hour break in the morning and two hours off in the afternoon.

One of the healthier crewmen kept nagging me to take some charcoal tablets. "Just take two. All your worries will be over," he said.

To get rid of him, I finally took a couple, the very first pills I had ever taken in my whole life. Like large black slugs, they moved slowly down my throat. Very shortly, I felt another surge of unpleasantness and rushed to the rail, where everything proceeded to come up again, only this time looking disgustingly black! Needless to say, they were the very last pills I ever took, too!

Despite the queasy stomach, I climbed out of my bed each day, clambered over all the boxes and crates and bags, fumbled in my sea bag for shorts and a shirt, threw water on my face and headed to the diesel-perfumed galley.

I had just about recovered from the *mal de mer* on the third day out and decided to get myself going with a luxurious hot bath in the sunken tub that came with my stateroom. Between cleaning up after lunch and beginning preparation for dinner, I used this break to fill the tub with steaming salt water and lowered myself slowly into it, down to my chin. "Ah, what a life," I sighed, as I leaned back against one end of the tub and breathed in the sweet sea-scented

Mess cook Bungy, a bit under the weather!

vapor. It was wonderful. I felt the last of the queasiness slipping from me in the delicious heat.

Suddenly, the boat took a long roll to port. All the water left the tub and washed across the deck. When the boat rolled back to starboard, the water rushed back, hitting me in the face with all the dirt from across the deck. From then on, I took showers in the officers' head. The tub turned into an excellent place to store things. The seasonable gray weather in which we began our voyage, lasted four days before we came into brilliant sunshine and set our sails to the trade winds. In the days to come, as the weather grew increasingly tropical, I spent those precious two hours off in the afternoon lolling around the deck, watching the wide oceans and far horizons.

Sometime during each day, I climbed the hundred-twenty-five-foot mast to the crosstrees, to survey my kingdom. Or took a trick at the wheel, just to feel the dominion of 134 feet of boat under me. As it got warmer, we all got into our bathing suits and threw buckets of sea water on each other. Sometimes the crew would hook up the bosun's chair, which is like a wooden swing, to one of the longboats' davits. We'd take turns hopping into the swing and being pushed out over the sea. The seat was on a pulley so the crew had great fun dunking anyone who tried this.

Under the warmth of the sun, and the soft, gentle breezes of the tropics, my days melted into one long, continuous adventure.

Helping Jack with the cooking was like attending a low-class culinary school. For the crew, we prepared only very basic dishes. Oatmeal, pancakes and sliced ham sufficed for breakfast; roast beef sandwiches carried us through lunch; and dinner consisted of great bowls of delicious steaming beef stew with your choice of white sauce or curry sauce on top.

I started the day by making fifty cups of coffee and waking the crew at 6:30. Since I worked harder and longer hours than the crew and they always complained about how hard their job was, I took great pleasure in waking them up. I stood outside the fo'c'sle entrance, taking a moment to look at the rows of bunks against the bulkheads, filled with all those snoring guys. Then I took a deep breath and yelled at the top of my lungs, "Good moooorning!" I have a very loud voice.

Pillows, shoes, books and anything else throwable flew my way, although I do not remember ever getting hit by anything. "Go away!" they shouted. "Shut up!" After two weeks they all signed a petition to the captain asking him to command me to stop. With a twinkle in his eye when he looked at me, he merely said to the crew, "Well, she gets you up in time for breakfast, doesn't she?"

I served the crew and cleaned up after they had eaten. After finishing breakfast duties, I scrubbed the deck, and when I had time, polished the brass. Gilbert and Sullivan's "She polished up the brass so carefully, that now she is the ruler of the Queen's navy," seemed an appropriate tune to sing as I worked, although I certainly never managed to rule over anything.

Our fresh food, like potatoes, apples, onions, lettuce and cabbage came in fifty-pound sacks or large crates. Every day, up on deck, I had to sift through every one of these, culling out the bad with all their slime and stink. If I did not do a careful job, the whole lot could go bad in a hurry. So, it really was an important job because when I looked around the horizon, I didn't see a supermarket!

Being the only girl in the crew had its disadvantages. No one had even heard the phrase "women's lib" in 1955. Adding to the gender challenge was the fact that, besides the captain, I again, was the only crew aboard who had actually gone to sea under sail before. Even the first and second mates had only worked at sea on freighters.

However, they had their officer's tickets, which the captain needed in order to carry paying passengers. Some of the men did not take kindly to my expertise. The first mate and the chief steward gave me my biggest challenges.

One night, the cook and I were trying to regroup the galley and recover after a particularly hard day. Squalls had hit us continually, throwing everything all about. We worked in 105° heat, exhausted and smelly. I had just finished the last deck swabbing of the night. It was around 9:30, and I was ready to hit the sack.

I leaned on my mop, sweat pouring off me, and groaned, "Whew!" The first mate walked in just at that moment and grumbled, "Well, if you can't take it, you shouldn't have signed on!" He poured himself a mug of coffee and left the galley, muttering, "Girls!"

He had no way of knowing how close he came to swallowing a mop with his coffee that night.

A similar night, just as I as about to shut down the galley, the chief steward walked in, ran his fingers over the galley's brass door knobs and door plates, saying, "Needs polishing!" and strolled off. That meant that I had to stay and get the job done, no matter how long it took! Hey! I was on my way to paradise, living my dream, and not even an officer with an attitude could spoil that magic!

I started as mess cook at $100 per month. Very soon, the captain moved me up a notch to cook's assistant, with a raise to $125 per month! The other crew members were a bit upset because this punk of a girl got a raise and they didn't. I only worked about a hundred times harder than they did, and the captain knew it. Whenever they complained, I just said, "You wanna change jobs?"

On board, we had five paying passengers and a photographer. The captain planned to use his photos for publicity to drum up clients for future voyages. The captain's gorgeous wife, Harriet, sailed with us, too. We also had a chief steward with two assistants to take care of the passengers. The stewards always dressed in crisp white uniforms. The chief steward came from Holland, but he had worked many years in food and beverage service at some of the big Hawaiian hotels. He did a great job of stocking the boat and seeing to it that everything pertaining to food and guests ran smoothly.

One slow, easy afternoon, as the boat made its way closer toward the South Seas, one of the guys and I had a little impromptu boxing match on deck. I had a really good punch I wanted to throw. I threw it and he dodged me. My hand went right into the iron bulkhead. We all heard a sickening crunch as the bones hit iron. Immediately, I put my hand down and went below and started studying my Bible and *Science and Health*, focusing on the fact that my relationship with God, who is all good, had to be all good. I realized that this thing that seemed to have happened appeared to be bad and, therefore, could not exist in my life. About fifteen minutes later I went back up on deck with the hand in perfect condition. The 23rd and 91st Psalms, which I had memorized in Sunday School, were always close and handy!

Another time, I had a serious accident in the galley. I worked in an apron, a sun-top, shorts and bare feet because of the almost unbearable heat. One day, I had a big five-gallon stockpot with about four gallons of water in it, boiling on the stove. I had to move it from the stove to the sideboard. I grabbed a couple of big towels in both hands and caught hold of the handles of the pot. Suddenly, the boat took a roll, and the boiling water went down the whole front of my body.

Instantly I gave God control of the situation and accepted that the all-powerful God had much more strength than what had just happened. I knew that because of God's power and love, this experience was impossible; it had no authority over me. I never experienced any pain. Within three minutes, there was not even any redness. Some of the crew saw this happen and they gave me, and my God, a great deal of respect after this incident.

The two officers were by far the worst officers I ever had to work under. They complained constantly and seemed to have no joy in their lives. Unfortunately, the chief steward had added the cleaning of the officers' head to my list of duties. They made such an awful, disgusting mess of the room that after a few weeks some of the crew, who had become a bunch of big brothers to me, got together and went to the captain and said, "We don't think this is fair for her to have to clean that head."

Capt. Darr nodded in agreement and asked, "Well, what are we going to do? It's got to be cleaned."

Amazingly, the crew offered to take turns. After that, about five of them took the shifts. They did this wonderful thing for me! I felt like I had the best brothers in the world!

On the other hand, I never figured out if it was because of my gender, or if some other factor clicked in, but my garbage and I became the bane of the engine room crew. The chief engineer's experience had been largely on freighters and tug boats and he was pretty tough. He had quite a colorful and vulgar vocabulary, using words I had never even heard before, but which I sometimes managed to figure out from the context. He also disapproved loudly of having a girl on board. "It's bad luck to have a woman on board," he said, agreeing with many of the old sailors of that time.

However, he knew engines and kept the engine room immaculate. Of course, that seemed quite easy to me, since we sailed almost all of the time. For weeks on end, the only motors running in the engine room were the generators.

Because I had so much to do, the big five-gallon rubber garbage bucket in the galley usually filled to overflowing by the time I got around to emptying it. In order to do that job, I had to drag the bucket over to the narrow iron ladder attached vertically to the bulkhead, directly over the main engine, lug it up the rungs (with the boat always in motion), drag it across the deck, heave the garbage over the side, tie a rope to the bucket and dunk it in the water several times to wash it out.

Each time I did this, the engineer came storming up after me, clutching hands full of potato peels or some such slop that had fallen out in my trek, messing up their spotlessly clean engine.

"Bungy!" the engineer shouted. "Look at this @*!@# mess! You've dropped @*!@# garbage all over the @*!@# engine again!"

"I'm so sorry," I replied meekly. "I'll try to do better."

"You've been saying that ever since we left port! No more @*!@# garbage! Or else!" he yelled, waving his fist at me. I never found out what he meant by "or else," but he sure had me scared.

About that time Jack generally appeared on the scene, cigarette dangling from his lips, his massive hairy chest bulging from an underwear T-shirt. "How about you guys giving Bungy a hand carrying the garbage topside from now on," he growled.

That usually silenced them for a while, until some particularly gruesome glob landed in their spic and span domain, and once more, they'd come up shouting and cussing.

Garbage at sea had a way of coming back to haunt me. Once, after I had dumped the bucket, half an orange peel lodged itself into the lee porthole directly over the passengers' dining table. The peel stayed there for days, as pressure of the seawater on the submerged starboard hull remained steady and constant in the trade winds. The poor guests had nothing to look at while they ate dinner except the ocean swirling by the porthole, and my half an orange peel.

One morning, for no apparent reason, the boat suddenly took a short tack, and then got back on its original course. "I wonder what that was all about?" I asked the cook. He shrugged incomprehension. As I manhandled the garbage bucket to the side a short while later, Capt. Darr came forward.

"Bungy. I wonder if you might just toss that garbage out a little farther aft from now on?" I nodded and complied with his kindly spoken request. After I had rinsed the bucket, I just had to take a peek. Sure enough, the orange peel had disappeared from the porthole. He had brought that huge sailing vessel around just to dislodge my orange peel. I do not know why I thought of it as "my" orange peel, except that throughout the journey, the buckets and buckets of slop seemed to take on a personality and I began to think of the garbage in a very possessive way.

267

During the mellow tropical evenings, we all sat on deck, passengers and crew. One crewman, a tall, handsome lawyer from Texas, softly strummed his guitar, singing *Jalisco! Jalisco!* while we watched the sun set in a blaze of gold and purple. Each evening, the Southern Cross rose higher on the horizon, while the North Star sank out of sight. Phosphorous in the dark water vied for brilliance with the stars.

Sometimes, out of the silence, we heard a soft, "Pffft. Pffft." We looked out to see the porpoises playing around the bow, with great leaps, the phosphorescence from the ocean flowing off their backs and sparkling into the sea for yards behind them. Then, as suddenly as they had appeared, they disappeared, rarely staying long.

The sails required only the minimum of attention, for once they have been set to the steady trade winds, they very rarely need changing, and the boat slips along at a good clip with the same rhythmic motion, day and night. We averaged about ten knots.

Occasionally, we saw squalls coming across the sea in the moonlight. They looked like tall, very dark clouds, spilling rain straight down. On either side of that, lightning streaks and brilliant moonlight silvered the scene. If the storm appeared to be heading our way, the captain shouted and we rushed to shorten sail. When it hit, we had a brief wild ride, galloping through the sea. This ride never lasted very long. The storm soon passed and up went the sail again.

Jack had cooked on different yachts all over the world. He stood about five-feet nine-inches tall with a great old gut sticking out front. His bald scalp sported just a fringe of gray.

Bungy, taking a trick at the helm on her off duty hours.

Throughout the trip Jack acted like a father to me. "Boys, that's enough of that now," he growled at the crew if the kidding got too heavy. When the work piled up, and I got buried under it, he rounded up a couple of the crewmen and got them to pitch in and help.

The boys told stories about Jack's prodigious swearing abilities, but I can remember him swearing in front of me only once the whole trip.

On this particular day, he had mixed up a beautiful peach cobbler with a feather-light crust and cinnamon sugar topping and we were carrying it over to the oven. He had made this concoction big enough to feed two-dozen people or more. The boat had run into a small squall. Jack and I made our way carefully across the bucking deck. Suddenly, a can of grease rolled off the stove, hit the deck and splattered all over.

Jack had one side of the big metal pan and I had the other. The grease got under our feet at exactly the same time the boat took a really big roll. Both of us slid sideways and banged into the big freezer at one end of the long galley. Then the boat took another roll and we took off for the other end, holding on to that pan of cobbler for dear life. We slid down the length of the galley, about twelve feet, and banged up against the pot sink.

With all that momentum, the peach cobbler just kept going on when we stopped. Like a huge slab of peach lava, it slid right out of the pan and into the sink.

"Damn!" Jack shouted.

With the boat still rocking and rolling, we very carefully scooped up all the peachy glop out of the sink and patted it back in the pan. Then we slid over to the oven and shoved it in. It was the best peach cobbler we ever made, and no one on board ever knew what had happened to it!

Jack taught me lots of handy things about cooking at sea. One of his best tips involved making two layers when baking a cake. He poured the batter into two very deep baking pans. Since the boat always sails at a tilt, the cakes always come out lopsided. Jack taught me to twirl the two layers around, matching deep side to shallow side, frost, and serve up the cake at the table looking perfectly level.

He was bound and determined that when I got off that boat I would know how to cook. But even something as simple as pancakes seemed to elude me. "If you pour your pancake batter on the griddle like this," he repeatedly told me patiently and quietly, grabbing the spoon to demonstrate, "then you get pancakes that are perfectly round that have no petticoats!" By the time he got to "no petticoats" he would be shouting. Petticoats were the frills left around the pancakes' edge that looked exactly like the frills on petticoats! I really and truly tried, succeeding about half the time. But to tell the truth, I always preferred sailing to cooking, and to this day, my pancakes still have those pesky little petticoats!

We soon got into the flat dead seas of the doldrums where we, at last, had to use the engines in order to make headway. In the days of the tall ships, the sailors dreaded the doldrums. The winds in that area could be so variable, or even non-existent for weeks on end. The big sailing ships took months to get through them, running out of precious water and supplies.

One afternoon, we arrived at the mysterious Equator, which is the line that runs around the middle of our earth. There is always a great ceremony initiating all the landlubbers who had never crossed this imaginary line, into the mysteries of King Neptune.

The always perfectly and spotlessly uniformed Chief Steward donned a mop for a beard, placed a colander on his head for a crown, and wrapped a long sheet around his chest. He held a longboat hook to represent King Neptune's spear.

All of the polliwogs, those of us who had not previously crossed the Equator, lined up on deck. Varadey spouted some kind of elaborately expressive folderol, while the shellbacks, the old, experienced hands who had crossed the Equator previously, pelted us with shaving cream and buckets of water. We then drank a toast of some absolutely awful mixture. To conclude the ceremony, Neptune presented us with official looking certificates declaring us "Official Shellbacks." Then, we all got to drink a couple of glasses of champagne, followed by singing and dancing. I enjoyed it all until I had to go below to help Jack prepare dinner.

Not long after, on one beautifully perfect tropical day, we saw land! The islands of the Marquesas group came over the horizon and what a wonderful sight to see those lush islands coming closer and closer after all those weeks at sea. The rich land smells grew stronger and stronger as we made our approach. We detected the unmistakable scent of earth mixed with the heady odor of the gardenia-like island flower, Tiare Tahiti. The Marquesas form a group of twelve islands just south of the equator. Their volcanic pinnacles point into the clouds.

My duties called, so the porthole over my pot sink framed my first view of them. John Greenleaf Whittier's poem popped into mind, "I know not where His islands lift their fronded palms in air; I only know I cannot drift beyond His love and care." I watched the dark natives paddle their canoes out to greet us, through the deep blue waters of the bay, framed in the rich, light green of coco palms from the beach to the dark, volcanic mountains soaring into the sky.

134" Te Vega cruising the South Seas, 1955.

Chapter 15

♪ *She's just the little brown girl in the little grass skirt ...!* ♫

We sailed into the Bay of Hiva Roa, surrounded by tall, craggy mountains with dark green tropical growth cascading down the sides to the blue, blue water of the bay. The palms glistened and swayed gently in the light breezes. Plumeria, bougainvillea, and jasmine scented the air. The anchor went down with a huge splash. The boat lay still for the first time since Newport Beach, California, over 3,000 miles away!

The sun was nearly setting behind the mountains by the time we had secured the boat. "Jump in for a swim," Capt. Darr said. "But put someone on shark watch." Apparently, the sharks were plentiful in those waters. One of the crew, who did not swim, climbed up the ratlines into the rigging with a pair of binoculars, where he would be able to spot any sharks approaching in the crystal clear, water.

The local mayor and other dignitaries came out to greet us in their canoes. The men all had on shorts or pareus of blue or red material covered with bright flower patterns pulled up between their legs and tucked in. Some of them wore white shirts, but most of them stayed bare-chested, their dark skin glistening with coconut oil.

Almost all of them, men and women, wore flowers in their hair, shell leis around their necks, or a crown of woven ferns on their heads. The women wore their brightly colored pareus wrapped around their chests like elegant sarongs. They all looked like Hedy Lamarr in one of the *On the Road* movies with Bing Crosby and Bob Hope.

All of the natives laughed and yelled as they approached the boat. They clambered aboard and the mayor greeted the captain in French. None of them spoke any English, only French or their native Marquesan, very similar to Tahitian. They invited us to a dance that night in our honor. We quickly learned that the hospitable islanders used any excuse for a party.

We had anchored in the middle of that huge bay, and had to row the longboats in to a concrete wharf to get ashore. The sea surged roughly in and out against the stone wall. Our timing had to be just right in order to jump ashore onto the jetty, because of the huge swell. We waited for a swell to lift our boat even with the dock, and with stomachs in our mouths, leaped across. Those who managed the maneuver first, reached out a helping hand to the rest of us, to keep us from landing in the water. It was really quite dangerous, but the sure-footed natives, who did this all the time, found our hesitation very amusing.

The longboat tossed up and down with the surge, repeatedly banging the rubber fenders we had hung along the side against the concrete pier. When my turn came, I stood up, stumbled to the dockside of the longboat and waited for a wave to lift me up to the level of the dock. With much trepidation, I leapt, landing unsteadily on solid ground, hands reaching to grab me before I fell back into the bay. One by one, we all made it ashore, except for the watch that had been left on board.

Before we left the pier, we set up a kerosene lantern to wave as a signal, to call the longboat to come and get us when we wanted to return to *Te Vega*.

Following the natives, we strolled down a path, to get to the dance. Actually, we didn't stroll because our sea legs had acquired a rollicking, bumping-into-each-other gait. We were all laughing and had to keep pulling each other back on to the path.

We arrived at a palm thatched pavilion right in the middle of the jungle. It had a palm woven roof, and open sides. The slight breezes from the sea kept everyone cool. The band consisted of two guitars and an empty five-gallon cooking oil can beaten with two hefty sticks. One of the crew asked me to dance and that broke the ice. Soon everyone twirled around the floor dancing foxtrots and jitterbugs. The "boys" grabbing the sarong clad girls, who always seemed to be happy and smiling.

We paused long enough in our dancing for the natives to give a demonstration of one of their traditional dances. Torches burned brightly, holding back the darkness of the surrounding jungle. They used only the metal oil cans to beat out the tempestuous rhythm of the dance of war. The dancers wore hula skirts decorated with shells and beads around the waist. Short cloaks woven from *lauhala* covered their shoulders. On their heads they wore elaborately woven coconut palm helmets decorated with more shells and beads. Their muscular bodies glistened with coconut oil. They carried long spears and flat carved wood weapons of various sizes.

Two opposing teams of dancers advanced and retreated and finally moved into a choreographed battle that grew more and more violent, crescendoing into a wild leaping and thunderous shouting. The primitive power of it reminded us that only forty years earlier these people had lived as cannibals!

When the festivities ended, everyone made their way back to the pier, except for a few of us who had received invitations to the mayor's private party, to be held at his house.

We took off over a jungle path behind a fast moving native who obviously knew the trail quite well. I stumbled along in the scary dark, brushing leaves away from my face and trying to keep up, wondering if this late-night trek was such a good idea.

However, we soon arrived safely at a real native thatched hut, lit with coconut-oil lamps, which consisted simply of halves of coconut shells filled with the oil pressed from the coconut meat. Natives sang and danced and played guitars. We sat between the musicians, on mats strewn on the ground inside the hut.

In the mid 1950s, the Marquesas were still unspoiled by the influx of tourism and the scene reminded me of descriptions straight out of Melville's *Typee*. Their only contact with the outside world was either a mail boat, which was the copra schooner that arrived every six months carrying supplies and trading for copra, or an occasional sailboat like *Te Vega*.

After the party, we stumbled through the jungle back to the wharf, and signaled with a lantern from the pier to have the longboat retrieve us. I returned happily to my own little bunk, amazed that I no longer had to dream of the South Sea islands. I was actually there!

We hauled up the anchor and hoisted sail, early the next morning. The sun just coming up over the tall, rugged mountains, spreading its gold everywhere. On to new adventures!

The crew was learning to sail bit by bit, but many still had no clue about how to set sails. One morning, about one o'clock, I awoke from a sound sleep, sensing a problem with the sails. I jumped up and in two seconds reached the deck, ready to work. A squall had split the main sail, and all of us who were on deck worked to haul it down as fast as we could, before it destroyed itself in the strong winds. If the pressure from a big sail like this is not controlled, it can even break the mast!

A lot of the crew took three to four minutes to get up there. It seemed that when there was a problem or change, they did not show up until the captain called them. It wasn't their watch! Some were learning the art of sailing, and some were along for the ride. We dragged up an old mains'l that had been stowed in the bosun's locker, and replaced the tattered one. Within an hour, we were racing along once more.

The next day, all hands were given sail needles, which are kind of like upholstery needles, and "palms" which is a tough item that fits over your thumb and into your palm, to help you push the needle through the heavy canvas, kind of like a thimble. It took two days to repair the damage. It was almost like making a brand new sail. By the middle of the second day, the old mains'l came down and the reasonably new one was hoisted back into place. All our sails were canvas, some heavy and some light. It was before Dacron.

We sailed west towards the Island of Nuku Hiva, which headquartered the French Administrator. From there, he governed all the islands of the Marquesas Group.

The bay where we threw out our anchors, had a golden sand beach running half way around it, with the ever present, graceful coco palms reaching into the sky, our longboats tied up to a regular pier.

The administrator came aboard ship and welcomed Capt. Darr and his guests to the island. A tall, handsome, lean fellow, he sported luxuriant black hair and a thick mustache. He stood there proudly twirling the ends of that well-groomed feature as he offered us all the hospitality in the world.

In English, with a charming French accent, he asked, "Would anyone care to go horseback riding?" One of the passengers and I leaped at the chance to ride in this gorgeous setting and we made arrangements to meet him the next morning.

Just before the sun topped the volcanic mountains, we climbed into our saddles ready to go. "*Vite!*" he shouted, and the horses took off along the hard-packed golden sand, with the sparkling sea to one side and the dark green-black jungle to the other. The horses, about the size of a large Welsh pony, flew along. "They live halfway up the mountainsides, roaming around on the cliffs and through the jungles," the administrator explained. "When we tire out a string, the locals take them back up the mountain and let them loose. Then they catch a new herd of fresh half-wild horses."

Between races along the beach, he shared his frustration with developing the island economically. "There are some really special coffee beans growing here in the mountains," he said. "If we could get the islanders to work the plantation, they would probably be rich." However, the Marquesans believed they already had everything without working, so why work? And they do – so they don't!

"The only time I can get someone to work on the coffee plantation is if they land in jail, and there's been no one in jail for six months! Our coffee bean supply is running short," he lamented.

That evening, the administrator invited the captain, his wife, the passengers, and officers to come to his house at the edge of the little village for a formal dinner. Somehow, I got invited, too. I suspect it was because I was a young, fairly attractive woman, and he was French. My status on the boat certainly had nothing to do with it. After all, as mess cook, I held the lowliest position on board.

The captain's wife, Harriet, came below earlier carrying my special invitation from the administrator in her hand. "It's too bad you can't attend the administrator's dinner, since you have so much work to do," she said. However, some of the crewmen working nearby heard her and immediately jumped in and volunteered to do my chores so I could go. She undoubtedly thought it something of an embarrassment to attend an important social function with the mess cook, but I looked forward to the dinner with pleasure.

An exotic Anglo-islander beauty, Harriet generally spent her days strolling languidly around the deck wrapped in a sarong, expertly entertaining the guests. She also liked to sneak up on me, checking to make sure I was not doing anything with the crew that I should not be doing. I never was, which probably only served to make her more suspicious.

I left my dishes to the crew, and climbed into a clean pair of white shorts and a Hawaiian shirt. We rowed ashore in the longboats and strolled through the village up to the administrator's gorgeous home, set on a high point, looking out to sea. We ate at a long formal dining table, with a small army of servants producing course after course of French and Polynesian dishes. After finishing the sumptuous feast and the final course of coconut pudding, called *haupia* in Hawaiian, our hosts ushered us out onto the huge veranda, and seated us in comfortable chairs made of native woods, facing a lush lawn rolling out to the sea that looked just like the John Wayne movie, *Donovan's Reef*.

The rest of the crew had come to the house to join us for a preview of the dancers this island planned to send to Tahiti in a few weeks, to compete in the big dance contests held during the Bastille Day celebration. Bastille Day, July 14, is the French equivalent of America's Independence Day and the islanders loved to celebrate it. People from all of French Oceania converged on Papeete, the capital of Tahiti, for this annual fling.

Flaming torches lit the freshly mown lawn. The dancers' bodies, greased with coconut oil, glistened in the wavering light. They began with several fast island dances and for the finale, performed the traditional Pig Hunt Dance. Unlike our experience on Hiva Roa, both males and females danced.

All the girls formed two rows in the center. The boys lined up on either side. They started slowly with very low grunts, with the rhythm set by the beat of a single drum. The drum stopped. The boys continued grunting in very low voices. So low, I almost doubted the sounds were human. The sound built slowly, growing ever louder and louder as the dancing got faster and faster. Jumping up and swirling rapidly around, brandishing their long spears, I easily imagined the pigs and the hunters right there in front of me. Then the final grunt sounded, with the imaginary pigs impaled with a powerful thrust of the spears.

Our host turned to me, bowed gallantly, and said with Gallic charm, "If you will be so kind as to take my arm, we shall lead the way through the village to the pavilion for a bit of dancing." He swept me off my feet! Of course, I would be so kind.

Five guitars and a couple of tin drums serenaded us. The whole island attended the event, all in the best of spirits. We danced and danced until early morning. The only one to get out of line was the local policeman, who had a little too much of everyone else's home-brewed spirits. He eventually went back to his own jail to sleep it off.

When we returned to the boat near dawn, I held back until everyone had made their way below to their bunks. As the sun began to push gold and pink into the sky above the black craggy mountains, I dove off the boat into the deep blue and green of the bay. I kept my strokes soft and gentle, to keep from breaking the stillness of the dawn. I swam in the brilliant colors of the sunrise, in water as perfect as a tepid bath.

Before long, I heard the crew clattering around on the boat and reluctantly made my way back to the rope ladder hanging down the side. Time to go to work and get breakfast on the table.

Later the following day, when I had finished my duties, another crewman and I borrowed a couple of those little mountain horses and went riding through the little village, where children and piglets played side by side. Banana, mango and papaya trees dripped with luscious fruit, and charming, smiling, old people sat together in perfect harmony. "*I ora na*," they called out to us, greeting us in Tahitian. We smiled, waved and returned the greeting.

We rode over little wooden bridges and across streams, where young native women laughed and sang as they pounded their laundry on rocks in the water of a stream that cascaded happily down the mountain and through the jungle growth.

We finally wound our way back to the beach where I tried to make my horse gallop. "*Vite! Vite!*" I cried. The best I ever accomplished was a half-hearted trot. The horses apparently did not understand my atrocious French accent. All my hours on deck, basking in the sun and practicing my pronunciation along with my Berlitz self-taught French book helped me communicate with the willing residents of the islands, but I never fooled a horse.

That evening, Capt. Darr returned the administrator's hospitality by inviting him and seven other residents to dinner. He asked me to serve and gave me a spanking white sailor suit to match the formal occasion.

The steward and Jack really did their stuff. We served cocktails and hors d'oeuvres. The main course included thick steaks from

283

our freezer, along with a huge baked potato and a fresh island fruit compote. A flaming peach cobbler completed the meal. The full moon provided dramatic lighting, accompanied by the brilliance of the southern sky full of stars and the glow of the phosphorescence of the sea.

As the dinner came to a close, the guests relaxed with their drinks, making quiet conversation.

We were lucky to have any alcohol to serve our guests at all. Our engineer kept finding ways to steal the liquor from the locked bar. At one point, the steward, who never did learn the identity of the culprit, had the culprit himself make a wooden bar with holes in it that fit right over the bottles and locked this with a padlock. That worked for a while and the steward took great pride in thinking of this brilliant invention. But before long, the even cleverer engineer fashioned a straw that fit right into the tops of the bottles while they remained firmly locked.

Each member of the crew received two chits a night to exchange for alcoholic drinks. Since I did not drink, the rest of the crew always tried to talk me out of my chits. I refused to play along, which really frustrated them.

As the evening wound down, one of the crew kept the music playing on the wind-up phonograph. A waltz began to play. The administrator came up to me, took the serving tray from my hands, bowed, and said, "May I have this dance?"

The idea of the mess cook dancing with the guests broke all rules of shipboard protocol. I was, after all, the low man on the totem pole of authority. In a panic, I looked over at Capt. Darr, and he nodded his head in permission.

In all my dreams of sailing, I had never imagined myself in the middle of the South Seas, on board a gorgeous sailing ship, waltzing under a full moon with a handsome Frenchman. *Ooo, la la*!

The next morning, with the entire population of the island either standing on the shore and waving goodbye, following us out in their canoes, or swimming alongside, we set our sails for the low lying atoll group, the Tuamotus, which lay southwest of the Marquesas. Most of the crew wore flower crowns and we all sang while we worked. Only in Hawaii do the natives give flower leis to their visitors. In the rest of the Pacific, the people make flower or fern crowns. If they really like a visitor, they will give a hand-made, intricately woven shell necklace. Feeling joyful, I had to fight the temptation to whistle as we worked our way out of the bay, since no true sailor ever whistles at sea. Whistling on a boat is one of the old sailors' taboos, as is never harming an albatross, or no women aboard!

Just before leaving, we took on huge stalks of bananas and hung them up in the rigging. The daily culling of the bananas, to throw out the rotten ones, got added to my list of duties. I grew up at a time when bananas were a luxury that we got to eat very rarely, and I just hated to throw the over-ripe ones into the sea, so I ate them. Those tree-ripened wonders tasted so delicious that I never got tired of eating five or six a day.

The flying fish began hitting the deck regularly, drawn to the boat at night by our white sails lighted by our running lights. Every morning we gathered them from the scuppers for the crew's breakfast. They made a welcome change from oatmeal and pancakes. On *Te Vega*, the paying guests ate the best, with their menus including even lobsters, steaks and roasts topped with delicious sauces. The crew's main bill of fare was the constant veal stew, with your choice of white or curry sauce. For variety, we laced that stew with catsup or Tabasco. In fact, we got so tired of stew that the crew finally petitioned the captain about it and he ordered the chief steward to provide more variety in the crew's menu when we got to Tahiti.

One night, while we served roast duck with wild rice to the paying passengers, Jack whispered to me, "Don't eat the stew." Wondering what mysterious plans he had, I served everyone, washed the mountains of dishes, pots and pans, and grew hungrier by the minute.

Finally, everyone hit the sack or went up on deck for their watch. We slipped quietly into the officers' mess where Jack had turned on the red nightlight to keep from waking anyone up. Jack sat on one side of the gimbaled table and I on the other. We had huge plates of the remains of the roast duck in front of us. We did not bother with forks and knives since very little meat remained on the carcasses. But we gnawed and sucked and smacked our way through those bones like two Henry the Eighths. We had grease from eyebrow to chin and ear to ear, while our stomachs bulged with satisfaction. Best meal of the entire cruise!

Jack smoked about three packs of cigarettes a day and I do not remember ever seeing him without one in his mouth. Even while he cooked the meals, the ash grew longer and longer on his cigarette, and it had no place to fall but into whatever he happened to be cooking and stirring at the time, usually the veal stew.

Jack never saw the ash drop, since steam from all the heat covered his glasses, so he just stirred it right in. It was always hot in the close, stuffy galley and he sweated profusely. His sweat ran down his forehead and dripped off his cheeks and nose and right into whatever pot stood on the burner, also. It took me a few days to get used to this, but life at sea makes a hard working sailor terribly hungry and soon it didn't bother me at all. The rest of the crew and the guests never knew.

One of my perks for working in the galley came when Jack baked a cake. I always got to lick the cake bowl and eat the leftover frosting. In fact, I ate any leftovers like a little pig. After my long, hard day, peanut butter and jelly on a slab of Jack's homemade bread tasted so good out on deck. I worked so hard that it was impossible to gain any weight!

After a few days of sparkling seas and steady trade winds, the Tuamotus appeared, long and low on the horizon. Unlike the volcanic islands we had just visited, with their tall, spiky, volcanic mountains, these atolls lie only seven feet at their highest point, created from coral built up from the bottom of the sea. We arrived in the late afternoon, so we had to keep tacking *Te Vega* back and forth just outside the coral reef that formed a curved arm of protection for the bay until the next morning. As the sun came up over the horizon, we lowered sail, and slowly motored into the small half-bay with a crew member constantly throwing the plumb line. "Thirty feet!" He yelled. "Twenty-nine feet!" When the call reached fifteen feet of depth measured by the line, the big anchor went down and we got to play in yet another South Seas paradise.

Jack and I had prepared big picnic baskets and the crew lowered the longboats as everyone anticipated an unusual day on this deserted atoll.

We rowed out into the middle of the sparkling green and white bay, where we anchored in crystal clear water only three or four feet deep. Below us, fantastic fish of every size and color darted through an underwater coral fantasy. Everything on the Tuamotus startled us, from the bright green of the plant life to the brilliant white of the beach sands. The water sparkled light, brilliant, green because of the pale coral below, unlike the dark blue waters off the volcanic islands we had visited.

We rowed towards a beach and dragged the boats up on the blindingly white sand.

For fun, we explored an old iron sailing ship that had gone aground in a hurricane around the turn of the century. The boys in the crew took great delight in chasing me with huge coconut crabs they caught on the beach. These awful creatures, with their one great claw clacking all the time, looked right at me with their unblinking, bulbous eyes.

Chate, one of the Tahitian crew members, told us we were going to eat our picnic in a beautiful garden. We jumped into the longboats again and headed out into the lagoon to a big coral bed in the middle of the bay with corals of every type, shape and color. We threw out our anchors and ate our picnic on top of that most unusual *garden,* with great gusto.

Just a bit before sunset, we all clambered aboard and set sail for the main atoll of the group. We arrived the next afternoon. That night, with duties finished, a bunch of us went ashore. We plucked the creamy tiare Tahiti flowers and put them behind our ears, feeling very native as we walked along the sugary white beaches and strolled along the white coral paths of the village, the coral made whiter with the brilliant, full moonlight.

We had anchored inside a small reef, and since the Mormon missionaries on the island did not want the natives to party, the Captain invited them on board *Te Vega* for a dance. Once again, we enjoyed seeing a skilled performance of authentic native culture. Soon they got us all up to join them and we had a happy, laughing time as we served them Kool-aid and cookies.

A hurricane had hit these islands just a few years before we arrived, wiping out every thing except the Mormon Church. The natives told us that before the hurricane, almost all the islanders had been Catholic, but after the storm the numbers reversed! They survived the storm by climbing the coconut palms and tying themselves to them. Many had not survived.

These atolls also had the best pearl divers in the whole Pacific. With only diving goggles hand-made from coconut shells and little pieces of flat round glass set in them, the divers went down a hundred-fifty to two hundred feet to harvest beautiful pearls, holding their breaths for what seemed like an impossibly long time.

Just before we were ready to leave, we spotted a small sailboat on the horizon. As it got closer we found it to be Paul Hurst, a sailing buddy of mine, who was a well-known yachtsman. He was also a multi-millionaire, who just had fun with his life! He and his crew rowed over and came aboard for breakfast. He spotted me, and got me aside, and said, "Why don't you jump ship, and come with me! I'm heading around the world, and will be gone a couple of years." Now, not only was this a grand compliment, but it was also one of those huge decisions that come along every once in a while. It was so tempting! I finally had to say, "No! I just can't leave Captain Darr in the lurch, thousands of miles from nowhere!" He understood, but said he thought I was too noble!

We bid a fond farewell to each other, and we upped anchor, as we sailed away from the Tuamotu atolls, heading for Tahiti.

Dawn came, and we could see a dark speck on the horizon. Tahiti! The famous painter Louis de Bouganville, in his diary, called this island, "The most beautiful of all spots on the surface of the globe!" As we drew closer, it was like a mass of towering green coming up out of the deep, blue water. A white glittering reef of coral surrounded Tahiti. It looked just like a strand of pearls. Lofty mountains peeked out above the clouds at the very top of the world.

Closer and closer we came, all of us silent, watching the beauty unfold. As usual, coconut trees circled the island. The smell of tiare Tahiti and rich earth filled us with the thrill and adventure of discovery.

The engine was turned on, and the sails furled. Slowly we made our way through the treacherous reef, using our sounding line to make sure we got in safely. We slowly backed into the quay that was right smack dab on the little main street. We had arrived at Papeete, the famed capital of Tahiti. The crew worked quickly to stow all the deck gear. I worked to square away my galley. We couldn't wait to get on shore.

The streets were dusty, and not too clean, but the Tahitians were so happy and friendly, in their colorful pareaus and lava lavas, greeting us with *Ia ora na,* and we answered them back with the same.

We walked down side streets filled with shops and houses that all had tin red or gray roofs, covered with bougainvillea and every other tropical flower imaginable. Vespas, the French motor scooter, were popular, with lots of them zooming here and there with one, two, or even three people riding and laughing on them. Papeete ran from the sea to nearly a half mile inland, so we could walk everywhere. The mountain soared high above at 8,000 feet over our heads. Waterfalls, made from the daily rains, looked like moving ribbons of silver, falling over the black volcanic rock. They fell hundreds to thousands of feet in successive drops.

The harbor of Papeete is the capital of Tahiti and surpasses all other capitals in natural beauty. Yachts from all over the world had sailed in for this special occasion and tied up, stern to, right in the heart of town. Two elegant white cruise ships from Europe floated calmly at the big wharf. Freighters had carried passengers from far places. The air filled with the sounds of French, Chinese, Tahitian and English.

Bright, flower-printed shirts and wrap-around pareus blended with the brilliant natural colors of the lush plumeria and bougainvillea.

With an afternoon off, I joined the crew and we made for the festival grounds. Vendors worked busily to construct row after row of booths made of quickly woven palm thatch. Islanders with flower-bedecked heads sat on the lush green lawns busily plaiting together the intricate patterns for the roofs. The Tahitians did all their work in leisure, but also with beauty and lots of laughter.

As soon as a vendor completed a booth, business began. The vendors hawked all kinds of games of chance and food, food, food. I cooled off with a delicious sweet sno-cone, and had a helping of barbecued fish that melted in my mouth. With a soft, warm sweet potato in hand, I walked over to a small Ferris wheel that rose up to the sky. Laughing adults filled the ride, all rocking their seats like mad. No one yelled at them, "Stop that swaying, or you'll have to get out!" No one seemed to care! Children had to wait in line for their turns while their parents took a ride. From every street came the sound of guitar music and singing.

That night, some of us went to see *Snow White and the Seven Dwarfs* at the local theater. It was dubbed in French. The moviegoers all dressed in white dresses or black pants with white shirts. Flowers adorned male and female alike.

We bought slices of chilled, juicy watermelon and slurped and hollered with the locals. No one sat quietly in this theater. We listened to a constant stream of conversation and laughter and talking back to the screen, along with plenty of eating and drinking. The smell of coconut oil, which everyone used profusely over their bodies and hair, hung like a cloud over the room.

Afterward, we all bought colorful ices and strolled through the happy crowds which showed no signs of winding down for the day. So, we decided not to wind down either. Instead, we headed for Quinn's Bar. Every book ever set in Tahiti mentions this world-famous bar. The boys all ordered Hinano beer, the local brew of Tahiti, which has a higher alcohol content than most of our American brews. Since I drank the ubiquitous Coca-Cola, they asked me to make sure they all got safely back to the boat and not to let them get into any trouble.

The room filled with the scent of French cigarettes, coconut-oiled natives and everyone's sweat. The band played French pop tunes and all danced, either with a partner, or alone. It didn't seem to make much difference.

After awhile, someone pointed me in the direction of the "facilities." I pulled open the burlap curtain that separated the toilets from the crowd of merry makers and paused. Latticed duckboard covered the floor. A galvanized half-inch pipe ran around the room. Water squirted out of small holes punched in the pipe. Standing men and squatting women had placed themselves near the squirting water "getting rid of their beer." They all grinned at me and pointed to the one water closet at the back of the room that had a door. They knew I was a tourist!

Within a very short time of our arrival in Tahiti, most of the crewmen had hooked up with beautiful Tahitian girls and spent every spare moment they had ashore. We often shut down the galley, with only sandwich makings available, so I had a lot of free time to tour around and have a good time, too.

William Stone, the most famous of South Sea Island authors of that time, had been a passenger on *Te Vega* coming home to Tahiti. He had married a beautiful Tahitian, and they invited us all to a feast. Their home was built entirely like a native *fare*, using pandanas, lauhala, and palm weavings, and koa wood. It sat right on the ocean and was completely open to the cooling trade winds. We ate, danced, laughed, and swam.

Soon, some of the crew, with their local girlfriends, started sliding down the slippery slope of *going native*. In fact, some even started talking about jumping ship and hiding out in the mountains until the authorities lost interest in them. This was not a new idea. Ever since its discovery by European explorers, Tahiti has exerted a powerful attraction to those who have landed on her exotic shores.

The two-week long fête contests began with a hundred-mile long, two-day around-the-island canoe race. The big twenty-foot long war canoes sped by the point of land where we stood to watch. The huge warriors, dressed in their colorful pareus, wearing fern crowns, chanting in unison with a deep, primitive grunting sound as they paddled furiously. At the back of the canoe, a man managed the steering paddle and called out the cadence for the paddlers. After they passed, we all raced down to a small bay to watch the finish. It looked just like a war party coming ashore. In the old days, the islanders ran away and hid at the approach of a war canoe. But this time, they greeted the boats with shouts of joy, with everyone splashing around the incoming canoes, giving the winners crowns of flowers.

Next, we checked out the javelin-throwing event that requires great skill and strength. Each entrant had three spears to toss. He had to throw them about fifty feet high up, trying to hit a coconut hanging near the top of the trunk of a coconut tree. Very few missed their targets.

Because I loved music and singing of all kinds, I looked forward every day to the singing contests or *hemenes*. These events took place on a lush, green lawn in the main square. Groups of about thirty singers, from each island in the French Oceania group—the Marquesas, the Tuamotus, Raiatea and Bora Bora—sat cross-legged on the ground, backs straight with heads bowed. Every choir I had ever sung with had instructions to stand up straight to create pure tones. But from this unusual position on the ground came the most beautiful *a capella* music I had ever heard. The choir masters carried long bamboo sticks and wandered among the bowed heads, listening for an off pitch. Any miscreant singer got thunked on the head with the long cane, and changed his tune in a hurry.

The dance contests came at the end of each day. The sounds and colors delighted my eye and amazed me over and over again. Groups from each island created their own distinctive costume and dance. The colorful dyed grass skirts had complex designs of seeds and shells woven into the tops. The dancers wore tall elaborate headdresses intricately woven and dyed to match. Group after group whirled and wriggled and jumped until my head whirled, too.

These contests went on for days, until the night of the grand finale of the fête, the Governor's Ball. A spacious outdoor dance floor of wood was set up in front of the Governor's Mansion. Colored lights draped from one great banyan tree to the next. Laughing Tahitians iced down crate after crate of champagne in large, old-fashioned, red commercial Coca-Cola boxes, strategically set around the dance floor.

We all dug into our sea bags for our finest for this event. My dressiest dress, the most seldom used article, usually stayed right at the very bottom, so I dug deep, pulled out that great no-iron dress and shook it out for the party. It was a miracle dress. After a month and a half rolled up at the bottom of that sea bag, it was wrinkle free!

The boys in the fo'c'sle had a bit of trouble coming up with complete outfits. Because they had no closet in the fo'c'sle, they had hung their jackets and pants on hangers on a pole that went down the center of the large room. To keep them in place and out of the way, they had tied them all together with rope. To the crew's horror, the constant motion of the boat had swung the suits back and forth all this time, and sliced some of the jackets and pants right in half. They had to borrow from each other and finally appeared on deck as a rather ill assorted bunch. But they had scrubbed until their faces shone and slicked down their hair. They looked quite fine.

We served dinner early on board and I gave some quick dancing lessons to the few fellas who had no idea what to do with their two feet. The hour came, and five fine looking gentlemen escorted me to the Grand Ball. Cinderella had nothing on me.

We danced and danced. When one band quit, another started, so the music never stopped all night. The orchestras knew all the old big band tunes from the 20s and 30s, so we waltzed and did the Charleston a lot.

Dawn came, its pearly colors spreading across the sky and we grabbed partners to swirl around the floor for one last dance.

"Let's go to the market!" someone suggested. We wandered up through the waterfront to the open-air market. Despite the all-night partying, business-as-usual started with the sunrise.

Natives came in with boatloads of fresh fish. Others walked down from the mountains with sweet island oranges. The Chinese baked fresh bread and rolls. Tough bartering and much good will went on for about two hours, then it all folded up until the next morning.

We bought mugs of hot coffee with fresh thick cream and raw island sugar. We added fragrant fresh baked chunks of bread lavishly spread with homemade butter. Then we wandered amidst the brightly colored fish of every size and shape displayed on ice, stalks of tiny sweet bananas hanging from rafters, stacks of green breadfruit and beautifully arranged baskets of bright oranges, making our way through crowds of laughing, bargaining natives.

Chate, introduced his wife and children. They insisted I go with them for a short walk. We came to a small store and they dragged me in with much laughter. Before long, they had dressed me in full Tahitian hula regalia, complete with the woven coconut palm helmet on my head. Then they led me back down the street. In no time, I had shell leis stacked up to my nose.

"Hey," someone shouted, "look at the time! We've got to get back to the boat. We're on duty in just a few minutes!" We raced to the harbor, jumped on board, dived into our work clothes and reported for duty just in time. Ho-hum! Another dreary day at the office.

Later that morning, we planned to set off for the neighboring island of Mooréa.

In Tahiti, and other ports here and there around the world, the authorities finally got smart and required visitors to have not only a passport, but also a return ticket. Nowadays, visitors need a plane ticket, but then we needed proof of a boat ticket. The officials did not care where to, as long as no one stayed on their island. Alternatively, a visitor may post money for such a ticket with the local gendarmes. Capt. Darr had to deposit enough cash for all of us, as a bond, until we left.

Officials checked all our passports against our incoming immigration papers and we had to match the pictures on our passports the last hour before departure.

The captain had to send a couple of the guys around the town to collect those who had completely lost track of time or had gone native. As we prepared to set sail, a handful of Tahitian girls in sarongs stood on the shore, holding flower crowns for their favorite crewman and crying voluminously.

"*Maururu a vau!*" they called. "Farewell, farewell!"

They got to wave and cry for a long time, because, unfortunately, as we left the quay and headed out through the bay, we ran aground on some sand and a coral head!

The bay held a scattering of small islands and coral heads. In these bays, the sand shifts around regularly but nothing ever gets marked on the maps. The captain, aware of the danger, had maneuvered the big boat between the outcroppings like a queen-sized ballerina tiptoeing through a minefield. We all jumped as we heard a loud scraping sound and *Te Vega* shuddered. We had hit one of the sharp, virtually indestructible coral heads and were firmly stuck.

Such an incident can be quite complicated. In foreign waters, if another boat comes up and pulls the boat off, the saving boat can claim the other boat as salvage. Harriet fluttered from one end of the deck to the other, wringing her hands and crying, "We're going to lose the boat! We're going to lose the boat!"

We did everything to get us off before the voracious tugs arrived. We could see them on the horizon, coming ever closer.

The engine roared into reverse, then back into forward. We spun the wheel this way and then that way, working with the engine, but nothing seemed to make any difference in our position. Coral heads are very sharp, so we worked as gently as possible to avoid damage to the hull. The captain sent two crewmen down below to pick up the floor boards here and there, to check for incoming water, in case the hull sprung a leak.

I decided that the best thing for me to do was to calm Harriet down to allow the captain to concentrate on the job at hand. I have never had much patience with crybabies, but I finally made some progress and got her settled below. When I came back up, I realized that no one stood at the helm, since we were going nowhere. Everyone moved busily all about the deck, looking over the rails, trying to come up with a solution.

First, I returned below and started reading The Books, just to clear my thoughts from the fear overtaking everyone on board. A verse from Psalm 21 came to me and I held it close, "The Lord shall preserve thy going out and thy coming in from this time forth, and even forever more." Then I got what I can only characterize as a "little angel message." I went up to the helm and gripped the big wheel. I just started singing a hymn about God caring for us all the time, "Trust the Eternal, when the shadows gather…." Within two to three minutes, that boat just slid right off that coral. With a big cheer from all hands, we set off for Mooréa.

When we arrived, we sailed into the deep, blue bay with no need to toss the plumb line, which is a line with a weight on it that measures the depth of the water. We slowly pulled in close to shore and threw our bow line around a coconut tree and lowered our anchor astern. Capt. Darr sent some of the crew down to inspect the hull wearing aqua lungs, or scuba gear, as it was later called. Jacques Cousteau and Emile Gagnan had invented these about ten years earlier and we were fortunate to have two crewmen with all the necessary diving apparatus and air tanks. They found no damage to the hull at all, just a few scratches in the paint. I thanked God and went off happily to wash the lunch dishes.

Mooréa Bay presented us with another spectacular view of all the usual tropical grandeur. A tall, sharply pointed mountain rose above the inlet, with a hole right through the top, like a sewing needle. The islanders told us a religious statue stood way up there, but after the Fête, none of us had the energy to climb, or indeed any money to pay a guide for a horseback trip up the precarious cliffs and through the thick jungle.

After cleaning up the boat and stowing and repairing all the sailing gear, we rigged up a siphon from a clear stream to fill the holding tanks on board. Once we completed that chore, the crew had the afternoon free. And after I scrubbed and cleaned the galley all "shipshape and Bristol fashion," I did, too.

Several of us strolled down a path through the jungle where brightly colored orchids dripped off the trees. Tropical flora and fauna pushed at us as we walked along. We hopped over small, clear streams and took off our shoes to ford larger ones. Waterfalls spilled into deep clear pools and we vowed to swim in them on our way back. We came out of the jungle onto a small cliff that overlooked another bay. A sailing canoe creamed along near the outside reef, and closer to shore a young girl and boy sat in another canoe, quietly fishing.

We made our way down the bluff to a local palm-thatched saloon where we found a Sunday afternoon jam-session in progress. The mayor of Mooréa and all his cronies waved us in with smiles and gestures and we soon joined in the fun. The usual guitars and oil cans joined a set of spoons played by a jolly fat fellow with fantastic rhythm. The fast beat of the music encouraged the dancers to jump up and dance a *tamure*, the fast Tahitian hula.

The girls grabbed me up and soon I stood in the center of the floor, trying my best to get my hips into circulation. They swept the boys onto the dance floor, too. It was not exactly like an elegant ballroom back home with someone like Lawrence Welk playing and bubbles floating around. It was better, and we certainly had a great time dancing on that hard-packed dirt floor.

When we took our leave, they sang the Tahitian farewell, "*Maururu a vau,*" in their traditional harmony that brought tears to our eyes.

Making our way back through the jungle, we heard some really off-key singing coming from behind some bushes. Pushing our way through, we found one of the crew sitting under a waterfall, bare-chested, wearing only a woven Tahitian pandanas hat and a bright red pareu tied around his waist, carefully hugging a large jug of the local wine beside him. We dragged him out, gathered up his "civilian" clothes and smuggled him back on board and into his bunk. The temptation to go native proved very enticing.

Next, we made a brief stop at the small island of Raiatea, where we went ashore long enough to poke through the little island shops and buy their famous finely woven white pandanas hats, much softer than the better known Panama straws. We also enjoyed ice cream cones from a teensy general store, in the only flavor they made, vanilla.

The boys bought whole long vanilla beans and bottles of brandy to sneak back on board. They inserted the beans into the brandy bottles and let the mixture sit for a few days. If anyone got careless and imbibed too much of this flavorful drink, the captain confiscated his brandy, so they were all very careful.

Our last stop, before turning north toward Hawaii, was Bora Bora, where we enjoyed outrigger canoe sailing, swimming under waterfalls, and walking along spectacular beaches lining sparkling lagoons. By this time, not one of us went ashore without a flower or fern crown. I even worked in the hot galley wearing a flower crown, usually made of sweet smelling tiare Tahiti blossoms that overcame the smell of burnt toast, which I frequently forgot I had cooking in the oven.

For less than a dollar, the islanders took anyone sailing on their ten-to-twelve-foot outrigger sailing canoes. I went so often with the same two young guys that we became friends and they wouldn't take my dollar any more! On our last day, I bargained with one of them for his outrigger, and we finally settled on the price of $100, almost a month's salary.

Then, I had to ask the captain's permission to stow the canoe in one of the longboats for the long beat up to Hawaii. He had consistently turned down lots of requests to haul large items, including a complete Model T Ford for the engine crew, back in Tahiti, so I did not have much hope.

The captain, without batting an eye, said, "Of course! Just make sure it will fit in the longboat and the canvas boat cover will still fit properly." His generosity caught me by surprise. Maybe he decided to reward me for all my hard work.

Unbeknownst to the captain, the engine room boys had bought the Model T for the grand sum of $25. They took it all apart on shore, and smuggled it piece by piece into the engine room, where they hid it heaven only knew where!

On our final night on Bora Bora, the natives put on a spectacular dance, with the most intricately woven of all the grass skirts we had seen in the islands. The girls had gotten hold of a Sears and Roebuck Catalog and ordered beautiful pink satin bras. They usually wore nothing on top, which was a bit disconcerting for conservative me. The other crew members obviously were not bothered by this!

The tiki torches flickered with the slight breeze. The surf pounded out on the distant reef. The drums started. The dance began, slowly. It built up to a crescendo, and ended with an abrupt stop. Nothing fake or touristy about this dancing!

After enjoying Bora Bora, we set off one delightful tropical morning for the two-week run up to Honolulu. The natives once more gave us a festive send-off, crowding around *Te Vega* in sailing canoes, double sailing canoes and single paddling canoes, all practically swamped with the load of humanity piled within. One finally did flip over, but the passengers all just laughed, turned the canoe back over, emptied it and climbed back in. As always in the tropics, the sun shone in a deep blue sky punctuated with a few small puffy clouds.

We sailed out of the reef and into the briny blue. A school of flying fish even appeared, to send us off. The Pacific Ocean's name implies that it is placid and calm, but it soon belied its name. The weather turned squally and going north we had to beat into the trade winds. In the galley, the diesel stove acted up and started smoking. Cooking over it smelled like riding behind a big city bus on a bicycle.

Jack and I struggled to shut the hatch over the stove as we were taking aboard a lot of white water. Waves crashed over the boat and rolled over the deck, sluicing into our open hatch and pouring down on top of the stove and us.

With the hatch closed, the galley got hotter and hotter, and smellier and smellier, until I could stand it no more. I dashed up the engine room stairs and hung over the rail. With my stomach somewhat relieved, I headed back down the stairs to help fry eggs.

The situation even got the best of Jack, and he had to make a run for the rail, too. Well, actually, he was too heavy and slow to make a dash, so he used the handy, dandy garbage bucket. Between us we managed to get breakfast and lunch, but the galley looked and smelled a mess. Rough seas had tossed pots and pans all over the place. Broken dishes and grease and food splattered all over the deck and bulk heads.

Since we had filled my trusty garbage bucket, we began to toss more garbage into a casserole pan that had some leftovers in it from the night before. It was the receiver of cigarette butts, broken glass and anything else that came to hand.

After lunch, we both collapsed into our bunks before facing the clean-up.

The chief steward, that real stickler for cleanliness, appeared in his clean pressed whites. "Jack," he said, with surprising compassion, "don't worry about the galley. I'll figure out something for dinner."

What a relief for us.

We took off an hour, and later, climbed out of our bunks feeling much better. We made our way to the galley where we found the spic-and-span steward pulling a magnificent looking dish from the oven.

Jack took one look and blanched.

The steward beamed. "I took that left-over casserole and beefed it up with all kinds of stuff, and now you can do the honor of serving it!"

We laughed for days at the look on his face when Jack told him what that beautiful concoction he had been about to serve to his elegant guests *really* contained.

Once the weather cleared, we spent many a night on deck, with the captain telling us stories about the South Seas, from the Easter Islands to the Fijis and every island in between.

One night, the crew waited for Chate, who had a great sense of humor, to get seated for dinner. Then they threw a live flying fish through the hatch above him, right onto his plate. Without batting an eye, he jumped up and yelled, "Fresh feesh! Fresh feesh! You cook, please?" and I cooked, please.

One easy sailing day, Capt. Darr decided to pull an abandon ship drill. When signing on, he had told us to check out the Maritime Rules posted on the bulkhead of the Officers Mess to learn our responsibility for this drill. I discovered that the mess cook, my title, had to haul up on the lines of one of the two davits that put the fourteen-foot longboat overboard and into the water.

Without warning, the signal bell rang and we all scampered around looking for our life jackets. Mine had gotten buried under all the dirty laundry in my stateroom and I ended up with one of the passengers in her stateroom, trying to find one for each of us.

We helped each other buckle up into the unwieldy jackets and I raced to my post. I grabbed the line, ready to start hauling up on the boat when the order came. Suddenly, the entire crew from our lifeboat started to laugh.

In the middle of the longboat, at six feet or more and weighing well over two hundred pounds, stood the biggest, most burly man in the crew. He held in his hand the tiny bilge plug which screws into the bottom of the lifeboat. His assignment on the proper Maritime Regulation Sheet was to plug the boat before it hit the water. And on deck stood Bungy, all five-feet six-inches of me, weighing about one-hundred-twenty pounds soaking wet, ready to haul up the heavy boat with all my might.

The captain bent the maritime rules with a few changes after that. I got the plug and the big guy got to haul the ropes.

After a long week of some good sailing, we reached the Hawaiian Islands and entered the Molokai Channel, one of the wildest bodies of water in the world. It was mid-morning of our last day at sea as we sailed near the island of Molokai, heading for Honolulu. The waves ran at about fifteen to twenty feet and a good stiff breeze pushed us along at around ten knots.

"Captain, can I go out on the bowsprit for a ride?" I begged. If I fell off, I would land in the safety basket under the bowsprit.

"It'll be so much fun!" I cried. "Please?"

With some trepidation, but with a twinkle in his eye, the captain nodded and advised, "Be sure the boat is heading up out of a wave and not down into it when you run out!"

I talked one of the crewmen into joining me while everyone else looked on in disbelief. We tied safety ropes around our waists, with the crew ready to haul us in, if necessary.

The bowsprit stretched about fifteen feet out to its tip and when *Te Vega* headed up a swell, we ran out to the end, threw ourselves down on it and wrapped our arms and legs around it tightly.

The lull ended in just a few seconds as *Te Vega* reached the top of a big swell. We went up into the clear blue sky. Then with heady speed, down we came, plunging maybe ten feet under the crystal clear water. And before we knew it, up again, into the dazzling sky, only to plunge again into the depths moments later. We had about fifteen minutes of this gloriously wet roller coaster ride before the crew pulled us back on board, soaked and exhilarated. To this day, when my life gets boring, I recall the mad beauty of that swirling water crashing around me, and the exaltation I felt, soaring out of that chaos into the sunshine, again and again.

When Honolulu, which appropriately means "protected bay," came into view over the bow of *Te Vega*, I knew I had a thousand memories of sailing the South Seas to add to the stories of my childhood. By afternoon, we sailed past Diamond Head and off Waikiki, arriving back at civilization and our final port, Honolulu's Pier 7.

A few days later, I signed off, received my final pay and bid farewell to the captain and crew that remained on board for *Te Vega's* next trip.

Making arrangements to have my canoe shipped home, I borrowed a truck from a friend at the dock and took it down to the Ala Wai Yacht Harbor where my sister and her husband, Nat, were living on the Barquentine California, with their brand new baby, Cala.

Bungy's Bora Bora outrigger canoe, with friends, in Newport Beach, California.

I got some help putting it back together in order to paddle it out to the boat. A friend and I, dressed in brand new *aloha* shirts, jumped in and began to paddle. It didn't go more than ten feet before it tipped right over! We were sopped, but laughing at our ignorance. We soon managed to right it and re-fixed the positioning of the *ama*, or arm, of the outrigger and I managed to have some fun with it for a few days before shipping it home on a Matson freighter.

I slung my sea bag over my shoulder, climbed aboard a bus and headed for the airport and home, where I found my life completely changed. No more Cove!

Chapter 16

♪ *M. I. C.   K. E. Y.   M. O. U. S. E.* *Mickey Mouse! Donald Duck!* ♫

When first arriving in Tahiti, we all dashed to the post office to see if we had received any General Delivery mail. There it was! A letter from home. But what a letter! It told of this new place called "Disneyland," where crowds of up to 28,000 people came daily to play in theme lands, like Fantasyland with a Sleeping Beauty Castle, and a magical carousel imported piece by piece from Europe; Frontierland with cowboys and Indians roaming the streets and shoot-outs at any time of the day or night, and where you could ride a huge Showboat, where Louis Armstrong sat in the bow with his band and played his wonderful jazz; Tomorrowland, where it was possible to take a rocket ride and believe you were living in a Sci-Fi book; and Adventureland, where people rode on Jungle Boats through a real live jungle filled with fake alligators, elephants and birds, and a big Bazaar where one could travel around the world with the different shops.

The letter said that we had left The Cove! We now lived in a farmhouse across the street from this odd place, in a big orange grove. We had three shops selling tikis, shells, and all of Daddy's South Sea Island imports! What was going on? It was too fantastic and I couldn't take it in. Here I was in Tahiti, and my other life had fallen apart. Well, I wasn't able to do anything about it right now. I still had at least another month before getting home, so I took the letter and stowed it in the bottom of my sea bag.

But here I was now, waiting at the LAX airport for someone to pick me up! I was full of questions when Ba pulled up and gave me a big hug of welcome.

"What's happening, Ba?" I asked.

She said, "I can't even begin to describe it. Seeing is believing!"

We arrived and parked in a big dirt lot, and came into what was obviously the "back stage" of this place. I began to see Indians in full regalia, and cowboys driving stage coaches pulled by big mules. There was even a Snow White wandering around. We pushed through great log gates and found ourselves in crowds of happy tourists. We finally arrived at The Bazaar in Adventureland, and The Island Trade Stores, which looked like the tropics I had just left! There was even a fourteen-foot tiki Daddy had been carving when I left many moons ago, standing in a corner. I was hugged, welcomed home, shown how to use the register, and immediately started taking money! "Ho ho ho, a pirate's life for me!" I never even had to sell. The tourists just stood in long lines, money in hand, ready to buy anything that had "Souvenir of Disneyland" on it. All the shops were ordering rolls of decals, and putting them on everything that looked like their particular theme. The best selling items for The Island Trade Stores were cannibal-looking salt and pepper shakers, with decals! We sold gross after gross of those. We

Newly opened Disneyland. Aerial photo, 1955.

Whole Puzzle of Adventureland, Disneyland, with Island Trade Stores located by arrow.

Original Puzzle Box. Note 29 cent marker!

1955 Public Opening Day

Opening:	Monday, July 18, 1955 at 10 am
Location:	1313 Harbor Boulevard, in Anaheim, California
Hours:	10 am to 10 pm seven days a week during the summer. Open 6 days a week in the fall, closed on Mondays.
Founder:	Walt Disney
Area Size:	Total area: 160 acres. Park: 60 acres.
Parking:	Parking lot size: 100 acres. Car capacity: 12,175.
Admission:	$1.00, including tax, for adults and 50 cents, including tax, for children 12 and under.
Food:	20 restaurants in all the four different lands.
Walking:	To visit every land, distance of 1.4 miles.
Personnel:	Over 1,000 employees.
Capacity:	Designed to handle 60,000 visitors daily.
Landscaping:	Plants from all over the world. Approximately 12,000 orange trees removed.

Schedule for Disneyland Grand Opening.

could hardly keep them in supply. This goes for a little two-inch tiki on a brown, plastic necklace, too. I've never seen even one of these items since! Some shops went out of business here and there, and Daddy would take over their lease. We'd fill the counters up with "Souvenir of Disneyland, Cactus mailed to your friends." Or the now famous Steiff stuffed animals. We were among the first to carry them on the west coast. We'd use it as overflow space for our shell and butterfly collectors. For a while we had a space where the sixteen-year-old girls we hired for the summer would stand, wearing an arrow-through-the-head, with a Zommerang in one hand, shooting the roll of red, white, and blue paper in and out, and a little pistol that shot candy into the mouths of passing children.

314

But the spot the girls groaned the most over was the one where we put live miniature turtles, in a big glass case. Every morning, the one assigned to the turtles for that day had to pick out the few dead ones and throw them away, and feed the rest. She then had to put Disneyland decals on their little backs, and she was open for business. None of us could stand doing this. Our hearts broke over those little turtles. We closed that moneymaking idea down in a hurry!

My life had flipped completely over! I had gone from owning the universe at the top of a mast, to helping thousand and thousands of tourists every day, working from ten in the morning, to closing down the registers at ten at night. I'd throw the moneybag into the basket of my bicycle, and ride out the front entrance and across a small, dark parking lot. I would ride through the orange groves, across Harbor Blvd., and home to the Farmhouse. The receipts for the day ran into thousands, but it was such a safe world!

My favorite cousin, Billie Lou, who was bookkeeper for the first year, showed me the books, and I, who had never done any bookkeeping at all, became, not only in charge of the books, but also hired, fired, and managed up to sixteen girls in the summers. I did payables and receivables, sales taxes, merchandise buying, accounting, payroll, and even Daddy's personal income taxes!

Those first few years at Disneyland were so new and hectic for all who worked there, that no one knew what to expect from day to day. There was excitement in the air. Walt Disney, the grand maestro himself, roamed the streets, making sure his idea was coming to fruition, greeting guests and us alike. All of Disneyland was filled

315

with employees ranging from sixteen to maybe twenty-five. And we all wanted to have fun. On breaks, all of us who worked in the park could go to any of the rides and jump on for free. It was quite a choice!

The Mouseketeers had been formed, and during Christmas, a real circus was performed, with a Disney theme, for two weeks. Those kids rode daily in the Grand Finale of the Big Top show. Extras were always needed to get into the Disney cartoon character suits and dance around after the stars, for the finale. I'd time my breaks for just that reason, dash over to the big tent, enter back stage, jump into whatever Disney character was left – a bear, a duck, an elephant – and off I'd go, dancing and waving around the Big Top!

The Farm House had a beautiful garden patio, and mother gave frequent parties. One time, she decided to give a really elegant dinner. She sent out invitations for forty, declaring that some would call and cancel, so we would end up with about thirty. No one canceled, and in fact, many called to ask if they could bring someone else! There were over sixty.

Now, at The Cove, many times we had over a hundred, but The Cove could handle that. And mother had it in her head, that she wanted a sit-down, place card party. For weeks, she had these little white cards with all the guests' names on them. She arranged and rearranged them in settings of four. Who would like to sit next to so-and-so? And, after figuring it out, a guest would call and ask to bring someone else, and she'd start all over.

She rented card tables and chairs. Our garden looked like a fairyland with kahili torches and candles twinkling in every corner. The guests arrived. Raymond Burr of Perry Mason fame, Jack Norworth of "Take Me Out to the Ball Game" fame, Roy Williams of Big Mooseketeer fame, Mad Man Muntz, the very first and most famous used car salesman to advertise on television fame, and Rudy Vallee, without his megaphone that he always sang through, before microphones. He asked me to waltz, and handed out fountain pens to everyone that said, "Truly yours, Rudy Vallee"! None of the guests sat at their place cards, but all had a great time!

At nine o'clock sharp, the nightly fireworks at Disneyland started. We had a clear view of them over our orange grove, because there were no motels in the way. They came later. It was practically like a Cove party. All came early and stayed late. The next morning, I was up and at 'em, and back to my post at The Island Trade Store.

It was summer, and Disneyland was booming, when I happened to look at the big antique glass battery jar where our real shrunken head from Peru was kept on display. He was gone! I alerted security, and it seemed like all Disneyland was put on the chase. It was the excitement of the day. But we never saw him again! Too bad. He was quite a draw!

I had sold my little eight-foot sailboat before going off to Tahiti, and got a call from an old friend saying he was going to be gone for a year on business. He wanted to know if I wanted to use his little 22-foot Block Islander, The Minada, during that time. You betcha! It was moored at one of the marinas on Terminal Island, about forty-five minutes from Disneyland.

When the weather was perfect, a gal friend and I would pack a picnic, get a couple of nice jungle river boat ride captains we'd been eyeballing, and take off in the evening, after Disneyland closed. The four of us would sail the huge Los Angeles Harbor, watching the great ships coming in and out, unloading and loading up. The lights on these big ships looked magical. The shouts from the stevedores sounded like a call from some strange exotic port, making me homesick for the top of a mast, any mast! Getting home as the sun was coming up, we'd grab a few hours sleep, and be back in harness as Disneyland came awake for another day. She was a sweet little day sailer, and later on I found a slip for her in Newport Beach, which was easier to get to from Disneyland than Terminal Island.

To move the Minada down to her new home, I got my gal friend and we found a couple of nice Disneyland guys who also had the day off, packed a picnic, and headed off. From my old slip, the wind was usually just right for sailing in and out, but I rented an outboard motor just in case I might need it for the new slip.

The sun was just about coming through the early morning coastal clouds as we set off. A bit of a breeze got us down the Harbor about halfway. It dropped, so we started the outboard and chugged along, passing big ships coming and going. A speedboat passed us, going too fast. His wake swamped the motor. But, no fear, the wind was bound to pick up – it always did!

Not this day. We crept along with a little breeze here and a little there, until we were practically out of the harbor. It was nine at night, by this time, and the boys were getting frantic. They had

318

college exams the next day! We flagged down a U.S. Navy tender, carrying their sailors to and from one of the big navy ships anchored out in the bay. They took the boys ashore, and promised to call our parents so they wouldn't worry.

As it got colder, we put on every piece of clothing there was on board. We ate every last bite of food, and drank every last soda pop from our picnic. And still no breeze. Little gusts of wind kept springing up, giving us hope, only to die again. We had to keep a watch, with one of us awake and the other sleeping all night, so we wouldn't get run over with the ship traffic, going in and out.

By the time dawn came, we were thoroughly discouraged, and decided we'd better flag down one of the big commercial fishing boats that were headed out for the day, or week. According to marine law, if you see someone in trouble you are supposed to stop and stand by until either you help them, or you call the Coast Guard, and they help them. We'd spot one of these big boats, scream and wave, and they'd pass right by. I suppose they were looking through their binoculars at two dumb girls without a brain in their heads, which were really not in serious trouble, and pretend they didn't see us. We could hardly blame them!

Finally, one got too close to get away, and they came alongside. "We'll help you, but we can't run you back in. We can take you to an oil drilling rig a few miles out, and they can tow you back when their tender comes in," they shouted to us. That sounded fine.

They brought us alongside the big oil barge, and dropped off our towline. All the oil rig crew started hootin' and hollerin', even though we looked so bedraggled by that time, there was absolutely no glamour left in us. They took us into the galley, and a nice, friendly cook gave us a huge breakfast. We felt like we hadn't eaten in days, and it had only been twelve hours!

We had a six hour wait before we could get a tow in with their shore boat, so when a pretty good breeze sprung up, we decided the calm was over, and we'd set off for Newport once more. The sea was sparkling in the sun, and the wind was perfect. That is, until it died in about an hour, and there we were again, but really worse off, because now we were out at sea.

In the distance we spotted a boat. We screamed and waved, and an old, rusty, twenty-foot long landing craft that belonged to some oil rig construction company, pulled alongside. The only guy onboard was really scraggly looking with a shaggy beard and dirty clothes, but he had a nice smile. He said he could take us nearly to Newport, so we tied up alongside, and climbed aboard his vessel. He had just came back from a few weeks of mountain lion hunting where he had fallen off a cliff and had lain there semi-conscious for a couple of days, until he was rescued. He wasn't as bad as he looked!

He took us all the way to the slip, and we were finally able to get home. We had exchanged numbers, and a few days later he called, wanting to know if I wanted to go dancing with him. Oh! The consternation! I couldn't turn him down, because he had been so nice, but what to tell my parents about this bedraggled date!

The big night arrived. I was ready for dancing with my flowy outy skirt and three inch heels. The doorbell rang. I opened it. There stood this handsome, clean-shaven guy, with a beautiful suit on!

He'd even brought me a corsage. Mother thought he was awfully nice. We left, climbed into his Jaguar convertible, and danced the night away!

That was the last of my sailing adventures. Oh! Wait! I forgot about the time, nearly twenty years later, when my husband, three kids and I were sailing a 32-footer from Hawaii to California for a $2,000 delivery fee. We were hit by storm after storm. We ran out of water. We were rescued by the U.S. Coast Guard when the steering mechanism broke. But, of course, that story is for another book!

Hand carved Tikis by Eli Hedley, Beachcomber at Island Trade Store.

OTHER HEDLEY FAMILY BOOKS

1. "How Daddy Became A Beachcomber" by daughter Marilyn Hedley. This book is a reprint of the original printed in 1947. It is the story of Eli Hedley, Beachcomber and his family, and how their love of the sea became a way of life and livelihood. Illustrations by Flo Ann Hedley and Marilyn Hedley.

2. Eli Hedley, Beachcomber's Original 1943 Catalog. This book is a reprint of items made from driftwood and sold at Trade Winds Trading Company in Hollywood. Photos of hand carved tikis by Hedley, added.

Printed in the United States
55162LVS00005B/1-87

9 781425 944100